A POLITICAL HISTORY OF ZAMBIA

A POLITICAL HISTORY OF
ZAMBIA

FROM COLONIAL RULE TO THE THIRD REPUBLIC, 1890-2001

Bizeck Jube Phiri

Africa World Press, Inc.

P.O. Box 1892
Trenton, NJ 08607

P.O. Box 48
Asmara, ERITREA

Africa World Press, Inc.

P.O. Box 1892
Trenton, NJ 08607

P.O. Box 48
Asmara, ERITREA

Book design: Saverance Publishing Services
Cover design: Ashraful Haque

Library of Congress Cataloging-in-Publication Data

Phiri, B. J.
 A political history of Zambia : from colonial rule to the third republic, 1890-2001 / by Bizeck Jube Phiri.
    p. cm.
 Includes bibliographical references and index.
 ISBN 1-59221-307-3 (hardcover) -- ISBN 1-59221-308-1 (pbk.)
 1. Zambia--Politics and government. I. Title.

DT3073.P48 2006
968.94'02--dc22

                        2005033214

To my late mother, Egereti Nyangulu, who laboured to see me through Primary, Secondary and University, and my late father, Jube M. Phiri, who did not live long enough to witness and share my achievements.

Table of Contents

LIST OF TABLES

Abbreviations

ALC	African Labour Corps
ANC	African National Congress
ANIP	African National Independence Party
ARC	African Representative Council
AZ	Agenda for Zambia
BNP	Barotse National Party
BSAC	British South Africa Company
CAA	Capricorn Africa Association
CAC	Central African Council
CAI	Capricorn Africa Institute
CAP	Central Africa Party
CAS	Capricorn Africa Society
CCMG	Christian Churches Monitoring Group
CCZ	Christian Council of Zambia
CO	Colonial Office
CP	Constitution Party
CPP	Conventional Peoples Party
DP	Democratic Party
EFZ	Evangelical Fellowship of Zambia
FAS	Federation of African Societies
FDD	Forum for Democracy and Development
FODEP	Foundation for Democratic Process
FUCA	Federal Union of Capricorn Africa
HM	Historical Manuscripts
LAZ	Law Association of Zambia
Legco	Legislative Council
LP	Liberal Party

LPF	Liberal Progress Front
MASA	Mines African Staff Association
MDP	Movement for Democratic Process
MLC(s)	Member(s) of Legislative Council
MMD	Movement for Multi-Party Democracy
MP	Multi-racial Party
MP(s)	Member(s) of Parliament
MPU	Micro Projects Unit
NADA	National Democratic Alliance
NAZ	National Archives of Zambia
NAZimb	National Archives of Zimbabwe
NCC	National Christian Coalition
NCDP	National Commission for Development Planning
NEC	National Executive Committee
NGO	Non-Governmental Organisation
NLP	National Lima Party
NOCE	National Organisation for Civic Education
NP	National Party
NPP	National Progress Party
NRAC	Northern Rhodesia Africa Congress
NRP	New Republican Party
PA	Party Archives
PF	Patriotic Front
PAFMECSA	Pan-African Movement for East, Central and Southern Africa
PAZA	Press Association of Zambia
PLP	People's Liberation Party
PRO	Public Record Office
PTA	Parents Teachers Association
RACM	Roan Antelope Consolidated Mines
RP	Republican Party
RRP	Rhodesian Republican Party
RST	Rhodesian Selection Trust
SACCORD	Southern African Centre for Constructive Resolution of Disputes
TSPP	Theoretical Spiritual Political Party
UBZ	United Bus Company of Zambia

UCAA	United Central Africa Association
UDI	Unilateral Declaration of Independence
UFP	United Federal Party
UNFP	United National Freedom Party
UNIP	United National Independence Party
UNRA	United Northern Rhodesia Association
UP	United Party
UPD	Unity Party for Democrats
UPND	United Party for National Development
UPP	United Progressive Party
VMI	Victory Ministries International
ZANC	Zambia African National Congress
ZAP	Zambia Alliance for Progress
ZDC	Zambia Democratic Congress
ZEC	Zambia Episcopal Conference
ZEMCC	Zambia Elections Monitoring Coordinating Committee
ZNBC	Zambia National Broadcasting Corporation
ZRP	Zambia Republican Party

Acknowledgements

Several institutions and individuals were generous enough to make this study a reality. I wish to thank the staff of the National Archives of Zambia for their generous co-operation. I wish also to thank the Director of the Research Bureau of the United National Independence Party (UNIP) Head Quarters for giving me permission to use the Party Archives in 1989. My thanks also go to the staff of the University of Zambia Library, particularly those in the Special Collections who made it possible for me to locate the Eileen Haddon Papers from a pile of unsorted mass of documents. I am equally grateful to the staff of the Political Museum.

I also wish to thank all those I have not mentioned by name who contributed to this work in one way or another. A number of organizations and individuals read through the manuscript and gave me useful information to perfect the work. However, whatever errors of judgement and interpretation there may be, are my responsibility alone.

Lastly, I thank my wife Jane and children—Chisomo, Chabala, Chimwemwe and Mushimba, for their support and encouragement as I tirelessly concentrated on the keyboard to accomplish the task I had set for myself.

INTRODUCTION

The Republic of Zambia, formerly Northern Rhodesia (1911-1964) is a land locked country in south-central Africa. It is bordered to the west by Angola, to the northwest by the Democratic Republic of Congo, to the northeast by Tanzania, to the east by Malawi, to the southeast by Mozambique, to the south by Zimbabwe and Botswana, and to the southwest by Namibia. It is a truism that the present is rooted in the past and thus our search of how things happened leads us to seek for ideas about how to understand our present world. Undoubtedly, therefore, a political history of Zambia can only be meaningful if the making of the country is explored and reconstructed from the colonial period for it is that colonial heritage which shaped the present.

While Zambia's political history can be divided into three periods,[1] it was the two periods in the colonial era that shaped the nature of the latter three periods: the First Republic (1964-1972); the Second Republic (1073-1991) and Third Republic (1992-2001). The two periods in colonial Zambia's political history are from 1890 to 1924 when the country was under the British South Africa Company (BAS Company), and from 1924 to 1963 when it was directly under the Colonial Office. Of the two periods, it was the second which was most significant in shaping the future of Zambia's political history.

Geographically, Zambia is situated in the southern hemisphere between 22^0 to 34^0 longitude east of the Meridian Line and between 8^0 to 18^0 latitude south of the equator. Through the process of the partition, and conflicts over originally imagined mineral wealth, Zambia's physical shape resembles a butterfly with its wings wide open. It is a landlocked country with no outlet to the sea, except through rail and road links via its neighbors.

The country is sparsely populated. Until the beginning of the nineteenth century most of Zambia's population was agriculturally based. Tribal hierarchy formed the basis for social heritage. Most tribes in Zambia trace their origins from the Luba-Lunda diaspora. The Ngoni of Eastern Province are an offshot of the Mfecane in South Africa. However, from the 1970s much of Zambia's rural population increasingly drifted to urban areas. By the late 1980s, Zambia was among the highly urbanized countries south of the equator. Over fifty percent of its population was living in the few towns along the line of rail from Livingstone in the south to the Copperbelt in the north, and in several provincial capitals and rural towns doted around the country. This urban population was nonetheless concentrated in Lusaka and the Copperbelt towns. This shift inevitably influenced the social, economic and political developments in the country.

Political developments that took place in Africa in the 1980s and 1990s necessitate a rethinking of the analysis and interpretation of the political history of the sub-continent and that of Zambia in particular. The political evolution that started during the process of colonization influenced the nature and pattern of colonial rule. That nature and pattern was "greatly influenced by the ideas of well-established white settlers from their territory south of the Limpopo River."[2] Through the transformation engineered by various forms of colonial administration, the previously traditionally independent rural African people were increasingly incorporated into the widening wage earning economy of the urban areas.

Much has been written about the process of urbanization in colonial Zambia, and the impact it had on the political, social and economic development of the country.[3] Undoubtedly, the process of urbanization was complex. As Epstein has suggested, its analysis required much in-depth research and views from various disciplines.[4] This study, therefore, does not deal with that aspect directly. Because nationalist politics, both during the colonial period and after were greatly influenced by the growth of towns, the political history of Zambia would be incomplete and illusory without a discussion of the impact of urbanization on that process.

Since 1890, when the BSAC began to effectively administer colonial Zambia, the colonial society began to experience division by many cleavages. The most dominant of these was that between Europeans and Africans in the emerging towns. Nonetheless, the colonial Zambian community also experienced cleavages that cut across these racial divisions. Consequently, it was not uncommon to witness coalitions between members of the different races in the territory. This was particularly so after the Colonial Office (CO) took control of Northern Rhodesian affairs. The "protectorate" status that came as part of the package was accepted, albeit reluctantly by the nucleus of white farmers and businessmen.

This book, therefore, seeks to show that despite these divisions between black and white, the two communities often worked together to achieve common objectives. This, however, has previously been down played by most nationalist Africanist scholars. The book also seeks to demonstrate that both settlers and African nationalists were, at different times and for different reasons, engaged in running battles with the Colonial Office. Both wanted to dislodge the Colonial Office from direct involvement in the affairs of the territory. It is from this perspective that it is argued in the book that liberal activism was, but one, avenue through which cooperation between Africans and whites, was actually achieved. As Epstein argued:

> Various devices in the form of economic barriers and social convention may serve to emphasize the separateness of the different racial groups, but there are also bonds of co-operation, which link Africans and Europeans together within a single field of social relations.[5]

It is from this point of view that the book emphasizes the moralizing effect of liberal activism on Northern Rhodesian politics during the era of decolonization. Consequently, the material from which this analysis obtains relates to both African and European communities in the territory.

This study begins by investigating the relevance and impact of liberalism on the "march to political freedom" in colonial Zambia. Second, it seeks to explore the extent to which "Africanism,"[6] as opposed to nationalism, determined the course of this march. "Africanism" rejected liberal ideology as an alternative approach to decolonization. The term "Africanism" was first used by Lord Hailey in his monumental *An African Survey*. He suggested that it seemed advisable at the time "to give prominence to the use of the term ` Africanism' rather than ` nationalism,'"[7] According to Lord Hailey, nationalism as understood in Europe was "a readily recognizable force, ... but as a concept it has associations which make it difficult of application in the conditions of Africa,"[8] He suggested that "taking the African peoples at large, the term "Africanism" seems to describe most nearly the movement which is now so much in evidence in many of the countries dealt with in the survey,"[9] He further noted that the spirit of

"Africanism" had two characteristic phases. One he considered more definite and in that sense more constructive than the other.

The more constructive phase envisaged the attainment of a government dominated by Africans. Such a government would express in its institutions the characteristic spirit of Africa as interpreted by the modern African.[10] This positive interpretation of "Africanism" contrasted with Capricorn Africa Society view, which regarded "Africanism" as one of the dangers facing Africa.[11] Capricorn argued that "the African people lacked the numbers, the technical skill, and the maturity to provide for the timely development of the continent."[12] The Society suggested that this development could be best achieved by combining, on a more extensive scale, western immigration and technology with the latent capacity of the African and other races. It was for this reason that Capricorn sponsored and championed the cause of multi-racialism.

Because this is not a study of trade unions *per se*, unions are discussed in relation to their role in influencing the development of political history of Zambia. Emphasis is, therefore, placed on the study of organizations that endeavored to deal directly with political issues and race relations in the territory.

The book is essentially a revised and expanded version of my PhD thesis that I successfully defended at Dalhousie University in 1991. The thesis covered the period 1949 to 1972 and largely emphasized the origins, growth and impact of liberalism on the decolonization process of colonial Zambia. The thesis demonstrated, not the futility of liberalism, but the usefulness and significance of liberalism in the decolonization of Northern Rhodesia. The current book maintains this central argument.

The book, however, covers a longer period. It starts with the establishment of colonial rule in Northern Rhodesia in 1890, and ends in 2001 when Zambia's Third Republic was ten years old. In this respect, the political developments, changes and continuities from the colonial period to Zambia's return to multi-party politics are discussed. Thus, unlike the thesis, the book covers periods not covered by the thesis.

The data for the book essentially comprises material collected during my fieldwork for the PhD thesis in 1989. The book also has benefited from my most recent research in the National Archives of Zambia (NAZ), the Political Museum and the research that I carried out in Eastern Province of Zambia as part of a team of researchers in 1996 and 1997. The research in Eastern Province was essentially concerned with people's participation or nonparticipation in elections. The focus of that study was the electoral process, especially after the reintroduction of multi-party political system in Zambia in 1991. Much of the material for the book, however, came largely from NAZ in Lusaka, the UNIP archives in Lusaka and the Public Record Office (PRO) in London.

The political History of Zambia is so vast a subject that no single volume can hope to be comprehensive. This book, therefore, is inevitably a small contribution to this vast subject. My aim has been to provide for students, academics and the general reader interested in the political history of Zambia an alternative interpretation.

The book examines multi-racial liberalism in Central Africa through the examination of the Capricorn Africa Society, a multi-racial organization founded in Southern Rhodesia in 1949. The study is situated in the context of nationalist fervor in colonial Zambia. Because Capricorn ideas generated debate about liberal democracy and political pluralism, the study examines Zambia's post independence period in order to provide an overview of the failure of liberal democracy, which is assessed in relation to the nature of the colonial experience and the way the colonial state functioned. The book is about the contribution of liberal activism. The main interest is the conception of liberalism as understood in the contemporary British Central Africa, and the crucial role it played in generating ideas about the future of liberal democracy.

This revisionist-post-nationalist interpretation of both Capricorn and liberal activism in colonial Zambia concludes that although liberalism had faded by 1964, Capricorn conceptions about democratic principles and the need for good governance continued to inform political processes. The book sees multi-racialism as an attempt to foster new forms of civil society that were capable of coping with demands of the colonial and postcolonial politics. The study also suggests that the failure of liberal democracy after 1964 reflects the legacy of colonial rule, and not necessarily a problem of postindependence political leadership. The book notes that the multiplicity of political parties after 1991 have generally worked against the consolidation of democracy in Zambia. It further examines the role of Non Governmental Organizations and civil society in the democratization process, and questions the usage of political ethnicity as tool for analyzing the political history of Zambia.

The study observes that the ruling Movement for Multiparty Democracy (MMD) was over represented in parliament during the first ten years of the Third Republic. Thus creating a *de facto* one party state, which in a developing country like Zambia has serious political implications for democracy. It is in this respect that the book suggests that mobocracy seemed to have taken root in the Third Republic and increasingly become prevalent in the Zambian political process across all political parties. This was particularly evident within the MMD and the United National Independence Party where the mob ideology seemed to dictate the political process. This was demonstrated by MMD's amendment of its constitution to facilitate President Chiluba's third term bid, and the leadership crisis in UNIP.

During the greater part of former President Kenneth David Kaunda's leadership, he attempted to lead the country through the principles of the Philosophy of Humanism. Although President Kaunda eloquently articulated the tenants of the Philosophy of Humanism and its implementation in Zambia,[13] the philosophy never gained support in the country. The Philosophy was never fully implemented, and consequently its impact on the political history of Zambia is minimal. Nevertheless, there is no doubt that President Kaunda's political behavior in the political arena was shaped by his strong belief in the Philosophy of Humanism. This study, however, has not attempted an analysis of the impact of the philosophy on Zambian politics.

To experts whose knowledge of sections of this book is wide, I acknowledge that the complexity of the problems and subtlety of arguments have been simplified. It could not have been otherwise.

Notes

1. Bertha Osei-Hwedie, "The role of Ethnicity in Multiparty Politics in Malawi and Zambia," *Journal of Contemporary African Studies*, 16, 2 (1998), p. 228.

2 Richard Hall, *Zambia 1890-1964: The Colonial Period* (London: Longmans, 1976), p.vii.

3 See for example, A.L. Epstein, *Politics in an Urban African Community* (Manchester: Manchester University Press, 1958).

4. Epstein, *Politics in an urban African Community*, p. xii.

5. Epstein, *Politics in an Urban African Community*, p. xii.

6. According M. G. de Winton, "To argue that the growth of "nationalism" hastened on political advance has no reality when applied to tropical African territories. The creation of a sense of national identity was one of the problems of nation building. A much more likely source of common motive was the spirit of Africanism, that is an understandable desire to get rid of the control of the white man." (M. G. de Winton, "Decolonization and the Westminster Model," in A. H. M. Kirk-Greene (ed.), *The Transfer of Power: The Colonial Administration in the Age of Decolonization*, Kidlington Oxford: Oxford University Press, 1979, p. 184). De Winton's concept

of Africanism is not far from Mazrui's pigmentational self-determination referred to earlier.

7. Lord Hailey, *An African Survey: A Study of Problems Arising in Africa South of the Sahara*, (London: Oxford University Press, 1957), p. 251.

8. Hailey, *An African Survey*, p. 251.

9. Hailey, *An African Survey*, p. 252.

10. Hailey, *An African Survey*, p. 252.

11. PRO, DO 35/3603/9, Acting President CAS to Secretary of State for the Colonies, Oliver Lyttelton, 2 November 1951, p. 5. According to Capricorn the "unhealthy and dangerous kind of African nationalism has been given additional fillip by the faulty timing of the Gold Coast experiment, the unfortunate behaviour of British politicians towards British settlers in this part of Africa..."

12. NAZ, NR 8/7/38, The Salisbury Declarations, 1952, para. 3.

13. Kenneth D. Kaunda, *Humanism in Zambia and a Guide To Its Implementation*, Part I and II (Lusaka: Government Printer, 1974).

Chapter 1

BRITISH SOUTH AFRICA COMPANY RULE AND COLONIAL OFFICE ADMINISTRATION ERA

INTRODUCTION

Two periods can be identified in the political history of colonial Zambia. These are from 1890 to 1923 when the country was acquired and administered by the British South Africa Company (BSA Company), and from 1924 to 1964 when it was under Colonial Office rule. It was one of the territories in Africa occupied by Britain during the late-nineteenth-century scramble for Africa. The initial inroads were made in Barotseland through the 1890 Barotse Concession to Cecil Rhodes' BSAC ostensibly as a representative of Queen Victoria.[1] Through a series of dubious treaties by BSAC representatives, the Company gained the rest of Northern Rhodesia by the end of 1891.

Although other European powers had by the end of 1891 recognized the BSA Company's right to occupy and exploit areas north of the Zambezi River, actual occupation was slow and at times violent.[2] At the request of the BSAC, Northern Rhodesia was split into North-Eastern Rhodesia and North-Western Rhodesia. They were linked to the outside world by different routes and had different origins. From inception Northern Rhodesia was conceived as a tropical dependency and not a settler colony. This decision had a considerable impact on the later political developments of the territory.

The imperial government assumed greater powers in North-Western Rhodesia than it did in North-Eastern Rhodesia. This was reflected through the imperial government's control over the appointment of the administrator and his officials. These were appointed by the High Commissioner at the BSA Company's recommendation and not by the BSA

Company.[3] By contrast, however, North-Eastern Rhodesia was directly under an administrator and officials appointed by the BAS Company, subject to approval only by the Secretary of State.[4] While the administrator of North-Eastern Rhodesia could legislate, subject to the approval of the commissioner for British Central Africa, his counterpart needed the assent of the High Commissioner for South Africa before he could legislate. In either case, however, the Secretary of State retained the right to disallow all legislation, while ensuring certain safeguards for Africans. Here we see the idea of the trusteeship policy already in place, though not clearly conceptualized.

Arguably, therefore, the imperial government had considerable powers on paper and in theory. Yet, in practical terms, the imperial government exerted very limited influence. Consequently, the elaborate constitutional differences between North-Eastern and North-Western Rhodesia proved to be of little value. This was largely because there was no close supervision on the ground because the imperial government did not have any officer in Northern Rhodesia until 1911. Furthermore, there were no staff in either Zomba or Pretoria to deal specifically with the affairs of Northern Rhodesia. As L.H. Gann has shown "In 1911 the High Commissioner's Staff at Pretoria consisted of the Imperial Secretary, a secretary, an accountant and ten typists and copyists. Most of the time of the office was taken up with the three British Protectorates in South Africa."[5] Thus in both North-Eastern Rhodesia and North-Western Rhodesia the imperial government relied entirely on information supplied by its commissioners who themselves were preoccupied with the affairs of South Africa and Nyasaland. Decisions were therefore based on reports submitted by the BSA Company administrators.

Colonial Zambia was officially created in 1911 when the separate administrations of North-Western Rhodesia and North-Eastern Rhodesia, first divided by the Kafue River and then by the railroad line, were amalgamated by the BSA Company to economize. In that year a resident commissioner who was answerable to the High Commissioner was appointed.[6] The territory was controlled from Livingstone near Victoria Falls.[7] The BSA Company ruled the vast region with financial supprt from Cecil Rhodes. However, its powers in Northern Rhodesia were in theory limited because of the negative effects of the Jameson Raid. The Colonial Office felt that it was not advisable to strengthen the Company's hand in Northern Rhodesia.[8]

However, as noted above, the BSA Company local administrator was virtually left with a great deal of independence. This was also necessitated by the fact that the Board of Directors in London left much of the administrative work to their administrators. The directors were more concerned with commercial matters and issues affecting the BSA Company's land and mineral rights. For almost three decades, therefore, the BSAC through the man on the spot ruled Northern Rhodesia for the British Crown.[9]

Initially, the BSA Company had little interest in Northern Rhodesia. Despite the Company's encouragement to settle white farmers in the territory, it was never envisaged that Northern Rhodesia would develop into a white colony in the same way as in Kenya, where European settlement was adopted as an official colonial policy as early as 1902.[10] Nonetheless, between 1904 and 1911 a total of 159 farms had been established between Kalomo in the south and Broken Hill (Kabwe) in the north. Yet, as Ian Henderson ably argued, Northern Rhodesia's "original *raison d'être* was as a labour reserve for the developing white areas of Southern Rhodesia and South Africa",[11] at least up to the mid-1920s.

The BSA Company faced financial problems during much of its administration of the territory. Therefore, in order to address this problem, it introduced the hut tax in 1900 and 1904 in North-Eastern and North-Western Rhodesia respectively. Initially, Africans resited paying. However, because the Company involved chiefs in the enforcement and collection of taxes, a considerable number of people paid their taxes regularly. It should be pointed out, however, that there existed much coercion in the collection of taxes.

By the 1920s Northern Rhodesia's position began to shift from that of a purely black colony like British colonies in West Africa to the uncomfortable middle position of a multiracial colony. The political development of Northern Rhodesia was shaped by Cecil Rhodes belief that the territory should be ruled by whites, developed by Indians and worked by Africans. This was essentially the philosophy behind British colonialism in Central Africa. Company rule was most unlikely to survive for very long because the Company was not really designed to rule. As a commercial company its desire was profit and not to spend on administration. Because Europeans had to be encouraged to come to Northern Rhodesia, they could not be heavily taxed. Doing so would have discouraged many from coming. It was in this respect that the development of the mining industry led to significant political and administrative changes in Northern Rhodesia. As Gann observed, "Northern Rhodesian enterprise was financed to some extent by mining interests with investments in the south; many of its mining pioneers had worked in Southern Rhodesia;

and the whole economy of Northern Rhodesia as of Southern Rhodesia came to depend on the development of its mineral resources."[12] Mining, therefore, became the backbone of Northern Rhodesia's social, economic and political development.

The discovery of large quantities of copper sulfide ores in 1925 at Ndola, in the area just to the south of the Belgian Congo border, allowed use of the so-called flotation process discovered in 1911, for the profitable mining of sulfide ores. The rise in copper prices in the 1920s made investment in the copper mines of Northern Rhodesia economically feasible. Large mining companies were attracted to the area, which developed into Northern Rhodesia's Copperbelt. The emergence of the Copperbelt had three important consequences.

First, it attracted increased white migration, including large numbers of skilled and semiskilled mine workers, many of whom came from South Africa.[13] Table I summarizes the composition of the European population in Northern Rhodesia by country of birth between 1911 and 1956.

Table 1: European Population by Country of Birth, 1911 to 1956

Country	1911	1921	1931	1956
Northern Rhodesia	83	397	1,291	11,319
Southern Rhodesia	43	193	906	3,398
South Africa	366	1,321	5,776	26,569
Great Britain	679	1,317	4,219	17,088
European Countries	205	217	798	3,955
Other Countries	121	189	856	2,948
TOTAL	1,497	3,634	13,846	65,277

Source: George Kay, *A Social Geography of Zambia: A Survey of Population Patterns in a Developing Country* (London: University of London Press, 1967), p. 29.

Many British-born persons crossed the Zambezi after spending some time in South Africa or Southern Rhodesia or both, and they were thus subjected for a period to the climate of opinion in a settler-dominated country before coming to Northern Rhodesia. Almost all shared the determination to protect their privileged financial and social position by preserving a white monopoly of the more highly paid jobs.

Second, copper mining stimulated trade, leading to considerable development not only on the Copperbelt towns but also of the whole area along the railroad line. The railroad line area, from Livingstone in the south to the Belgian Congo border in the north, became an area of intense economic development and white domination. Uneven development grew as the railroad area flourished while most of the country remained poverty-stricken, though much less directly affected by white domination and racialism.

Last, the development of the Copperbelt attracted a large African labor force, first for short periods, but later many settling almost permanently in compounds that were developed in the mining towns. Because of cultural differences and the superiority complex of the white labor force, Africans were generally treated with disrespect. Gann, for example, thought it understandable that white foremen "considered a severe discipline, backed sometimes by corporal punishment" a suitable remedy.[14] Undoubtedly, this perception by whites, irrespective of their origin, made mining unpopular among Africans in the early years of the development of the mining industry.

Africans near the mines preferred to sell grain to raise tax money instead of working in the mines. To assist the mines acquire the much-needed African labor, in 1909 taxation was raised from 5s to 10s (£1/5 to £1/2) in the Copperbelt area. Thus, political pressure instead of economic incentives was used to force Africans into wage labour in the mines and elsewhere. Because the system never really benefited Africans, shortage of African labor was a major constraint in the early years.

The demand for skilled and semiskilled labor, with competition from neighboring mines, led to labor stabilization on the Copperbelt. J.W. Davidson estimates that about 30,000 Africans worked in the mines in 1930.[15] The urbanization process had began. Women and children were part of the Copperbelt population.[16]

With insufficient white workers in Northern Rhodesia during this period, some African workers had better opportunities in skilled and clerical work than was the case in the countries to the south. African participation in the labor market, both in the mines and in the clerical ranks of the civil service, led to the eventual emergence of a "small elite with the education to understand modern political methods" and ready to take a lead in the development of modern African nationalism.[17]

With this increased European population came an increased European participation in local politics. The white population of Northern Rhodesia sought membership on various quasipolitical bodies from which they sought and secured great influence on the colonial officials toward the colony. It is worth noting that European participation in local politics developed over a long period and that the process itself was influenced by both fear and the desire to be free from BSA Company administration.

BRITISH COLONIAL POLICY AND SETTLER POLITICS, 1924-1954

Colonial Zambia's political history, therefore, is essentially a story of race relations characterized by the doctrines of paramountcy, then partnership; European demands, first for amalgamation with Southern Rhodesia and later for a federation of the two Rhodesias and Nyasaland; and African responses to these initiatives. The stage for these political events was largely the Copperbelt and the railroad line that formed the economic base of the territory. However, it was in Livingstone that whites first showed any interest in politics at all. Nonetheless, the initial political dispensations were the work of one man, L.F. Moore, who started a newspaper, the *Livingstone Mail*, in 1906. He used the paper to air his political views. Administrators were forced to begin listening to the views of the whites.

Though the seeds of African and European nationalisms were sown as the territory developed and as the two communities became increasingly interdependent, it was the European[18] assault on the doctrine of paramountcy and the demands for closer association of the Rhodesias that gave prominence to the two nationalisms. The emergence of liberalism as a political force in the late 1940s and early 1950s was an attempt to bridge the gap and provide a middle ground in the racially polarized political development of the territory.

Therefore, to appreciate the development of liberalism, with its commitment to multiracial politics in colonial Zambia in the late 1950s, it is necessary to examine the period before 1953. In this earlier period the economic, political and social structures that determined Zambia's colonial and postcolonial political history were established. The colonial state[19] *par excellence* emerged after 1924 with the Colonial Office takeover of Northern Rhodesia from the British South Africa Company. The African colonial state was a particular form of imperial dependency and existed largely as an appendage of sovereign European states.

> It lacked a pre-existing revenue base; was organised swiftly in an intensely competitive imperial environment; contained a more extensive cultural project than most other forms; and was organised at an historical moment when European states themselves were far more comprehensive, institutionally and doctrinally elaborated polities than in earlier centuries.[20]

During the formative stages of the colonial state, many changes occurred in British colonial policy in Northern Rhodesia, especially between 1924 and1948. These changes included the deemphasizing of paramountcy of African interests and the adoption of the partnership principle as a prelude to multiracial liberal politics.

The changes also reflected the entry of Africans into wage labor that created new relationships and attitudes among Africans themselves. These new relationships and attitudes not only determined how efficiently Africans worked but also their relationship with employers of African labor and the colonial administration. By the 1940s African workers had discovered their power that forced colonial officials to begin thinking of articulating "a forward-looking colonial social policy—while trying to contain workers' reactions to the strains of their daily lives."[21] Indeed, the change from African paramountcy to partnership should be assessed in terms of officials' belief that "Africans could be modern."[22] From an earlier belief in the superiority of the "untouched" rural Africans over the urbanized, semiskilled, semiliterate and semi-Europeanized officials gradually changed their attitudes and developed an increasingly negative view of Africans who were not modern. Thus "the focus on social and economic development legitimized the European standards of living as a reference point for the aspirations of Africans",[23] as well as a basis for partnership.

When the Colonial Office assumed administrative responsibilities in colonial Zambia in 1924, the white population was relatively small. However, this was soon to change. The man responsible for this change was the first governor of the protectorate after the BSA Company had relinquished its rule on 1 April 1924. Governor Herbert Stanley, who began his African career in South Africa, envisaged a large white-controlled dominion stretching from the Cape to Kenya in which the Rhodesias were to play a key role. To encourage white settlement in Northern Rhodesia he set aside blocks of land for European use.[24] Governor Stanley put in place measures that encouraged white settlement in the territory. Inadeventantly, as the numbers of white settlers increased, they began to demand a share in the political administration of the territory. This development soon brought them into direct conflict with African social, economic and political aspiration and interests.

CONSTITUTIONAL DEVELOPMENT, 1924-1954

While African nationalism in colonial Zambia was a post-World War II development, it was white nationalism that played a key role in the constitutional development of the territory since the 1920s. When the Colonial Office took over the administration of colonial Zambia from the BSA Company administration in 1924, it replaced the Advisory Council that had been established in 1918 by a Legislative Council (Legco) with a color-blind franchise with property qualifications and limited to British subjects, which ensured that few African voters would qualify given that virtually all were British Protected Persons. The color-blind franchise effectively guaranteed control of the five elected seats in the fourteen-member house to the tiny group of white settlers.

The constitution of colonial Zambia was laid down by Her Majesty's Government in an Order in Council of 1924 and provided for an Executive Council and a Legislative Council. Constitutional development over the years gave the unofficials (European settlers) first an equal strength (in 1938) and later a majority (in 1945) on the Legco. Special representation for Africans was not introduced until 1938 when a European member (Sir Stewart Gore-Browne) was nominated by the governor, according to the constitution, to represent African interests in the Legco. It was not until 1948 that two Africans were first appointed on the Council to represent African interests. In the same year the number of European unofficials nominated to represent African interests was reduced to two, thus bringing the total number of members representing African interests to four. During the same period there were ten elected European members and ten officials on the Legco. In 1954 the number of African members on the Council was increased to four. This brought the number of African representatives to six, including the two nominated European unofficials.

There is no doubt whatsoever that European settlers were in a powerful position on the Legco. Nonetheless, "the formal power of the whites on the Legislative Council was not so important as their informal power, through public opinion and through membership of government advisory committees."[25] or through interest groups such as the Capricorn Africa Society (CAS). Table II summarizes the changes in the composition of the Legislative Council from 1924 to 1954.

Table 2: Legislative Council, 1924-1954

	1924	1929	1938	1940	1945	1948	1954
Official Members	9	9	8	9	9	10	8
Unofficial Members: Elected	5	7	7	8	8	10	12
Nominated	-	-	1	1	5	2	2
African	-	-	-	-	-	2	4
TOTAL	5	7	8	9	13	14	18
TOTAL Members	14	16	16	18	22	24	26

Source: PRO DO 35/4636/333 Revised Draft White Paper, February 1958.

It is evident from Table II that the frequent constitutional changes since 1924 had one major purpose and consequence: the increase of European unofficial participation in the Legco. It is plausible to suggest that the Colonial Office was using the Legco arithmetic to prevent the emergence of a simple majority of European elected unofficials, which would have made responsible government seem obviously the next step.

The position on the Executive Council was equally revealing. Until the end of 1939, when European unofficial members were first appointed to the Executive Council, the government was conducted entirely by officials. It was ten years later that an unofficial first held a portfolio. Their number was increased to four in 1954 and they all held ministerial positions.[26] Table III summarizes the composition of the Executive Council from 1924 to 1954.

Table 3: Executive Council, 1924-1954

	1924	1929	1938	1940	1945	1948	1954
Official Members	4	5	5	5	5	7	5
Unofficial Members without portfolio	-	-	-	4	3	4*	-
Unofficial Members with portfolio	-	-	-	-	-	-	4*
TOTAL MEMBERSHIP	4	5	5	9	8	11	9

Source: PRO DO 35/4636/333 Revised Draft White Paper, February 1958.

* Including one member of Legco nominated to represent African interests. Two elected members undertook portfolios in 1949. None of the members of the Executive Council was an African during this period.

Until 1958 the franchise law in Northern Rhodesia practically excluded Africans, all of whom (save for those who had been granted naturalization) had the status of British Protected Persons. Further, the qualification for registration as a voter remained almost unchanged since 1925. Although the value of money in 1954 was much lower than it was in 1925, the income qualification of £200 a year was very much above the earning power of the vast majority of the African population. This, coupled with the requirement that a voter must be a British subject, resulted in the somewhat ludicrous figure of only eleven Africans on the voters' role.[27] Consequently all seats on the Legco filled by direct election were occupied by Europeans. African members on Legco were returned through an electoral college system culminating in the African Representative Council (ARC). The governor was bound to appoint those whom the ARC selected from among its members to be members of Legco.

Inevitably, the franchise law was among the most contentious issues in the constitutional development of colonial Zambia. In fact, the nature of constitutional development regarding the franchise pointed the political direction of the country. That was the essence of the dilemma between continued racial representation on the Legco or the introduction of modern Western democracy.

Perhaps it ought to be pointed out that party politics never really developed in colonial Zambia during this period.[28] The race question therefore dominated the constitutional development of the country. Racial representation on the Legco was not exactly conducive to party politics. The Northern Rhodesia African Congress formed in 1948 was inspired more by the closer association issue than by territorial politics.[29] This is why in 1944, when Gore-Browne suggested that Africans should be elected by African Representative Councils for nomination as African representatives on the Legco, Governor Eubule John Waddington thought that suggestion premature. The governor argued in his response that the proposal if accepted would necessitate canvassing, thus importing "politics" into "native" representations prematurely. He further pointed out that if elections were adopted many Africans would want African rather than European representatives and that it was also premature to expect them to represent themselves effectively on the Legco.[30] Simply stated, Governor Waddington did not think that Africans were ready for a modern form of constitutional democracy because Africans and the few Europeans in the territory had not yet met the requirements of the "cardinal principle of British policy": that colonies with politically advanced populations could not continue to be administered from London.

The settlers on the Legco believed otherwise. As far as they were concerned they were sufficiently prepared to shoulder the responsibilities of self-government. Actually they were already exercising a disproportionate influence in the politics of the territory.[31] In fact, whatever the feeling of the government about settlers, it was already giving them an increasing share of political power. Despite this, settlers continued to demand responsible government.

Throughout 1949 and 1950 the question of franchise for British Protected Persons dominated debate in both the ARC and the Legco. Unofficials were instrumental in opposing the enfranchisement of British Protected Persons because they felt that doing so would be detrimental to the development of the country. They consistently argued that not many Africans were able to take an intelligent part in politics.[32] Although this may have been true, the real reason, however, was the fear by white

settlers that extending the vote to British Protected Persons would ultimately remove their political dominance. Therefore, from 1945 onward,
the constitutional changes that took place in colonial Zambia reflected
that objective.

The Colonial Office was equally reluctant to give political power to
what they believed were "politically immature" Africans. The grant of an
unofficial majority in 1945, though designed to buyoff settler demands
for amalgamation with Southern Rhodesia, certainly gave momentum to
the process of settler ascendancy to political power in colonial Zambia.
It was felt that the gentleman's agreement during the war, by which unofficials did not raise the question of amalgamation, was not going to hold
for very long. In anticipation, the United Kingdom government decided
in 1944 to grant a new constitution that gave the unofficials a majority
on the Legco.[33] Later the Secretary of State for the colonies informed the
Northern Rhodesia governor that Africans would continue to be represented by members nominated by the governor until the recently created
regional councils had gained sufficient experience. Once a territorial
council was set up it would send African members to the Legco.[34]

It was hoped the ARC would provide the necessary training to
Africans before entering national politics. The idea was to inculcate into
ARC members values and principles of parliamentary democracy on
the Westminster model the parliament was the supreme representative
body. Its members were elected on the basis of universal adult suffrage.
The emphasis was squarely placed on multiracial politics so that ARC
members could emerge as champions of liberal politics in the country.[35]

Yet another limiting factor in the constitutional development of colonial Zambia was the dilemma between adopting a modern form of franchise on the Westminster model and maintaining racial representation.
The former option would have led to African voters swamping European
voters (a threat to European dominance), while the latter would have led
to an "arthritic condition" for Africans.[36] The 1953 constitutional talks in
London failed to resolve the initial dilemma and the talks failed. Africans
and Europeans wanted diametrically opposed changes in the constitution. During the preliminary and private talks, Africans put forward to
the Secretary of State for the colonies "extreme" demands that would
have given them a complete majority on the Legco. Africans wanted the
enfranchisement of British Protected Persons and an African majority on
the Council.

When the Secretary of State asked Africans to modify their demands,
they settled for parity with the elected members. Although parity was

an eventual goal of colonial policy toward colonial Zambia, it was not considered practical politics in 1954 and was therefore rejected. On the other hand elected members opposed the admission of British Protected Persons to the common voters' roll. They in turn wanted an increase in the number of elected members of Legco by two and a reduction of officials on the Executive Council from seven to four.

Because the views of the two sides were irreconcilable, Colonial Secretary Oliver Lyttelton made an arbitral award that both sides asserted was highly unsatisfactory, as was perhaps inevitable under the circumstances. The award involved no political transfer of power as such—officials still held the balance between unofficials and Africans. The award made the following provisions:

(a) Legislative Council

Elected Members (Europeans) were increased from ten to twelve and African Members from two to four (and a fifth would be nominated as one of the unofficials when it was appropriate to do so). Officials were reduced from nine to eight.

(b) Executive Council

All members of the Executive Council were to hold portfolios.

Lyttelton argued that the performance of African members on Legco was rather unimpressive and that therefore they should not join the Executive Council, which effectively formed a government front bench in the Legco.[37]

A communiqué issued after the talks announcing the award revealed the long-term objective of the United Kingdom government, namely that it looked forward to the day when racial considerations in the affairs of the territory would sink to a negligible level. Then it would be possible to move toward a democratic system based on a widened franchise.[38] Essentially the Colonial Office was advocating a system by which Africans advanced gradually towards equal representation. Meanwhile property and education qualifications would be adjusted from time to time to avoid one race (Africans) swamping the other.[39] This emphasis on qualified franchise as opposed to universal adult suffrage was to become the basis for the development of liberalism in the country.

Although under this arrangement the *status quo* would be maintained and effectively safeguarded, Roy Welensky still complained and threatened to resign from the government to form an opposition to fight for settler political power in the country. He saw the award as an act of appeasement toward Africans and an affront to Europeans.[40] Sokota and Dauti Yamba, the two African members of the Legco, were equally unhappy with the contents of the award, which they saw as a surrender to the settler community in the country. Worse still, they were disappointed that the award made no provision for an African to join the Executive Council.[41] Evidently, both camps returned to colonial Zambia quite dissatisfied and ready for a showdown.

Sokota and Yamba did not waste time. In early 1954 they proposed that British Protected Persons should be enfranchised without first becoming British subjects, as was currently the constitutional requirement. In response, the colonial secretary pointed out that Africans could not have it both ways: They were asking for the franchise to be extended to them while asking for guarantees that there should be no increase in qualifications. In this regard the colonial secretary observed that:

> Both races were necessary to the country and capital should not be frightened away. Advance must come by evolution and should be worked out.... Universal adult suffrage would add nothing to Northern Rhodesia. Capital would go. That was not to say that there would be no change, but Africans could not have it both ways and must see the difficulties. It was absurd for Africans to seek a majority on the Executive Council. Our problems could not be solved by reiteration of ideas that would mean ruination of Northern Rhodesia.[42]

This statement was significant for two reasons. First, it reflected the economic concern of the Colonial Office, and the responsibility of the colonial secretary to ensure that colonies were developed for the benefit of the empire and of the world economy.[43] Hence the reluctance to recommend constitutional changes that would "frighten away" capital.

Second, the statement reflected the liberal character of the Colonial Office regarding the process of change and devolution of political power in multiracial colonies—hence the emphasis on carefully worked out evolutionary advancement of Africans. The African representatives were not at all impressed and wanted to discuss further constitutional changes, but they were told that they had to wait for 1959 when further constitutional changes would be considered. Meanwhile they were advised that they had five years to show their maturity, learn to get used to being unpopular and saying "No."[ar]

ORIGINS OF AFRICAN NATIONALISM, 1923-1948

African nationalism began essentially as a reformist movement, which "sought not the overthrow of the system, which appeared secure and permanent, but its liberalization."[45] According to Ibbo D.J. Mandaza, African nationalism developed as a political response to imperialism and its racial ideology of white supremacy.[46] Mandaza added that:

> For all its apparent militancy and anti-colonialist stance, African nationalism is essentially a liberal ideology. This is not surprising since liberalism itself is part of the capitalist ideology and as the capitalist mode of production is dominant in the colonial society, it follows that the capitalist (or bourgeois) ideology is also the dominant ideology—as the ideology of the ruling class—in such a society, and penetrates the entire fabric of the colonial society, through economic, political and social structures, which emerged during colonisation. More specifically, liberalism (as part of the capitalist ideology) is imparted into the colonised through the colonialist educational system, the Christian religion and various other forms of cultural and ideological expressions of colonial life.[47]

Few can deny that initially African nationalism was essentially a struggle for individual rights by African emerging elites. They were mainly interested in some limited access to power—both political and economic.

However, settler demands for self-government on the Southern Rhodesia model, before Africans achieved even limited access to power, transformed what was really a reformist movement into a militant organization, which adopted a seemingly populist ideology. This transformation gained currency because of the specter of federation that Africans feared and opposed.[48] Nonetheless, there was never a clear break with the past. In spite of its "apparent militancy and the anti-colonialist stance," African nationalism expressed itself through liberal rhetoric as a struggle for the inalienable rights of man. Yet, the extent to which liberal rhetoric by nationalist parties was a reflection of the influence of liberal organizations has so far been ignored. Instead, liberalism has continued to be summarily dismissed as "Africa's lost cause."[49]

FROM WELFARE SOCIETIES TO POLITICAL PARTIES

It is a truism that World War II greatly altered labor relations in the Rhodesias and helped to precipitate nationalist consciousness. In response to the imperial cause, many whites joined the imperial forces. Many Africans, too, were enlisted and shipped to South East Asia where

African troops were used in the Burma campaign. In colonial Zambia, the departure of some white workers opened up some jobs, previously reserved for whites, to Africans.

On another level, the Northern Rhodesia government greatly expanded public information services; publications in African languages, as well as in English broadcasting,[50] and mobile cinemas mixed propaganda films with Charlie Chaplin.[51] The propaganda was intended to enlist African sympathy for the imperial war effort. Inadvertently, as Rosaleen Smyth argued, the war news and propaganda "hastened the emergence of an African political voice."[52] The government began to pay more attention than ever before to African opinion. The imperial authorities, on their part, were eager to show and perhaps prove that they were custodians of the ideas of liberty. In a parliamentary statement of 13 July 1943 Oliver Stanley defined his goal as "self-government within the framework of the British Empire."[53] The famous Hailey Report vividly described the rising tide of "African racial consciousness" in the absence as yet of nationalist movements. He suggested that there was an urgent need to create an African political class that was more capable of managing a modern state than the existing native authorities and local councils.[54] In colonial Zambia the concern was addressed through the establishment of the ARC in 1946. The ARC was expected to provide the training of African politicians as much as it was intended to inculcate into them liberal ideas and values.[55]

Meanwhile the settler community, whose contribution to the war effort had earned it enhanced influence within the colonial state, began to claim more political power and responsibility for African affairs. In fact the shortage of manpower during the war led to the appointment of settlers to important civil service jobs.[56] On another level they intensified their campaign for a federation of the Rhodesias and Nyasaland in the interest of economic development and political stability. These developments, together with the awareness aroused by war propaganda, gave rise to modern African nationalism—first to resist settler demands for responsible government in colonial Zambia, and to oppose European proposals for closer association of the Rhodesias, and later to demand independence. The Africans' vicarious experience of war accelerated the ripening African political consciousness in colonial Zambia. War propaganda further made Africans familiar with the grammar of Western politics, thereby making them politically strong.

Nonetheless the origins of nationalist activity in colonial Zambia are fluid. As in West Africa, nationalist activities were in response to Colonial

Office policy as well as to local conditions. Lord Hailey observed in 1938 that there was a noticeable absence of nationalists, ("emergent Africans" as leaders of development) while the future of the trusteeship system that relied on Native Authorities (Indirect Rule) appeared bleak.[57] The Native Authority system was deemed less efficient as an agent of development and called for urgent revamping if it were to fit in any scheme involving an elected legislature. In colonial Zambia the Native Authority system was first introduced in 1929. It was later extended to the Copperbelt in 1938 when Urban Advisory Councils were established.[58] The Urban Advisory Councils on the Copperbelt were composed of members partly elected by tribal representatives and by boss boys, and partly of members nominated by the District Commissioner. The function of these councils was to keep the District Commissioner in touch with African opinion, to advise him on matters of African welfare and to make government policy known to Africans generally.

In keeping with the concerns raised by Lord Hailey in his 1940-1941 report, submitted in November 1940 and partly "to enable Africans to contribute more effectively to the development of general, as distinct from purely local policy," eight regional councils were formed in 1943-1944. The regional councils were composed of urban delegates elected by Urban Advisory Councils and of rural delegates chosen by Native Authorities. The sessions of these Regional Councils were chaired by provincial commissioners. The system was further developed in 1946 with the creation of the African Representative Council for the whole territory. Its membership was drawn from the eight regional councils. In 1948 the ARC began to elect two of its members for appointment by the governor to the Legislative Council.

Meanwhile, alongside these government initiatives, mission-educated Africans developed their own political bodies that sought to participate in the political process. As Henry S. Meebelo suggested, "the seed-pot of the thrustful African politics in post-war Northern Rhodesia" was in 1923 when mission-educated Africans formed the first Native Welfare Association at Mwenzo in the Northern Province.[59] The association lasted only for five years; nonetheless, this was not the end of the movement. Some migrant workers from the Northern Province became leading champions of the movement in urban areas of colonial Zambia. In May 1946 representatives of fourteen welfare associations scattered across the country met at Broken Hill and formed the Federation of African Societies of Northern Rhodesia (FAS).[60] The meeting elected Dauti Yamba, a schoolteacher of Luanshya, as the first president of FAS, which was established in order

> to create cooperation and mutual understanding between
> constituent societies of rural and urban areas in Northern
> Rhodesia ... to speak for and on behalf of Africans ... and ...
> to cooperate as much as possible with the Government of
> Northern Rhodesia with a view to the continuance of good
> government ... to promote and support any work which is
> calculated to ensure good feeling between Europeans and
> Africans in general.[61]

The fundamental aim of FAS was to secure improved positions for its members within the colonial system. FAS was not a nationalist movement in the strict sense of the word. It served only as the base upon which the first African nationalist party was to be built.

FAS held its first general meeting in Lusaka in late October, after which a deputation met the Assistant Chief Secretary for Native Affairs to request official recognition by the government and five seats on the newly formed ARC. The government was reluctant to give the FAS official recognition, though the Executive Council "decided that a special effort should be made not to antagonize the Society's leaders."[62] In the end, however, the demands were rejected after the government's position was personally explained by the Secretary for Native Affairs. Nevertheless, there was always an overlap between the officially instituted bodies and those that arose purely from African initiatives. Most of the founders of the FAS were also associated with various Provincial Councils and Urban Advisory Councils.

FAS spent the next two years dealing with two explosive issues: the settler demand for self-government and for closer association with Southern Rhodesia. African nationalism was given a jolt in January 1948 when Sir Stewart Gore-Browne, who since 1938 had served as one of the unofficial members in the Legco nominated to represent African interests, surprised both Africans and the government by mking a motion demanding responsible government for Northern Rhodesia. The demand was coupled with a threat that unofficials might be forced to use their existing power to paralyze the government if their demands were not met.[63]

In March, Gore-Browne again shocked Africans when he came out in support of federation between the two Rhodesias as the only arrangement that would satisfy Central Africa's whites, protect the rights of Africans and secure the advantages of mutual cooperation.[64] These demands antagonized both the ARC and FAS. Both organizations condemned them. A nominated member representing African interests might be forgiven for exercising his personal judgment when and if African opinion was split and divided on any issue. However on no other issues could

Africans have been more united than opposing responsible government as then envisaged and federation. Gore-Browne symbolized the arrogance of "the white man knows best". Africans became convinced that settlers could not be trusted.

FAS held its second and last general meeting in July 1948, during which it was decided by a unanimous vote to rename the organization the Northern Rhodesia African Congress (NRAC) with Godwin Mbikusita Lewanika, an aristocrat from Barotseland, as the first president. The other officials of the congress were Robinson N. Nabulyato, a schoolteacher at Kafue Training Institute (General Secretary), Mateyo Kakumbi (Treasurer), L.M. Lipalile (Vice-President), J. Richmond (Assistant Secretary), and George W. Charles Kaluwa (Assistant Treasurer).[65] This was the first political party formed by Africans in colonial Zambia.

In spite of the circumstances that precipitated the founding of the Congress, the organization remained essentially reformist. It sought not the overthrow of the system, but its liberalization. The N.R.A.C. became the African National Congress (ANC) in August 1951 when Lewanika was replaced by Harry Mwaanga Nkumbula following a nineteen-to-five-vote victory for the party leadership. Lewanika's defeat was attributed to his lukewarm attitude toward the closer association proposals of that year. While the Congress opposed federation, it still affirmed its loyalty to the British Crown and "very politely asked for some petty reforms."[66] It was not, therefore, until after 1953 that Congress attempted to become a radical political party.

Nationalist activities during the period up to 1948 were generally aimed at securing the rights of the emerging African elites. These were essentially interested in some limited access to both political and economic power. All evidence points to the fact that it was settler demands for self-government on the Southern Rhodesia model, before Africans had achieved even the limited access to power that radicalized African nationalism in colonial Zambia. Furthermore, African nationalists adopted a populist ideology to strengthen their demand for immediate independence.

Notes

1. See Richard Hall, *Zambia 1890-1964: The Colonial Period* (London: Longmans, 1976).
2. See Richard Hall, *Zambia* (London: Pall Mall Press, 1965), pp. 89-90.
3. The North-Western Rhodesia Order in Council of 28 November 1899, *Statute Law of North-Western Rhodesia 1899-1909* (1909).

4. North-Eastern Rhodesia Order in Council of 29 January 1900, *Statute Law of North-Eastern Rhodesia 1909-11, of North-Western Rhodesia 1910-11, of Northern Rhodesia 1911-16* (1916).

5. L.H. Gann, *The Birth of a Plural Society: The Development of Northern Rhodesia Under the British South Africa Company 1894-1914* (Manchester: Manchester University Press, 1961), p. 64.

6. Northern Rhodesia Order in Council of 4 May 1911, art. 8.

7. Peter Slinn, "The Role of the British South Africa Company in Northern Rhodesia, 1890-1924," *African Affairs* 70, 281 (1971), p. 367.

8. Gann, *The Birth of A Plural Society*, p. 62.

9. See L. H. Gann, *A History of Northern Rhodesia, Early Days to 1953* (London: Oxford University Press, 1964); Hall, *Zambia*, pp. 34-49.

10. See Levi I. Izuakor, "Kenya: The Unparamount African Paramountcy, 1923-1939," *Transafrican Journal of History*, 12 (1983), p. 33.

11. Ian Henderson, "The Limits of Colonial Power: Race and Labour Problems in Colonial Zambia, 1900-1953," *Journal of Imperial and Commonwealth History*, 2, 3 (May 1974), p. 295.

12. Gann, *The Birth of a Plural Society*, p. 117.

13. PRO CO 537/5896/16 Acting Governor, Northern Rhodesia, to Secretary of State for the Colonies, 28 July 1950.

14. Gann, *The Birth of a Plural Society*, p. 122.

15. J. W. Davidson, *The Northern Rhodesia Legislative Council* (London: Faber and Faber, 1948), p. 19.

16. See Jane L. Parpart, "Class and Gender on the Copperbelt: Women in Northern Rhodesia Copper Mining Communities, 1926-1964," in Claire Robertson and Iris Berger (eds.), *Women and Class in Africa* (New York: Africana Publishing, 1986), pp. 141-160.

17 J. D. Omer-Cooper et. al., *The Making of Modern Africa: Vol. 2 The Late Nineteenth Century to the Present Day* (London: Longmans, 1971), pp. 285-286.

18. The term "European" as applied to the white community in Central Africa included white South Africans. Further, throughout this study, the terms "European" and "white" will be used interchangeably.

19. For a detailed discussion of the nature and characteristics of the colonial state, see Crawford Young, "The Colonial State and its Connection to Current Political Crises in Africa," draft paper given at a conference on African Independence, University of Zimbabwe, Harare, January 1985, or the published version, "The African Colonial State and its Political Legacy," in Donald Rothchild and Naomi Chazan (eds.), *The Precarious Balance: State and Society in Africa* (Boulder: Westview Press, 1988), pp. 25-66.

20. Young, "The Colonial State," pp. 1-2.

21. Frederick Cooper, "From Free Labour to Family Allowances: Labour and African Society in Colonial Discourse," *American Ethnologist: The Journal of the American Ethnological Society*, 16, 4 (November 1989), p. 746.

22. Cooper, "From Free Labour to Family Allowances," p. 757.

23. Cooper, "From Free Labour to Family Allowances," p. 758.

24. Jane L. Parpart, *Labour and Capital on the African Copperbelt* (Philadelphia, Temple University Press, 1983), p. 17.

25. Henderson, "The Limits of Colonial Power," p. 298.

26. PRO, DO 35/4636/333 Revised Draft White Paper, February,1958.

27. PRO, DO 35/4636/282 Brief for Secretary of State's visit to the Federation of Rhodesia and Nyasaland, December 1956-January 1957.

28. The first political party, the Northern Rhodesia Labour Party, was founded by Roy Welensky in 1941. It contested and won five of the eight elective seats during that year's Legco elections. Welensky wanted to ensure the protection of the interests of white workers and to introduce party politics into the council to which hitherto all unofficials were elected as independents. (J.R.T. Wood, *The Welensky Papers: A History of the Federation of Rhodesia and Nyasaland* (London: Oxford University Press, 1984), p. 72).

29. See Wittington Sikalumbi, *Before UNIP: A History* (Lusaka: Neczam, 1977) p. 3.

30. PRO, CO 595/133 *Northern Rhodesia Constitution*, 1944.

31. PRO, CO 537/4690/19 Stanley to A. Creech Jones, 16 February 1948.

32. NAZ, HM 53/2/Legco 2978 Nightingale to R. P. Bush, Secretary for Native Affairs, 16 August 1950.

33. PRO, CO 795/130, Minute by Creasy, 16 March 1944.

34. PRO, CO 795/130/19 Telegram from Secretary of State to the Governor, Northern Rhodesia, 29 June 1944.

35. Gabriel Musumbulwa, Interview, 15 May 1989.

36. PRO, CO 1015/1014 "Northern Rhodesia's Dilemma" by Oliver Lyttelton, Secretary of State, 13 January 1954.

37. PRO, DO 35/4635 Statement by O. Lyttelton, 13 January 1954.

38. PRO, DO 45/4634/11 Telegram from Commonwealth Relations Office (CRO), 15 September 1953.

39. PRO, DO 35/4634 Minute by D. Williams, 21 December, 1953.

40. PRO, DO 35/4634/37 Northern Rhodesia Constitution: Notes of meeting with Sir Roy Welensky, 21 September 1953.

41. PRO, DO 35/4634/35 Telegram from African National Congress (ANC) to Secretary of State, 22 September 1953.

42. PRO, CO 1015/1013 Discussion with Sokota and Yamba, 11 January 1954.

43. PRO, CO 537/6685, Responsibilities of the Colonial Office in the economic field, 1950.

44. PRO, CO 1015/1013, Secretary of State for the Colonies, discussion with Sokota and Yamba, 11 January 1954.

45. Richard Hodder-Williams, *An Introduction to the Politics of Tropical Africa* (London: George Allen and Unwin, 1984), p. 69.

46. Ibbo Day Joseph Mandaza, "White Settler Ideology, African Nationalism and the ' Coloured' Question in Southern Rhodesia/Zimbabwe, Northern Rhodesia/Zambia and Nyasaland/Malawi, 1900-1976," D. Phil., University of York (UK), 1978, p. 813.

47. Mandaza, "White Settler Ideology," p. 817.

48. African protests against federation are well documented. For example see, Robert I. Rotberg, *The Rise of Nationalism in Central Africa: The Makinf of Malawi and Zambia1873-1964* (Massachusetts: Yale University Press), pp. 215-302.

49. George Keith, *The Fading Colour Bar* (London, Robert Hale, 1966), p. 64.

50. For a detailed discussion on this see Rosaleen Smyth, "War Propaganda During the Second World War in Northern Rhodesia," *African Affairs*, 83, 332 (July 1984), pp. 345-358.

51. John D. Hargreaves *Decolonization in Africa*, (London: Longmans, 1988), p. 57.

52. Smyth, "War Propaganda During the Second World War in Northern Rhodesia," p. 345.

53. Hargreaves, *Decolonization in Africa*, p. 57. Although there was no thought of independence then, Britain was concerned with the state of colonial rule and what would happen after the war.

54. Ronald Robinson, "Andrew Cohen and the Transfer of Power in Tropical Africa, 1940-1951", in W.H. Morris-Jones and George Fischer (eds.), *Decolonization and After: The British and French Experience* (London: Frank Cass, 1980), p. 52.

55. Interview with Gabriel Musumbulwa at Luanshya, 15 May 1989; Dot L. Keet, "The African Representative Council 1946-1958: A Focus on African Political Leadership," MA Thesis (University of Zambia, 1975), p. 13. PRO CO 795/130 Oliver Stanley to Arthur Creech Jones, 7 May 1945. The ARC was the apex of political institutions created by the colonial government to provide platforms shared by the educated elite and traditional elites. In time the educated elite were to replace the traditional elite.

56. Wood, *The Welensky Papers*, p. 72.

57. Lord Hailey, *An African Survey: A Study of Problems Arising in Africa South of the Sahara* (London: Oxford University Press, 1938, Revised Edition 1957), p. 252.

58. J.W. Davidson, *The Northern Rhodesia Legislative Council*, (London: Faber and Faber, 1967), p. 21.

59. Henry S. Meebelo, *Reaction to Colonialism: A Prelude to the Politics of Independence in Northern Zambia 1893-1939* (Manchester: Manchester University Press, 1971), p. 235.

60. Welfare associations had been in existence in the territory since the 1920s, ostensibly as avenues for addressing African problems that arose in the racially polarized political system. For a good discussion see Robert I. Rotberg, *The Rise of Nationalism in Central Africa*, pp. 115-134.

61. NAZ, SEC NAT/353 Minutes of the Meeting of the Executive Committee of the Federation of African Societies, 18-19 May 1946, cited in Rotberg, *The Rise of Nationalism in Central Africa*, p. 207.

62. David C. Mulford, *Zambia: The Politics of Independence, 1957-1964* (London: Oxford University Press, 1967), p. 15.

63. John B. Stabler, "Northern Rhodesian Reaction to 1948 Responsible Government Proposals: Role of Sir Stewart Gore-Browne," *Journal of Southern African Affairs*, 3, 3 (July 1978), p. 295.

64. Mulford, *Zambia*, p. 16.

65. Kaluwa was one of the Mazabuka African community that attempted to form the Northern Rhodesia African Congress in 1937. The 1937 Congress was denied sanction by the Secretary for Native Affairs.

66. Sikalumbi, *Before UNIP*, p. 2. Sikalumbi was a founding member of the Congress.

Chapter 2

LIBERAL POLITICS AND THE CENTRAL AFRICAN FEDERATION, 1949-1963

INTRODUCTION

The creation and disintegration of the Central African Federation (1953-1963) received considerable study and several attempts were made to explain "how an error so interesting and surprising, so large and portentous, came to be made."[1] There is a consensus in these studies that Africans overwhelmingly opposed federation (or its earlier form, amalgamation) and that federation was a mistake. Yet studied from the perspective of the 1990s, particularly considering the formation of the Southern African Development Co-ordination Conference (SADCC) in 1979 (now the Southern African Development Community (SADC) since 17 July 1992), the principle of federation does not seem necessarily to constitute such a mistake after all.[2] The federation was an excellent idea—except that its timing was bad and it reinforced the political power of the white settlers. That was the mistake. Indeed, it is plausible to suggest that a worse mistake was the unscrambling of the federation in 1963. A closer examination of the objectives for the creation of the Federation of Rhodesia and Nyasaland and the objectives for the establishment of SADC reveal that both aimed at maximizing economic growth of the region as well as promoting common political values, systems and institutions. It can be further suggested that the Capricorn idea was even closer to the SADC idea than the federation idea.

As W.F. Gutteridge pointed out, the idea of federation or amalgamation was as old as Rhodesia itself. It was the protectorate status of colonial Zambia and Nyasaland that proved to be the stumbling block.[3] The advantages of contiguous territorial expansion had been articulated by the British South Africa Company as early as 1905 when the BSA Company sought permission to amalgamate North-Western and North-Eastern Rhodesia.[4]

This initial request was not granted until 1911 when both the Colonial Office and the paramount chief of the Lozi (particularly the latter) accepted the Company's assurances that the Barotse Valley would be reserved against white settlement. There is a sense, therefore, in which the Colonial Office established a tradition of consulting (however defined) the indigenous community before granting requests by the local administration.

The origins of amalgamation or federation are well documented. This study does not, therefore, dwell on the debate that preceded the creation of the Central African Federation, except insofar as it relates to the role of liberal activism (represented in this study by the Capricorn Africa Society), and African responses to liberal activism and the closer association issue. The emergence of the Capricorn Movement in Central Africa is closely associated with the rise of African nationalism in the region. Both emerged around the same time and were galvanized by similar forces. Initially both movements sought the creation of a multiracial democratic government as the ultimate goal.

The Capricorn Africa Society and African nationalism constantly influenced each other. Both emerged in response to the changes initiated in the Colonial Office—popularly known as the colonial reform movement that began in 1938-1939 and was revitalized by the Cohen Report of May 1947,[5] which looked to the future of colonial development and attempted to match economic needs with political requirements.[6] The 1947 report was an ambitious Colonial Office strategy of nation-building in Africa. It was this colonial reform movement and the "constitution-mongering" it inspired that, in part, accounts for the rise of both Capricorn and African nationalism in Central Africa. This chapter seeks to show, not the futility of liberalism, but its utility in championing the cause of both federation and early African nationalist activity.

THE ORIGINS OF THE CAPRICORN AFRICA SOCIETY

Capricorn was Southern Rhodesian in origin, but its philosophy and ideology were Central African in orientation. Its history is therefore relevant to colonial Zambian social, economic and political history during the years leading to federation and decolonization. Capricorn's history unfolded in two main phases: the first phase lasted from its formation in 1949 to 1953 when the Federation of Rhodesia and Nyasaland was created; the second phase lasted from 1954 until about 1963 when the Society was officially dissolved.

The formation of the Capricorn Africa Society raised much excitement and hope, both in the United Kingdom and Central Africa. Joseph H. Oldham wrote in May 1955 that "in the strictest confidence the Colonial Office, from the Secretary of State downwards, is prepared to take the Capricorn Africa Society seriously".[7] He later wrote in his book published in 1955 that:

> For the first time since the beginning of the fateful contact of Europe with Africa, there has come into existence on African soil and on a substantial scale a joint endeavour by members of different races to create an inter-racial integrated society in which differences of race and colour will cease to have any significance.[8]

The Society came into existence in Southern Rhodesia in 1949 under the leadership of Colonel David Stirling, "the Phantom Major" of World War II.[9] The origins of Capricorn can be traced back to the short-lived Federal Union of Capricorn Africa (FUCA), which was formed in July 1947 in Salisbury, Southern Rhodesia. FUCA's main objective was to campaign for a federation of Southern and Northern Rhodesia instead of the long-desired yet unobtainable amalgamation.[10] Very little is known about FUCA, except that it emerged two years before Capricorn and that Colonel David Stirling was associated with it.[11] On 22 and 23 November 1948, Sir Godfrey Huggins, the Southern Rhodesia prime minister, held discussions with Stirling and General Sir Francis de Guingand who were both representing FUCA. The aim of the meeting was to formulate strategies for influencing British colonial policy that was believed to be out of touch with current developments in the multiracial colonies. The presence of Stirling on FUCA is the only evidence linking the two organizations.

The Capricorn Africa Movement, of which the Capricorn Africa Society was one of the three wings and the most prominent, was founded with four aims and objects in mind:

1. the cultural, political and economic establishment of Capricorn Africa as an integral part and pillar of Western civilization;
2. the development of Capricorn Africa mainly by large scale European investment and immigration;
3. the political and economic closer association of all Capricorn Africa;

4. the promotion of a just Race Relations policy, based on the Southern Rhodesian Two-Pyramid policy, and adaptable to the changing needs of time and place.[12]

The four aims and objects formed the basis of the Capricorn Africa Movement's philosophy and ideology, namely to encourage all races to develop and advance along Western cultural standards, albeit with constant adjustments to suit the changing circumstances. The movement chose to call itself the *Capricorn* Africa Movement because the territories with which it was most directly concerned were situated largely within the Tropic of Capricorn. According to the *Capricorn Handbook for Speakers*, although Capricorn Africa consisted of territories that lay south of the Sahara and north of the Limpopo, the scope of the movement was limited to Kenya, Tanganyika, Northern Rhodesia, Southern Rhodesia and Nyasaland.[13]

The Capricorn Africa Movement was essentially a pressure group launched by a "small group of men" who "formed themselves into a founding committee in 1950."[14] The founding committee then decided that the most effective organization would be a three-tiered one: the Capricorn Africa *Society* (CAS); the Capricorn Africa *Institute* (CAI); and the Capricorn Africa *Association* (CAA). The Capricorn Africa Society originally consisted of a few individuals in the important centers of Capricorn Africa "chosen by election." These individuals were expected to give a good deal of time and effort to the Capricorn cause as well as "undertaking to give their first loyalty" in all public matters to the promotion of the movement. These exacting demands obviously precluded any general appeal for membership.

The Capricorn Africa Institute on the other hand was to be established as funds became available, first in Salisbury, and then branches were to be opened in London, New York, Nairobi, Lusaka and other suitable centers. The Institute was envisaged as a center for the collection and dissemination of economic, political, industrial, geographical and historical information relating to Capricorn Africa. It was never established as planned.

Last there was the Capricorn Africa Association, which was open to all those who supported or sympathized with the aims and objects of the movement, and wished to help in promoting them. The subscription for Association membership was set at £1 per annum.

The organizational structure of the Capricorn Africa Movement was impressive, but lack of adequate funding could not sustain the three-tiered structure. In the end Capricorn assumed the roles that were to have been played by CAI and CAA. The latter merged with the United Central Africa Association (UCAA) in 1952, which had begun by then to campaign for federation, having abandoned amalgamation as its objective.

From its inception in 1949 Capricorn, like the parent body, remained essentially a pressure group predominantly under European leadership. The guiding philosophy was the need to define a "nationality" for the territories in which it operated—a "nationality" based on the principle of "equal rights for all civilized" people. The founders of the Society were predominantly post-World War II European immigrants who had come to Southern Rhodesia to start a new life.[15] These individuals were (on the average) more liberal than most prewar settlers in their attitude toward members of other races. As such they were ridiculed by most of the old-timers. One such settler wrote:

> When we came here (S[outhern] R[hodesia]) the Natives were like wild animals living in caves and running for their lives if they saw a stranger. To-day they are educated, live decently and many of them are extremely well off. Who accomplished this? It was the pioneers and their children, not the new comers who know nothing of the Native and want to make him the social equal of the Europeans who have only reached their present stage of civilisation after thousands of years.... at Chipinga meeting we passed a motion of no confidence in the CAS, because we want nothing to do with people who want integration of the races. We are all for the advancement of the Native, but in his own sphere.[16]

The society was evidently not welcome among most old settler communities.

Nonetheless there was a liberal element in Southern Rhodesia that belonged to the pioneer stock but remained outside Capricorn like Holderness. Most of these tended to be in the Labour Party. Others like Eileen Haddon and Mike Haddon who came to Southern Rhodesia in 1948 belonged to other multiracial organizations and remained outside Capricorn. There were evidently divisions among the established settlers and the post-World War II immigrants.

David Stirling is generally regarded as the founder of Capricorn. After World War II Stirling joined his brother in business in Southern Rhodesia, where he soon became convinced of the economic potential of East and Central Africa. Stirling was hardly the first nor the last to have such notions. His uniqueness lay in the way his plans were conceived and implemented. From the start his goal was to arouse local and metropolitan interest while simultaneously dampening fears of settler exploitation of Africans.

The Society was, however, managed by a governing body called the General Council, which included a chairperson, three vice chairpersons, a treasurer, a secretary and six representatives from each branch of the movement.[17] The president of the Society was, by virtue of his office, the chairperson of the General Council. This meant that for the first eight years Stirling was president of Capricorn and chairperson of the General Council, hence the contention that during that period Capricorn and Stirling were inseparable. The Council had complete control over all matters concerning the Society as a whole. It interpreted the rules and principles and established committees as they were needed.

Nonetheless, Stirling found important associates who shared his belief that economic development and political stability rested with the creation of a large political and economic union of Capricorn Africa. In Salisbury (Harare) the most important was N.H. Wilson, a resident of Southern Rhodesia since 1906. He was almost single-handedly responsible for the formulation of Capricorn's philosophy.[18]

Most of the founding members were recent arrivals who had come to Southern Rhodesia to start new economic ventures, but were appalled by the "parochialism of the small-town society" they encountered. Among them was Brian O'Connell, an accountant, who was angry about the "useless drift and the living-in-the-pastiness," which he believed was characteristic of the administration and the European community in Southern Rhodesia.[19] O'Connell was also critical of the Colonial Office for its "ignorant political grip" over Central Africa and for the "misguided and highly dangerous experiment" of promoting African self rule. Then there was John Baines who joined Capricorn because it "seemed good business to build a Central African Federation." They were both "practical men who brought to Capricorn the capacity and determination to get things done."[20] Initially the intention was to limit membership to one hundred, and to exclude other races and women. This position was abandoned because it made the society too restrictive and contradicted its general liberal ideology.

Nonetheless, during the first three years, the Society's activities were shrouded in secrecy. As a pressure group, Capricorn did not seek to take over the government but to influence its policies. This explains its lack of direct involvement in politics during the initial phase, although the issues it was dealing with were largely political. As such, it never attempted to become a mass organization. The founders concentrated on investigating the racial problems of Capricorn Africa and trying to find solutions.

In London, the most important acquisition was Joseph H. Oldham, who became the special advisor to the Society. His book, *New Hope in Africa*, which he described as a "faithful interpretation of its aims and purposes" reflects Oldham's influence on the Society.[21]

CAPRICORN PHILOSOPHY AND IDEOLOGY

Where did the need for a Capricorn Africa Society brand of liberalism originate? The general tendency of liberal thought and activism when applied to Africa was to readjust the ideological hegemony of the West to changing African conditions. What attempts did Capricorn make to facilitate this readjustment? What was the perception of Capricorn about change?

The driving force behind the founding of the Capricorn Africa Movement was the belief that "a policy for Africa must come from within Africa" and that such a policy must be "sponsored by members of all races living in Africa." On 25 March 1952 the *Rhodesia Herald* published an article entitled "A Policy in Between" which summarized the Society's philosophy and ideology.[22] The philosophy involved the creation of a delicate balance between the interests of Africans on the one hand and those of the whites on the other. The ultimate objective was to achieve a true partnership between the races by promoting the spiritual, economic, cultural and political progress of the different races.

The balance was to be created through a partnership of prominent people representing both races. The Society therefore sought to recruit Africans who were thought to be making a positive contribution to the development of their territories. African teachers, civil servants and traders were the obvious target because they were deemed capable of understanding and furthering the Society's ideology.

The Society was committed to establishing a Federation of East and Central Africa. As Stirling explained in 1953 in a letter to General Sir Francis de Guingand:

> The ultimate purpose of CAS is to establish a United States of Capricorn Africa founded on a political philosophy or ideology embracing the aspirations of all races and founded on a common citizenship open to all those of any race who have attained the qualifications necessary to protect Western civilisation and standards.[23]

The emphasis on protecting Western "civilization" was the bedrock of the Society's philosophy and explains why Capricorn sought to attract only those Africans who were believed to have acquired Western values and were prepared to defend them.

This was a departure from white settler ideology of white supremacy that permanently relegated "Natives" to the lower echelons of society irrespective of the level of their education, whence the term "educated Native." Capricorn was prepared to accept educated Africans as social and professional equals.

Nonetheless, the use of the concept "Western civilization" as a yardstick brought much condemnation and controversy to the objectives of the Society. While Capricorn sought to attract Africans imbued with Western values and believed that harnessing those Western liberal values would make it possible for democratic principles to operate in Capricorn Africa, it dreaded the thought of transferring political power to an African ruling elite that would abuse it. It was in this respect that Stirling wrote to the *Times* in 1951 saying:

> The Colonial Office policy will result in handing over of administrative responsibility to the Native before he is capable of sustaining that responsibility, thereby risking a situation in which the superficially educated Native will exploit his more backward brethren in a form of autocracy which will not even have the safeguard of the old tribe system.[24]

African nationalists did not take kindly to these views because they challenged the very foundation to their claim for greater political representation. The more radical African nationalists became increasingly suspicious of liberalism and moderate Africans. The African National Congress responded by replacing moderate leaders in 1951.

However, Roy Welensky and Godfrey Huggins supported this approach. Huggins later pointed out, regarding the nationalist demand for universal adult suffrage, that the idea of democracy did not normally take into account the quality of those qualified to vote. He argued that in a true democracy the quality of the voters was more important than the mere numbers. Thus Capricorn's view of democracy fitted well with that of Southern Rhodesia at this time.

Although African nationalists were not yet demanding one man one vote, the insistence on a qualitative, as opposed to a quantitative franchise by Capricorn significantly contributed to the unpopularity of liberalism as an ideology for the transfer of political power to a local elite. This emphasis on a qualitative franchise was consistent with official colonial policy during this time. The Secretary of State for the Colonies explained in 1951 that the responsibility of the United Kingdom government in Central Africa was to prepare the region for

> self-government within the Commonwealth, but self-government must include proper provision for both Europeans and Africans. We have set Africans on the path of political, social and economic progress and it is our task to help them forward in that development so that they may take their full part with the rest of the community in political and economic life of the territories.[25]

African nationalists initially accepted this position, but later began losing patience when promises of shared political power did not materialize.

Tafataona Mahoso suggests that the emergence of "expatriate liberal groups" (Capricorn included) after World War II represented a massive intervention in the Rhodesian affairs.[26] Mahoso refuses to see Capricorn as a locally initiated liberal group and therefore maintains that it was just another imperialist front seeking to perpetuate imperialism and colonial rule. There is no evidence to suggest that Capricorn was in any way prompted or manipulated by British forces, even less by the Colonial Office.

The term "expatriate" normally applies to groups operating temporarily within a society and not intending to live there permanently. The elements that formed Capricorn were recent immigrants seeking permanent settlement and wishing to expand the local economy. There is simply no basis for applying complex center-periphery theory, as Mahoso does, to explain their behavior and more liberal political attitudes when simpler explanations serve better.

John E. Flint has shown that World War II brought a considerable liberalization of popular and official attitudes to race in Britain,[27] while attitudes in the colonial service remained ossified and isolated. One may apply this contrast even more forcefully to white settlers in Central Africa, who remained cut off from British influences during the war. The new immigrants after 1945 were naturally of a more liberal standing than most settlers of the prewar vintage.

However, it is also plausible to suggest that most of the post-1945 immigrants came into contact with urbanized Africans who were adequately conversant with European ways. Unlike the early arrivals, these new immigrants could easily find common cause with the educated urban Africans. Thus not only were the post-1945 immigrants of a more liberal stamp than most pre-1945 immigrants, but the urban Africans were also of a different type—educated and semieducated. This accounts for the easy mixing that followed, leaving the impression that post-1945 immigrants were more liberal than early arrivals. It has to be remembered also that because most of the early post-World War I settlers came to Northern and Southern Rhodesia after spending several years in South Africa, they were subjected to the climate of opinion in a settler-dominated country. Most of them therefore shared a commitment to protect their privileged position.

N.H. Wilson supplied the philosophy of the society. His basic contention was that Capricorn Africa could become the key to the world's prosperity and help to protect the British Empire and other democracies from communism.[28] Capricorn lacked faith in the ability of Africans to uplift themselves without European assistance. Thus the white minority, with its "superior" culture, was expected to provide leadership until Africans, through European assistance, had gained enough experience to exercise that role without looking to sectional interests.

It is important to realize that Capricorn was opposed to the "barren racial" policy that was in force in the Union of South Africa. The society was committed to accepting advanced Africans as equals. Between 1949 and 1952 Wilson's writings expressed the Society's early ideas: the confidence in the moral superiority of Western civilization and the British Empire, and the need in Africa to defend both; the emphasis on the material advantages of uniting East and Central Africa; and the proposal to encourage white immigration into the area to help economic development while encouraging African advancement.[29] Hancock argues that Capricorn never intended to encourage African advancement—it would only acknowledge it when it occurred.[30] What Capricorn really objected to was African advancement for its own sake. Capricorn favored and emphasized individual ability as the criteria for advancement.

In the political area Capricorn was already aware of the shortcomings of trying to concentrate political power in the hands of one racial group. Capricorn was also beginning to develop its own ideas about how African nationalism could be diverted away from its extremist stance. It therefore envisaged the development of multiracial politics by encouraging liberal activism in which members of different races participated.

Capricorn also sought to contribute toward the efforts of the mining companies and the Northern Rhodesia government in promoting some advancement of Africans in the mining industry. It was this commitment to industrial harmony that led some mine management officials to make financial contributions to Capricorn programs.[31] At the request of Sir Ronald L. Prain, chairman of the Rhodesian Selection Trust (RST), W.V.

Cornellius sent a check for £500 to Stirling that was drawn from the RST chairman's funds.

Ideologically Capricorn was opposed to the policy of racial exclusiveness (apartheid) that was being pursued by the Union Government of South Africa, which it recognized as dangerous and an impediment to the development of the British way of life in Central Africa (or Capricorn Africa). Capricorn also rejected extreme nationalism based on race—both African and European—as well as the communist ideology that it identified as the second and third enemies to be eliminated in Capricorn Africa. Capricorn's ideology was based on the philosophy that:

> All men, despite their varying talents, are born equal in dignity before God, and have a common duty to one another ... the difference between men, whether of creed, or colour are honourable differences ... we wish to dissociate ourselves from the barren philosophy which determines racial legislation in lands beyond our boundaries.[32]

Although this was the guiding philosophy of Capricorn since its inception in 1949, it was only in 1952 that it was clearly propounded in the Declarations. The belief in this philosophy—equal rights for all men before God—enabled liberal Capricornists to accept individuals from other racial groups as equal partners in the pursuit of racial harmony in Central Africa. Nevertheless, Capricorn recognized that European immigration in Northern Rhodesia and Southern Rhodesia had resulted in trade union practices that were designed to protect the European from the "unfair competition" of the African with his "lower standard" of living. Because the Society believed in the preservation of European standards, it regarded the principle behind that attitude as inevitable. Also because the Society never favored the "horizontal color bar," it sought to harness emergent Africans by creating advanced opportunities for them in both open and Native areas.[33] Capricorn believed in the theory that the training which Africans received should be for the benefit of the rural areas where most the African population lived.[34]

The Society looked to the development of an African middle class with common interests with Europeans so that together they would strive for prosperity and political stability through the rejection of the principle of paramountcy of interests based on race. Because Capricorn believed in the "moral superiority of Western civilization and the British Empire" and was motivated somewhat by the "need to defend both in Africa", Africans accused Capricorn of being an imperialist front for the preservation and consolidation of the colonial state. On the contrary, considering the general acceptance that the model of the constitutional state was the ideal polity to be replicated in the postcolonial state, Capricorn was justified in demanding the establishment of liberal democracy, albeit temporarily based on a qualified franchise. After all, not even the African nationalists were contemplating the abolition of the model of the colonial constitutional state. They wanted to step into the shoes of those who ran the system, but through universal adult suffrage.

CAMPAIGN FOR FEDERATION, 1949-1953

In order for Capricorn to participate in the campaign for the creation of the Central African Federation, it had to find a common ground with protagonists of federation in both Central Africa and the United Kingdom. The United Kingdom government had resisted settler demands for amalgamation for over two decades.[35] Colonial Office resistance was based on the unwillingness to relinquish control over the northern territories. After the war, the settler community revived its campaign for closer union of the Rhodesias. New arguments emerged to strengthen the case for federation. The coming to power of the Nationalist Party in South Africa and the adoption of apartheid as that government's official policy in 1948 gave momentum to the federal cause. Alongside this fear was the argument that although African nationalism was increasingly becoming vocal, the Africans as a community by themselves were not, and could not, for some time to come, effectively resist Union influence. Since amalgamation had been ruled out several times before and it was unlikely that Whitehall would change its stand on it, federation became the object of settler policy.

In a calculated move to undercut economic arguments for amalgamation the British government had decided in 1944 that it was going to implement one of the Bledisloe Commission's[36] recommendations and announced that it would establish a permanent interterritorial council to coordinate policy in the three territories.[37] The 18 October announcement by Oliver Stanley, the Colonial Secretary, establishing the Central African Council (CAC) was the "death knell of amalgamation." The CAC was intended to undercut the economic arguments for federation. The CAC held its inaugural meeting on 24 April 1945 in Salisbury.[38]

Although the CAC lacked executive powers and was mainly advisory, its performance within these limitations was so impressive that Governor Sir Gilbert Rennie reported in 1948 that:

> We are making useful progress under the Central African Council set-up, that each of the three territories concerned has

so much on its plate that all of us should get on with the work of development to which we are committed, and that, so far as Northern Rhodesia is concerned, we have so few men available and offering themselves for public service that it would be difficult to find the personnel for membership of any form of Central Assembly, if such were established in addition to membership of Legislative Council.[39]

Evidently, economic arguments for closer union were no longer as forceful as they were before the establishment of the CAC. The Northern Rhodesia government was obviously satisfied with the operation of the CAC. However, by 1950 the Southern Rhodesia government, more desirous of federation, had decided it would no longer cooperate in the affairs of the CAC because of the supposed "shortcomings of the Council."[40] The case for federation again came to the fore. These developments led the United Central Africa Association, which had been campaigning for amalgamation for some time, to begin supporting federation. The ever-perceptive Andrew Cohen, who was then head of the Africa Division of the Colonial Office, received the information with relief and recorded that a very "important development in the political alignments in Central Africa" had taken place. The association, "sensibly enough" was "putting forward federation as a political aim."[41] Cohen confessed that he had himself for "some time taken the view that federation" should be the "ultimate aim of policy", but had felt that federation could not come until the Africans in the north were "able to take an intelligent decision on the question and to play an effective part in the federal arrangement."[42] He began to wonder whether the Colonial Office was really right not to attempt a step forward toward federation.

Capricorn considered the creation of the Central African Federation as only the first step toward the eventual establishment of a larger Federation of East and Central Africa or Capricorn Africa. Its leaders were therefore anxious to further it in any way possible. Yet, while Cohen appreciated the urgency of the issue in view "of the Afrikaner menace", he pointed out that "Until we can be sure that we can protect Central Africa from erosion and infiltration from South Africa it would surely be unwise to say the least, to suggest any constitutional link between East and Central Africa."[43] Consequently, in February 1952, Capricorn explained its new program to Sir Godfrey Huggins. Stirling also held unofficial talks with members of the Colonial Office and Commonwealth Relations Office at the latter's office on 8 February 1952, at which the Society agreed temporarily to shelve plans for the larger federation.[44] The strategy was threefold: (1) merging the Capricorn Africa Association with the United Central Africa Association; (2) raising funds for the campaign to win votes for the referendum in Southern Rhodesia; and (3) establishing solid African support not only for federation but for all the objectives of Capricorn.[45]

Meanwhile Northern Rhodesian settlers led by Roy Welensky intensified their campaign for federation. The debate emphasized political advantages as opposed to economic ones (these were no longer forceful because of the success of the CAC). The one major political factor that determined the course of events was the South African threat. Capricorn had already singled it out as enemy number one. In Colonial Zambia some Afrikaners were already becoming politically noticeable. Their pro-South African views threatened imperial interests in the region.[46]

Therefore, when Capricorn emerged proclaiming that it stood for "the closer association of the two Rhodesias and Nyasaland as a first step toward its greater aim," it obviously was making an important political statement that inevitably entangled it in the politics of the scheme. Capricorn spokesmen were among the most effective lobbyists for federation. The Society enjoyed the personal confidence of the Colonial Secretary of the time, Oliver Lyttelton, not to mention that of Cohen. The cordial relationship was evidenced through exchange of information regarding the federal scheme. For example, after his tour of Central Africa in 1952 Lyttelton wrote Stirling about African attitudes toward federation:

> Large numbers were completely disinterested in the question altogether. Others said that they would be content if the Colonial Office told them straight out what was best for them and they would follow it with confidence. On the other hand African opinion on official representative bodies was opposed to federation.[47]

This exchange of views suggests very strongly that Capricorn was taken seriously within the Colonial Office.

Cohen became even more supportive of the role of Capricorn in the region. Although he did not agree with the Society's scheme of a federation of six East and Central African territories, he nevertheless acknowledged that Capricorn was important in the political development of Central Africa and justified his four "long meetings" with Stirling. Cohen wrote:

> Stirling represents a liberal and potentially valuable group among Southern Rhodesian Europeans and I have felt that there is everything to be gained from making close contact with him and his liberal efforts and at the same time seeking

to influence him away from courses which are not likely to be profitable from our point of view.[48]

Cohen's views on Capricorn were consistent with Colonial Office liberal ideas of the time. Cohen, in many ways the archetype of colonial reform policies as revived after the war, appears to have recognized in Capricorn a useful ally. As elsewhere, the Colonial Office lost no opportunity to attempt to influence potentially "sound" political groups or movements in the "right direction." While Cohen tried to influence Capricorn, the process was of course double edged. Entry as advisors in the corridors of power in Whitehall was bound to enhance the status of the movement in Central African politics. For a while, therefore, Capricorn and the Colonial Office held a communion of interests.

Yet the Colonial Office decided to keep an officially neutral position on the question of federation. Colonial Office officials carefully worded their responses to letters from Capricorn to conceal their enthusiasm and support for the Society's efforts.[49] The Colonial Office therefore not only created the impression that it ignored Capricorn, but missed the opportunity to influence African opinion effectively toward the scheme. As F. Joelson of the newspaper *East Africa and Rhodesia* pointed out, "the pretence of neutrality" was neither wise nor did "it help African leaders to understand the position properly."[50] Nationalists grabbed the opportunity and their views influenced the less articulate, amid threats and intimidation.

Stirling also enjoyed a certain amount of support among settler leaders in the region. Capricorn could play a useful part in educating the public on the advantages of federation, argued Stirling. Therefore, when the Society offered its services in this capacity to the Southern Rhodesia Prime Minister, Sir Godfrey Huggins, he urged them to lose no time in starting their operation.[51]

Capricorn kicked off the campaign for federation with the establishment of a Special Appeal Committee that included several leading settler politicians. The committee immediately set to work, mounting advertisements in leading papers in Northern and Southern Rhodesia advocating support for the federal scheme. Its target was African opinion, and contrary to Harris Sondashi,[52] Capricorn never once ignored African opposition to the scheme. Capricorn acknowledged the fact that the vast majority of Africans opposed the federal scheme, but felt this was "in large measure due to deliberate misinterpretation of the proposals by the vociferous but small group of Native `intellectuals' present in all the territories."[53]

Furthermore, Capricorn pointed out that it abhorred the Colonial Office assumption that it could impose federation against the unanimous opposition from Africans. "We, of CAS," declared the statement, "are most adamantly against this line of thinking."[54] Capricorn believed that European leadership in Africa could not "endure" and did "not deserve to endure," unless it was "capable of carrying with it in major decisions affecting their common destiny, genuine and substantial African support."[55]

The Society maintained that African and European interests were indivisible and as such sought to deal with those aspects that created suspicion between the two races. It is incorrect to suggest that Capricorn "completely ignored African opposition"[56] to the federal scheme. Capricorn recognized the difficulty and therefore decided to deal with the "vociferous" African opposition. At the suggestion of John Baines in January 1952, the Society embarked on a training program for Africans who accepted Capricorn principles and favored the establishment of the Central African Federation. These cadres would be dispatched to rural areas in Southern Rhodesia, Northern Rhodesia and Nyasaland where they would hold meetings with local Africans and impress upon them the advantages of federation. Baines suggested that each of these cadres would be paid £50 a month to provide "moral courage" in the face of expected hostility.[57]

A Capricorn meeting of 31 January 1952 approved Baines' plan, set up a budget of £5,000 but decided to reduce the payment to each African cadre from the proposed £50 to £25 per month. However, on 25 February the Finance Committee arranged to pay Abel Nyirenda £40 a month for six months to deliver the profederation message to Northern Rhodesian Africans.[58] Regarding the £25 payment, Mahoso commented that "in a country where the majority of African workers made less than £2 per month, £25 per month was a great deal of money and could indeed make an organization seem necessary in the eyes of many Africans. The sincerity of some of these members is questionable."[59] Mahoso suggests that those Africans who became cadres under this scheme did so as a survival tactic because they had been, to borrow his phrase, "denied positions in the regular economy commensurate with their `learning.'" While African grievances about the job market were real, the argument that Africans who joined Capricorn were self-seekers is purely an assertion.

Nonetheless, the literature on the nationalist period has condemned the role that liberal Africans played and relegated them to paid agents of Europeans. Rotberg, for example, wrote of the Northern Rhodesian government's decision in 1952 to step up its campaign for federation among the Africans that "Welensky subsequently paid Frank Kaluwa, an agent of the Capricorn Africa Society, to `sell' federation to rural Rhodesians."[60] Yet he knew nothing about Kaluwa's political convictions. Historians have scarcely deigned to imagine that Africans supporting federation might themselves have had genuine liberal views, or for that matter any individually thought out positions of their own.

One such person was Abel Nyirenda.[61] He was a medical assistant at the Native Disease Hospital in Salisbury when he first came into contact with Capricorn. This was a prestigious occupation for Africans in those days. Africans referred to these medical assistants as "doctors" and they were widely respected. Therefore, Nyirenda's decision to take Capricorn's banner to colonial Zambia should not be taken lightly. Evidence suggests that he genuinely believed in the Capricorn philosophy. He was perhaps the only Northern Rhodesian Capricorn member to have kept a record of his activities while "crusading" for the Society.[62] Historians will never know what his full experiences were as a Capricorn member. The little that remains of the diary tells the story of a person who honestly believed in the Capricorn ideology.

N.H. Wilson was in charge of the orientation program for the cadres who were taken on in March 1952. At the completion of the orientation program, Nyirenda was sent to the Eastern Province of colonial Zambia with instructions to get in touch with Africans on the Legislative Council and educated Africans. He was specifically asked to try to influence the African National Congress policy toward federation.[63]

On his way to Fort Jameson, Nyirenda attended a meeting of the African National Congress, after which he held "intensive" talks with Harry M. Nkumbula, leader of the ANC, who "for the first time" told Nyirenda that federation was good but that as leader of ANC he was not "allowed to air his own views on federation."[64] Nyirenda also talked to Safeli H. Chileshe, a former teacher who was then running his business enterprise in one of Lusaka's African residential areas.[65] Chileshe told Nyirenda that Africans who understood federation and were willing to see it come were afraid to support federal proposals openly because they feared harassment by the ANC.[66]

Nyirenda also toured the Copperbelt, holding more meetings and talking to Africans on the advantages of federation. While in Mufulira, he recorded in his diary that African opposition to federation on the Copperbelt was not as strong as it was in Lusaka. Several people he talked to were willing to become members of Capricorn: Mansford B.C. Mussah,

Moses Mwale, L.B. Ng'ambi and J. Zulu were among those who showed interest in Capricorn and said they would encourage others to join.[67]

Nyirenda's campaign was somewhat effective. In Fort Jameson, F.C. Moore wrote to Wilson:

> I am taking Abel Nyirenda to Lundazi. I am sure that he has done some good here and if the Africans of this province turn back again to favour federation it will be a terrific setback to the Congress and it is quite probable that other districts, or even Provinces may follow the lead.[68]

It was certainly going to be a "terrific setback" for ANC if Capricorn had succeeded in its campaign for federation and had drummed up enough African support for that cause. Already Godwin Mbikusita Lewanika had been replaced as leader of the Congress because of his favorable attitude toward federation. ANC leadership therefore took the Society's campaign seriously and stepped up their campaign to oppose Capricorn and Federation.

AFRICAN OPPOSITION TO CAPRICORN AND FEDERATION, 1951-1953

The emergence of the Northern Rhodesia African Congress in 1948 as a political party was stimulated more by African fears that amalgamation of the two Rhodesias would permanently ensure European domination than by African desire to wrestle political power from white hands. Africans in Colonial Zambia disliked the Native policy in Southern Rhodesia, which had been a self-governing colony since 1923. They feared amalgamation would eventually lead to the extension of Southern Rhodesia's Native policy into the protectorate and therefore dilute the powers of the Colonial Office, especially with regard to its Native policy. Initially African nationalists fought against giving more political power to settlers on the Northern Rhodesia Legislative Council. They were not successful in this, especially after 1945 when the Colonial Office became more committed to increasing unofficials' political power.

Until 1953 the Congress was committed to preventing the establishment of the Central African Federation, which it believed was merely a stepping-stone toward amalgamation. For Congress, therefore, anyone or any organization that advocated the creation of federation became an enemy. While there was not much that could be done about European proponents of federation, African supporters (few as they were) faced a real danger.[69] This aspect has been overlooked by scholars as a major contributing factor for the low African membership in Capricorn and other liberal organizations. As Gabriel Musumbulwa pointed out, being an African liberal was not easy: there was even a risk of death.[70]

W. Sikalumbi wrote many years later of the way in which Congress dealt with people who supported the federal scheme. Congress formed a Supreme Action Council whose mandate was to organize opposition and spread propaganda against federation and it

> trained Africans to ridicule people who were either lukewarm about federation or did not attend Congress meetings. They even went to the extent of training Africans to hate African civil servants and Africans who had responsible positions in private or with Native Authorities. As a mark of division those Africans who were not Congress supporters were called "Capricornists." Later these same type of people were called "informers."[71]

Under these circumstances it required great courage for an African to sympathize openly with Capricorn ideas, let alone accept Capricorn membership. Many Africans who were prepared to discuss federation were either "temporarily forced into oblivion" or left politics altogether. For example, A.B. Kazunga[72] and Thomas M.D. Mtine[73] were reported to have "insist[ed] that if federation proposals were to be rejected, they should be rejected on reasonable grounds."[74] Both men were members of Congress, though favorably disposed to the economic arguments of federation. Eventually they directed their energies into business and Mtine became the first Zambian indigenous millionaire. Small wonder that when Nkumbula wrote a circular letter[75] to several people asking them to confirm their membership in Capricorn and whether they were in favor of federation, he was flooded with letters denying such membership or preference for federation. The social and political cost of supporting federation was too high for most Africans.

L.B. Ng'ambi's letter to Nkumbula was characteristic of such disclaimers. He wrote: "Nyirenda is proving to be a traitor to his own chieftainship and is also trying to damage other peoples names. TELL THE CAS THAT I AM NOT THEIR MEMBER AND SHOW THEM MY LETTER REFUTING THE STUPID ALLEGATION."[76] Several other people who had recently held talks with Nyirenda took it upon themselves to "clear" themselves of the Capricorn stigma with the ANC president. Mansford B.C. Mussah said he had discussed federation with Nyirenda but strongly denied being a Capricorn member.[77]

Amid these denials P. Chizuma and Frank Kaluwa, both known Capricorn members, were threatened with violence "with intent to murder"[78]

The two lodged a complaint with the District Commissioner against .the Munenga community for threatening them. Threats of this nature were not isolated incidents. Jeremiah Kabalata, a schoolteacher in Maramba Township in Livingstone, experienced similar threats for writing to the *Livingstone Mail* expressing support for the federal scheme.[79] His letter appeared in the paper on 15 August 1952.

The Livingstone African Welfare Association took very strong exception to the contents of the letter and called a meeting on 8 October at which it was decided that if Kabalata was not dismissed from his teaching job, they would withdraw their children from the school. Things got out of hand when the district commissioner told the meeting that he did not think Kabalata had committed any offense; he was merely expressing his personal views on the issue, which he thought they should have been doing. Some even went as far as suggesting that Kabalata was not a Northern Rhodesian, but an Angolan and should be deported. The district commissioner then told the meeting that their threats "only showed why Africans were afraid to speak their opinions."[80] The Kabalata Affair became so serious that police were deployed to patrol Maramba compound for a few days to maintain peace and order.

Then there was the case of Chief Musokotwane whose "misfortune" began on 19 August 1952 when he traveled from his "palace" to Livingstone to pay his respects to the former British Prime Minister, Clement Attlee. Attlee was on a tour of Central Africa to find out for himself African opinion on federation. It is not clear what Chief Musokotwane said during his meeting with Attlee. Afterward when he traveled to Lusaka to attend a meeting organized by the Congress, he was assaulted for being in favor of federation after a session of the meeting addressed by Nkumbula. He was accused of being a member of the Capricorn Africa Society, which Nkumbula accused of being responsible "for spreading lies about intimidation."[81]

Chief Musokotwane was so shaken by the incident that when he was later interviewed by A.T. Williams (Native affairs), he said Congress was using witchcraft on him. Consequently, on the advice of A.T. Williams the Colonial Office decided that the incident "was not good propaganda" from their point of view and ministers were advised not to cite the incident in their public speeches.[82] In the end, the Colonial Office reduced the incident to acts of witchcraft. D. Williams of the Colonial Office, therefore, minuted on 13 September that "Chief Musokotwane far from having been beaten up for favoring federation was in all probability neither beaten up nor in favor of federation."[83] There should be no mystery about the incident once it is realized that Congress had recently formed a Supreme Action Committee whose duties, among other things, was to "ridicule people who were lukewarm about federation."[84]

Nevertheless, reports of harassment and intimidation, amid accusations that some Africans had become agents paid by Capricorn to campaign for federation, could not be ignored by Colonial Office officials and politicians in London. James Johnson MP (Member of Parliament) gave notice that he was going to ask the Conservative Secretary of State for the Colonies on 29 October "if he was aware that CAS was paying 2s. 6d. to every African who signed a statement supporting federation." On receipt of the notice, the Colonial Secretary telegraphed the three governors in Central Africa on 23 October asking them to confirm whether they had any information on the allegation by 9.00 hours, on 27 October.[85] Governor Sir Gilbert Rennie telegraphed his reply to the Colonial Secretary on 25 October and said in part that:

> One person thought to be a representative of the Capricorn Africa Society has been discussing Federation with Africans in the Territory. He is reported to hold an honest belief in the advantages of Federation and he is trying to persuade his fellow Africans to accept it. I have no (repeat no) information about attempts to obtain signatures, or alleged payments to persons giving such signatures.[86]

The reply from Southern Rhodesia was brief, but pointed out that while ministers had found nothing to support the allegation, "if true, it was preferable to intimidation." With this information, the colonial secretary accordingly dismissed the allegations during his reply in Parliament. Nevertheless, the stigma remained, especially among Africans for whom Capricorn was a dirty word. Kenneth Kaunda was to remark many years later that "Capricorn was dirty because of the people using it."[87]

The Society's spread to Colonial Zambia coincided with rumors about encounters with vampire-men (*Amunyama*) who were allegedly involved in capturing people and sucking their blood until they were dead.[88] Reports about *Amunyama* had begun to appear in the press in late 1951 and continued in early 1952.[89] *"Acapricorn"* became synonymous with *Amunyama*, and an African was politically dead if identified with that term. Those Africans who were associated with Capricorn were considered to have been captured, but were turned loose to capture others for the European vampire-men, otherwise why would they become members of Capricorn.[90]

The rumors that *Acapricorn* were vampire-men spread like bush fires. They gained some "legitimacy" because for the first three years the Society's activities were shrouded in secrecy. Rumors were the single most effective propaganda against Capricorn. Africans became suspicious and impervious to liberal ideas that Capricorn was trying to spread about the advantages of federation.[91] Coupled with this propaganda was the harassment of those who saw through the propaganda and decided to participate in the liberal cause. The effectiveness of these rumors, aided by intimidation tactics adopted by militant nationalists, resulted in most Africans remaining ignorant of the truth about Capricorn during this period.[92] Furthermore, the low level of education among most Africans made them easy targets for nationalist propaganda of the type discussed above.

African rejection of Capricorn was further strengthened because Africans wrongly identified people like Welensky and Huggins as Capricorn leaders. Sikalumbi, for example, wrongly identified Welensky as a founding leader of the Society.[93] Because Africans in the territory had long identified Welensky, leader of the settlers in the Legislative Council, as the main stumbling block to their political advancement, they could not imagine him supporting an organization that would be beneficial to Africans. The general idea of what the Society was and for what it stood was never correctly understood by most Africans. Evidently African suspicion and rejection of Capricorn was therefore not a response to and rejection of Capricorn ideology, but largely based on fear of the occult, or of harassment, or both.

CAPRICORN AND CAPITALIST INTEREST

Thus far this examination of Capricorn has illustrated the Society's commitment to the individual within the collective. While its political philosophy did not neatly conform to the classical meaning of liberalism as known in Europe, at the economic level Capricorn sought to defend the freedom of capital and laissez-faire economics. Capricorn believed in the ideals of free enterprise and its economic policy was formulated with that object in mind. The founders of Capricorn were generally well-placed Europeans "linked to the political and financial elites in London," who hoped to attract North American endorsement of the federal scheme. The Society felt that "it was possible to reconcile economic development and the proper trusteeship of Native interests."[94] Among the founders were people who did not like the way the settler colony was being administered. John Baines, for example, had founded an investment company and decided to join Capricorn because its economic agenda was attractive—it made good business sense in terms of the long-term interests of "enlightened" entrepreneurs. People like Baines felt that the settler population was holding on to discriminatory policies of the prewar era and had failed "to see the enormous economic potential of the African as a wage-earner and a consumer."[95]

The Society's economic agenda was particularly attractive to mining interests in colonial Zambia. The Rhodesian Selection Trust, mining subsidiary of American Metal Climax, was particularly supportive of Capricorn. Sir William Murphy, who sat on the Board of RST, was a member of Capricorn. Sir Ronald L. Prain, chairman of RST, used his position to arrange several anonymous financial contributions to further the activities of the Society. In 1952, for example, he gave Capricorn £1,000 on condition that his name was not mentioned.[96] Why did business concerns find it attractive to support Capricorn financially? Capricorn played an important role in the racially polarized geopolitical economy of Central Africa. The mining companies believed that the Society's liberal program would have a mollifying effect on the radicalized African mine workers who had begun to challenge the color bar seriously in the industry through strike action.[97] Both the colonial state and the mining companies could no longer ignore the question of African advancement on the mines. Capricorn therefore was seen as the only opportunity there was "of pre-empting opposition by reconciling the black middle class" with their white counterparts in the post-World War II period. In the words of Parpart, "the mining companies planned to neutralize labor protests ... by among other things counting on the growing support among liberal whites and Northern Rhodesian Government officials for the establishment of a black middle class."[98]

Capricorn was also attractive to mining interests in colonial Zambia because of its support for the principle of equal pay for equal work. Capricorn favored ending job reservation by skin color—a principle that was too expensive for the mine owners. Ending the color bar would have given mine owners greater flexibility in recruitment and would have inevitably led to a reduction in wage levels. In fact, this policy became one of the pillars of mine management's labor strategies in the 1950s.

Notes

1. Ronald Hyam, "The Geopolitical Origins of the Central African Federation: Britain, Rhodesia and South Africa, 1948-1953," *The Historical Journal*, 30, 1 (1987), p. 145. On the origins of the federation see also Prosser Gifford,

"Misconceived Dominion: The Creation and Disintegration of Federation in British Central Africa," in Prosser Gifford and W. R. Louis (eds.), *The Transfer of Power in Africa: Decolonization 1940-1960* (New Haven, CT: Yale, 1982), pp. 387-416; Harry Franklin, *Unholy Wedlock: The Failure of the Central African Federation* (London: George Allen & Unwin, 1963); and J.R.T. Wood, *The Welensky Papers: A History of the Federation of Rhodesia and Nyasaland* (Durham: Graham Publishing, 1983).

2. On the Southern African Development Co-ordination Conference, see Christopher R. Hill, "Regional Co-operation in Southern Africa," *African Affairs*, 82, 327 (April 1983), pp. 214-239; Roger Leys and Arne Tostensen, "Regional Co-operation in Southern Africa: The Southern African Development Co-ordination Conference," *Review of African Political Economy*, 25 (January-April 1982), pp. 52-71.

3. W.F. Gutteridge, "The Debate on Central African Federation in Retrospect," *Parliamentary Affairs*, 10, 2 (1957), p. 213.

4. John B. Stabler, "The British South Africa Company Proposals for Amalgamation of the Rhodesias, 1915-1917: Northern Rhodesian Reaction," *African Social Research*, 7 (June 1969), p. 494. The territory north of the Zambezi was initially divided into two administrative units; North-Western and North-Eastern Rhodesia, with the Kafue River and later the railroad as the dividing line.

5. See John E. Flint, "The Failure of Planned Decolonization in British Africa," *African Affairs*, 82, 328 (1983), pp. 389-411.

6. Ronald Robinson, "Andrew Cohen and the Transfer of Power in Tropical Africa, 1940-1951", in W.H. Morris-Jones and George Fischer (eds.), *Decolonization and After: The British and French Experience* (London: Frank Cass, 1980), p. 62.

7. National Library of Scotland, ACC. 7548/340B, Joseph Oldham to Jim Dongall, Foreign Mission Committee, Edinburgh, 1 May 1955. I am indebted to Jane Parpart for bringing this communication to my attention (Personal Communication, 29 April 1991).

8. Joseph H. Oldham, *New Hope in Africa* (London, Longmans, 1955), p. 13.

9. David Stirling was born in 1915 of Roman Catholic Scottish landed gentry. He joined the army in 1939 and in 1940 established the Special Air Services Brigade (a guerrilla organization raiding air bases behind Axis lines in North Africa). It was during the war that he earned the nickname "Phantom Major" because of his cheek and bluff while carrying out the raids. In 1946 he went to Southern Rhodesia and joined his brother Bill in business. He then founded and led the Capricorn Africa Society from 1949 to 1958. In 1967 Stirling founded Watch-guard International Limited which was a political security agency offering African heads of state a counter-coup service. In 1974 he founded the "GB 75"—a volunteer strike-breaking force.

10. Wood, *The Welensky Papers*, p. 114.

11. Wood, *The Welensky Papers*, p. 126.

12. NAZ NR/11/121/19 Greater Rhodesia, 1951.

13. *The Capricorn Africa Society Handbook for Speakers* (Salisbury: CAS, 1955), A 1. My research interest is confined to Central Africa, with special emphasis on Northern Rhodesia.

14. NAZ, NR 11/121/19 Greater Rhodesia 1951.

15. Ian Hancock, "The Capricorn Africa Society in Southern Rhodesia," *Rhodesian History*, 9 (1978), p. 44.

16. Microfilms of papers of the Capricorn Africa Society held at the Center for Research Libraries, Chicago (originals are held at the J.B. Morrell Library, University of York, England) hereafter referred to as CAS Papers., File No. 80, Letter to the Editor in *Umtali Post*, 20 December 1957.

17. CAS Papers, "Constitution of the Capricorn Africa Society," p. 2.

18. N. H. Wilson, "Standing on the Threshold: Capricorn Africa in the Global Structure," *The Northern News*, 31 October 1950; "Standing on the Threshold: Natural Resources of Capricorn Africa," *The Northern News*, 7 November, 1950; and "Standing on the Threshold: Capricorn Africa as the Key to the Future," *The Northern News*, 14 November 1950.

19. Brain O'Connell to Stirling, 4 January 1951, cited in Hancock, "The Capricorn Africa Society," p. 44.

20. Hancock, "The Capricorn Africa Society," p. 45.

21. Oldham, *New Hope in Africa*, p. 7.

22. Anonymous, "A Policy in Between," *The Rhodesia Herald*, 25 March 1952, CAS Papers, File No. 66.

23. CAS Papers File No. 50, Stirling to General Sir Francis de Guingand, 10 June 1953. A similar letter was sent to Secretary of State for Commonwealth Relations Office Patrick Gordon Walker on 11 June.

24. PRO, DO 35/3603/ Copy of letter to the *Times*, 18 May 1951.

25. PRO, CO 537/7203 Statement made in the House of Commons by the Secretary of State for the Colonies, 13 June 1951.

26. Tafataona Pasipaipa Mahoso, "Between Two Nationalisms: A Study in Liberal Activism and Western Domination , Zimbabwe 1920-1980", PhD Thesis, Temple University, 1987, p. 161.

27. John E. Flint, "Scandal at the Bristol Hotel: Some Thoughts on Racial Discrimination in Britain and West Africa and its Relationship to the Planning of Decolonization, 1939-47," *Journal of Commonwealth and Imperial History*, 12, 1 (October 1983), pp. 74-93.

28. N.H. Wilson, "Capricorn Africa in the Global Structure," *The Northern News*, 31 October 1950.

29. N.H. Wilson, "Standing on the Threshold," *The Northern News*, 31 October, 7 and 17 November 1950.

30. Hancock, "The Capricorn Africa Society," p. 44.

31. CAS Papers, File No. 30, Harold K. Hochschilds to David Stirling, 20 November 1956; W. V. Cornellius to David Stirling, 16 November 1960.

32. CAS Papers, File No.134, The Capricorn Declarations, Salisbury 1952.

33. Open areas were largely in the urban and industrial centres where the Europeans were expected to be in control but in which advanced Africans would be accepted. Native areas were to be closed to Europeans except to perform duties that were directly to benefit the Africans. This reflected the "two-pyramid" policy of the Southern Rhodesia government.

34. This reflected the labour policies that evolved in the 1920s and 1930s.

35. See Robert I. Rotberg, "The Federation Movement in British East and Central Africa,1889-1953," *Journal of Commonwealth Political Studies*, 2, 2 (1963-1964), pp. 141-160.

36. The Bledisloe Royal Commission was appointed in 1939 to inquire on "whether any ... closer cooperation or association between Southern Rhodesia, Northern Rhodesia and Nyasaland is desirable and feasible, with due regard to the interests of all the inhabitants, irrespective of race ... and to the special responsibility of Our Government ... for the interests of the Native inhabitants." *Rhodesia-Nyasaland Royal Commission Report*, Cmd. 5940 (1939), cited in Robert I. Rotberg, *The Rise of Nationalism in Central Africa: The Making of Malawi and Zambia 1873-1964* (New Haven CT: Yale University Press, 1965), p. 111.

37. Wood, *The Welensky Papers*, pp. 90-94.

38. For a detailed discussion of the Central African Council and its dissolution, see Wood, *The Welensky Papers*, especially pp. 90-149.

39. PRO, CO 537/3608/23 Governor Rennie to A.B. Cohen 17 July 1948.

40. PRO, CO 537/5885/101 A.B. Cohen to H. Nigel Parry, 2 August 1950. and CO 537/5885/114 Memorandum on Closer Union of Central African Territories, 1950.

41. PRO, CO 537/3608 Minute by Andrew B. Cohen, 16 July 1948.

42. PRO, CO 537/3608 Minute by Andrew B. Cohen, 16 July 1948.

43. PRO, DO 35/3603/12 Andrew B. Cohen to G. H. Baxter, 6 November 1951. Cohen was advising the Secretary of State for the Commonwealth Relations through the Secretary of State for the Colonies on Capricorn's envisaged federation of East and Central Africa.

44. CAS Papers, "Notes on Meeting Between Members of Colonial Office and Commonwealth Relations Office," 8 February 1952.

45. Joan Lorraine Watson, "The Capricorn Africa Society and Its Impact on Rhodesian Politics," PhD Thesis, St. John's University, New York 1982, p. 51.

46. PRO, DO 35/3603/12 Andrew B. Cohen to G.H.Baxter, 6 November 1951; CO 1015/70/43 Stanley N. Evans to Oliver Lyttelton, 21 April 1952.

47. CAS Papers, Oliver Lyttelton to Stirling, 4 August 1952. See also Oldham's views in *New Hope in Africa*.

48. PRO, CO 1015/70 Minute by Andrew B. Cohen, 23 November 1951.

49. PRO, CO 1015/70/11 Secretary of State for Commonwealth Relations Office to Norman Hughes (CAS), 18 December 1951. The letter was written on behalf of the Colonial Secretary; CO 1015/70 Note by A.B. Cohen, 11 December 1951. Cohen minuted that "I am sure that it is right to encourage Colonel Stirling and his friends and to show the most friendly sympathy towards them... But ... I prefer that Colonel Stirling were not congratulated `very much indeed.'

50. NAZ, NR 11/121/56 F. Joelson to Sir Gilbert Rennie (n.d.).

51. CAS Papers, File No.8 Stirling to Colonial Secretary, 22 November 1951.

52. Harris B.K. Sondashi, "The Politics of the Voice: An Examination and Comparison of British Pressure Groups (Capricorn Africa Society, the Africa Bureau and the Movement for Colonial Reform) Which Sought to Influence Colonial Policies and Events: The Case of Central Africa, 1949-1962," MPh Thesis (University of York, 1980), p. 6.

53. CAS Papers, File No.8. A.B. McNalty, to Secretary of State for the Colonies, 22 November 1951.

54. NAZ, NR 8/7/51/1 CAS. Central African Federation and the Salisbury Declarations, 30 May 1952. For details of the Salibury Declarations, see Appendix III.

55. NAZ, NR 8/7/51/1 Capricorn Africa Society: The Central African Federation and the Salisbury Declarations, 30 May 1952.

56. Sondashi, "The Politics of the Voice," p. 6.

57. Hancock, "The Capricorn Africa Society," p. 46, fn. 14.

58. Hancock, "The Capricorn Africa Society," p. 47.

59. Mahoso, "The Politics of the Voice," pp. 189-190.

60. Rotberg, *The Rise of Nationalism in Central Africa*, p. 244. This is the only place where Rotberg mentions Capricorn in the entire book, and offers no evidence of the allegations that Welensky paid Kaluwa to support federation.

61. Abel Nyirenda was a son of Chief Tembwe of Lundazi District, Northern Rhodesia.

62. Pages of the diary are located in the Party Archives, Lusaka, File ANC 3/24. What is noticeable about his diary is that it appears to have been deliberately tampered with. Many of its pages are missing, resulting in an incomplete record of Nyirenda's activities in Northern Rhodesia. It is plausible to suggest that the missing pages contained information that might have confirmed Capricorn's claims that some influential Africans went along with its ideas.

63. CAS Papers, File No. 29, Report on Africans, 31 March 1952.

64. PA, ANC 3/24 Abel R. Nyirenda to N.H. Wilson, 8 October 1952.

65. Chileshe was vice treasurer and chairman of Lusaka branch of ANC (1951). In August 1951 he was reported in the press to be pro-federation when he said "reasonable" Africans in Northern Rhodesia would give the Closer Association Report and the Proposals on Federation their earnest consideration. *The Northern News*, 3 August 1951. A few years later (1956) his shops were boycotted because of his pro-federation views.

66. CAS Papers, File No.8, Wilson to Colleagues, November 1952. According to Monica Fisher in her book *Nswanga-The Heir: The Life and Times of Charles Fisher a Surgeon in Central Africa*, (Ndola: Mission Press, 1991), pp.184-188. Safeli H. Chileshe was among Africans who participated in Capricorn activities in Northern Rhodesia.

67. PA, ANC 7/83 Correspondence on CAS, Extract from pages of Nyirenda's Diary, 24 July 1952.

68. CAS Papers, File No.8, F.C. Moore to Wilson (u.d.).

69. Interview with Gabriel Musumbulwa at Luanshya, 15 May 1989.

70. Interview with author, 15 May 1989. Musumbulwa was one of the few Africans who accepted multi-racial politics. In 1957 he became a founding member of the Constitution Party. In 1958 he was appointed minister of African education, having been elected to the Legislative Council on a United Federal Party (UFP) ticket. Nonetheless, throughout the interview Musumbulwa carefully avoided discussing Capricorn, especially his role in it.

71. W.K. Sikalumbi, *Before UNIP: A History* (Lusaka, Neczam, 1977), p. 15.

72. Kazunga was a trader, member of the Ndola Urban African Advisory Council and of the African Representative Council.

73. Mtine was a bookkeeper, member of the Ndola Urban Advisory Council's working committee on federation proposals and vice-chairman of the Ndola branch of the African General Workers Union.

74. *The Northern News*, Friday, 24 August 1951, p. 3.

75. PA, ANC 7/83, Nkumbula's letter, 21 November 1952.

76. PA, ANC 7/83, L.B. Ng'ambi to Nkumbula, 26 November 1952. Ng'ambi was a headmaster at Upper Middle School in Mufulira (his capitalization).

77. PA, ANC 7/83 Mansford B.C. Mussah to Harry M. Nkumbula, 18 December 1952. Mussah was a trader in the African township.

78. PA, ANC 7/83, Letter to District Commissioner, Mazabuka, 4 March 1953.

79. NAZ, SEC 5/113 Closer Association: The Kabalata Affair, 1952.

80. NAZ SEC 5/113 Closer Association: The Kabalata Affair, 1952.

81. Wood, *The Welensky Papers*, p. 298; NAZ, SEC 5/112/175/2 J. Lennon, District Officer in Charge to All Chiefs, 26 August 1952.

82. PRO, CO 1015/142/22 D. Williams to R.L.D. Jasper, 13 September 1952.

83. PRO, CO 1015/142 Minute by D. Williams, 13 September 1952.

84. Sikalumbi, *Before UNIP*, p. 15.

85. PRO, CO 1015/71/72 Telegram from Secretary of State to Governor, Northern Rhodesia, 23 October 1952.

86. PRO, CO 1015/71 Telegram from Governor Rennie to Colonial Secretary, 25 October, 1952.

87. Fergus MacPherson, Kenneth *Kaunda of Zambia: The Times and the Man* (Lusaka: Oxford University Press), 1974, p. 115.

88. For a detailed discussion of vampire-men, see Mwelwa C. Musambachime, "The Impact of Rumour: The Case of The Banyama (Vampire-men) Scare in Northern Rhodesia, 1939-1964," *The International Journal of African Historical Studies*, 21, 2 (1988), pp. 201-215.

89. *The Northern News*, 14, 18 December, 1951; 16, 23 January, 1952.

90. Peter Frankel, *Waileshi*, (London: Weidenfeld and Nicolson, 1959), p. 201.

91. NAZ, SEC 5/185/19/1 Godwin M. Lewanika's Address to the Central Africa Sub-Group of the Conservative Commonwealth Council, Wednesday, 1 August 1956.

92. I found during my fieldwork in Zambia in 1989 that many politically active Zambians were still reluctant to discuss Capricorn openly. For many, their evidence was heavily clouded with the *Amunyama* stories. Terence Ranger, who was briefly a member of CAS, thought "there was not much point in researching Capricorn.." Personal communication, 3 January 1989 (erroneously dated 1988).

93. Sikalumbi, *Before UNIP*, p. 14.

94. Ian R. Hancock, *White Liberals, Moderates and Radicals in Rhodesia, 1953-1980* (New York: St. Martin's Press, 1984), p. 30.

95. Hancock, *White Liberals*, pp. 30-31.

96. CAS Papers, File No. 12, Stirling to Arthur Stokes, 8 December 1953.

97. For details see Ian Henderson, "Wage-Earners and Political Protest in Colonial Africa: The Case of the Copperbelt," *African Affairs*, 72, 287 (1973), pp. 288-299; and also his "The Limits of Colonial Power: Race and Labour Problems in Colonial Zambia, 1900-1953," *Journal of Imperial and Commonwealth History*, 2, 3 (May 1974), pp. 294-307.

98. Jane L. Parpart, *Labour And Capital on the African Copperbelt* (Philadelphia, Temple University Press, 1983), p. 137.

Chapter 3

AFRICAN OPPOSITION TO CAPRICORN AND FEDERATION, 1951-1953

Our country, Padre, is faced with very difficult problems. In a way they are not peculiar to ourselves, but the point is a solution must be found to this peculiar problem and that is why I take a genuine interest in trying to meet you and others like you so that through discussion and mutual exchange of ideas we might find a way out of our present difficulties. As things are, *we all live in one and the same country, but entirely un-understanding of each other's point of view.*

I would be the last to disagree with what you said to me during one of those visits you paid me in prison, that there is a danger in an African nationalist leader of my standing being called all sorts of names if he frequently met Europeans. This is very true and yet I sincerely believe that it is essential for me at least to get to know what it is that is responsible for this sad state of affairs in this country. I believe too that one of the ways of getting a lasting solution is by this free exchange of ideas.... I do wish to know quite frankly what there is to fear where Europeans are concerned, in establishing constitutional democracy in this country.[1]

Kaunda's dilemma expressed in his words quoted above was also Capricorn's dilemma, though for different reasons. The Capricorn Africa Society wanted to win over the emergent moderate African elite to the grand political design of the 1950s—multiracialism, which the British conceived as the panacea for all their problems in East and Central Africa. Though elements of multiracialism already existed among Africans in colonial Zambia as early as 1946 when the African Representative

Council was established, there was very little dialogue between Africans and liberal Europeans. The Society's role in the campaign for federation had made it extremely unpopular among Africans. Since the success of the multiracial panacea depended on the willingness of the African educated elite to participate in multiracial party politics, it was imperative that Capricorn should yield gracefully to nonwhite pressure and drop its original ideas.[2]

Two themes, therefore, dominated the Society's activities during the period 1954 to 1957. First, Capricorn engaged itself in a process of rethinking its ideas and principles. This process culminated in the Salima Convention of 1956. Second, after the Salima Convention, Capricorn moved into its next stage, which was characterized by the establishment of two branches in colonial Zambia and the formation of the Constitution Party in 1957. Both developments were aimed at publicizing the Capricorn philosophy to increase African involvement in the liberal cause. It is necessary, therefore, to examine the significance of this change of policy to explain the emergence of Capricorn's liberal activism in Colonial Zambia. "Colour-conscious" African nationalism in Colonial Zambia made a certain impact on Capricorn, and was simultaneously affected by Capricorn liberal philosophy.

CAPRICORN AFRICA SOCIETY AND THE FEDERAL GOVERNMENT

Before discussing the rethinking that preoccupied the Society for nearly two years after 1953, an understanding of the position of Capricorn in the federation is essential. Once federation became a reality, Capricorn looked forward to a period of cooperation between itself on the one hand and the federal government on the other. In this respect David Stirling urged Welensky:

> I do hope now that Federation is in the process of consolidation, you will feel that our Society can be of real value to you, in achieving our long-range objectives in Africa which I am convinced we all share. Looking back on last year, I feel that the activities of our Society and particularly myself ... must have exasperated you with our apparent deviation from taking first things first, at a time when you felt that federation was the first thing of the moment.... But from now on, I really hope that you will regard us as your potential agents working in a dimension which would be dangerous for you to work in as a political leader.[3]

Yet things did not work out as expected for Capricorn. The federal government was uncomfortable about associating itself with the Society too much at this stage. Capricorn's support for federation had made it unpopular among Africans. Welensky and other federal leaders were anxious to gain African confidence and did not think continued flirtations with Capricorn would help.

Under these circumstances Capricorn began to rethink its position, ideology and the role it was to play in the federation. During the first period, preceding and including 1953, Capricorn had remained essentially a Southern Rhodesian organization, occasionally sending emissaries to the north to campaign for federation. It had no branches in colonial Zambia, even though the Society was already part of the political vocabulary among Africans and non-Africans alike—for Africans in an increasingly pejorative way. Part of Capricorn's response, therefore, was to open branches in the north as well as to recruit more members from all races. Capricorn also sought ways of removing the negative image it had acquired during the campaign for the Central African Federation.

On 26 February 1954 Capricorn placed advertisements in leading newspapers of East and Central Africa explaining its new ideology and its intention to recruit up to 100,000 members.[4] According to Tafataona Mahoso, the 1954 manifesto was basically a documentation of the general principles and assumptions that had guided Capricorn since 1949.[5] Nonetheless, the manifesto was also a means of guiding and gathering new ideas from those who were provoked into discussion. The aim was to build a platform for the 1956 convention.

CAPRICORN MANIFESTO

The Capricorn Manifesto superseded the Salisbury Declarations[6] as the Society's policy statement. While the Salisbury Declarations had emphasized two things: (1) that the attainment of administrative and economic unity between British Capricorn African territories in some form of political federation could and should precede the achievement of unity and integration between the races within each separate territory; and (2) that the effective support of European political leaders in Africa could precede the widespread backing of the rank and file of all races for the aims of the Society,[7] the manifesto emphasized striving for multiracial liberal partnership between the races within each territory as more important than the success of the federation.[8] Now Capricorn wanted to consolidate partnership in the individual territories before striving for a larger political unity. The Society observed that Africa was suffering from deep wounds inflicted by fear and mistrust between races. It therefore saw an urgent need for the development and nurturing of a new spirit in the form of a patriotism stronger than racial or any other loyalty. While Capricorn still believed in the larger federation of East and Central Africa as the ultimate objective, it now proposed to work for the improvement of race relations in the individual territories as the immediate goal.

The manifesto suggested that Africans and Europeans were members of one body and therefore racial cooperation should have been a natural process. Capricorn now chose as its crest a zebra on the map of Africa and argued that although a zebra had black, brown and white stripes, it was one animal. If the zebra was pierced to the heart, it would die irrespective of the stripe through which it was stabbed. Capricorn sought to build the image of the multiracial society as a single organic community in which each race depended on the other for life. In the past Capricorn had been

> content merely to distinguish between an emerging urban elite and the rural peasantry, and to declare themselves for accepting the one and protecting the other, the Manifesto called for positive efforts to encourage and enlist those Africans considered suitable for membership of a multi-racial society.[9]

The idea that Africans and Europeans were members of the same body was not original, at least in the colonial Zambian context. As far back as 1946 Moses Mubitana had stated during the first session of the African Representative Council meeting that Africans and Europeans were members of the same body (Northern Rhodesia) and "that each part of the body, even the simplest, has a little contribution to give for the prosperity of the whole body."[10]

Godwin Mbikusita Lewanika, then president of the Northern Rhodesia Congress, expressed the same idea of society as an organic whole in 1950:

> The Motto of Congress is now "Eendrag" (Unity Through Team Work). We not mean unity only amongst the Africans themselves, but also unity with European settlers, Indian settlers, and Euro-Africans for the benefit of Northern Rhodesia. Experience has taught us that Northern Rhodesia will never go forward with other progressive countries if we are divided and suspicious of one another.[11]

Thus, it was not only individual Africans who subscribed to the ideology of multiracialism, but the Northern Rhodesia Congress as well. The significance of the proposals in the manifesto lie in the fact that they represented a major shift in policy by the Society, which reflected the ability and flexibility of Capricorn to adapt to the changing political circumstances, and not "inconsistency of policy."[12] The original Capricorn philosophy had reflected the colonial social ideology in which the upper rungs of society were reserved racially for the white community. Now Capricorn was prepared to open the upper rungs of the colonial society to "civilized" members of the black race.

CAPRICORN REVISES ITS APPROACH

The experience of the campaign for the Central African Federation and the fact that Africans were more than ever before determined to fight against federation influenced Capricorn to review and change its philosophical approach to the political problems confronting Central Africa. Now the Society believed that what Capricorn Africa needed most was "not discussion in political terms of any wider federation but closer understanding on human terms between Africa's different races."[13] That same experience taught Capricorn that there would be no racial harmony in a wider federation founded on "grounds of economic or administrative expediency" alone. The Society was now convinced that its new role would be to arouse an irresistible weight of multiracial public opinion that would in turn gradually lead to a natural desire for closer union between those territories that would have adopted the new Capricorn order of common citizenship.

The new policy was founded on two closely related assumptions. The first was that to have political stability, priority should be given to the creation of a common patriotism and the establishment of a society in which there was no discrimination on racial grounds, where opportunity was open to all and where human capacity and merit were the only criteria for responsible participation in public affairs. The second assumption was that although in multiracial territories all development depended on the interaction of an advanced civilization and one that was less advanced, there was, nevertheless, need to maintain "civilized" standards in Capricorn Africa.[14] These assumptions formed the basis of the Society's activities for the next five years.

Although the announcement of the new policy was not followed by much positive response from the public, the first Federal Prime Minister, Sir Godfrey Huggins, gave the new policy a guarded approval in *The Times* when he said:"The general idea behind CAS is an ideal that few could object to. It deals however, with subjects that have been a live issue for years in multi-racial countries, and will only be solved by evolutionary development."[15] Roy Welensky was somewhat more supportive of the new policy because it came close to the partnership policy.[16] He was quoted in the *Rhodesia Herald* as having said:

> In my opinion the objects of CAS are worthy of the support of all of us who are anxious to find a solution to the racial problem of our Federation. They are in short, the fulfillment of the principles embodied in the preamble of the constitution, the preservation of and advance of western standards of civilization and culture, and the achievement of a common citizenship by those who can bear the attendant responsibilities.[17]

However, the positive attitude adopted by Huggins and Welensky toward the new Capricorn policy was undermined by opposition from within the Society, championed by one of the veteran members, N.H. Wilson.[18] On 27 February Wilson published a number of charges in the *Rhodesia Herald*. He alleged that the text of the new Capricorn policy had not been communicated to or approved by the Society. Wilson claimed that the new policy was essentially a one man show by David Stirling. In protest, Wilson resigned from the Society.[19] By the end of March, Stirling was worried by the number of hostile press reports. He wrote to Jack A. Couldry that the Society was running into opposition initiated by Wilson, whom he described as the "old rogue ... doing his utmost to sabotage the Society."[20]

In reality, Wilson's departure from Capricorn was an opportunity for Stirling. On 28 September 1953, he had written to Arthur Stokes that while he did not wish to hurt "the old boy's feelings" in view of his "immense contributions" in the past, he hoped Wilson would leave Capricorn because of his association with the white supremacist Confederate Party.[21]

The Society minimized the negative publicity by deliberately playing down the press. There is no doubt, however, that the new policy was launched at an inopportune moment in the history of Central Africa. In colonial Zambia especially, nationalists were becoming more militant and anti-European than ever before. The Society therefore now sought to deal with these problems by consolidating itself in the Rhodesias. The process of consolidation was, however, preceded by a two-year period in which a new philosophy enshrined in the Capricorn Contract was developed.[22]

This process of consolidation was undermined further by staff resignations from the Society's administrative body, the Executive Council. J.G.M. Bernard, a former secretary of Huggins' United Party, who had joined the Executive of Capricorn's Central African Branch on its formation in 1954, resigned because he saw the new platform as "utterly unrealistic" in its basic assumption that the educated African represented his "primitive brethren."[23] Colonel A.S. Hickman, former commissioner of the British South Africa Police, who had become Southern Rhodesia chairperson of Capricorn in August 1956, indicated his intention to resign in January 1957. Meanwhile, K.L. Stevens who had taken over as executive officer for Southern Rhodesia on 1 October 1956 was to end his duties officially on 31 December 1956. Hickman said that while he completely endorsed the principles and ideas of the Society, and would remain a private member, he felt obliged to resign from differences of opinion with the president about administration.[24]

Although these resignations were immediately followed by recruitment of new members who saw a viable role for Capricorn, David Stirling's tour of colonial Zambia was affected. Dorothy Lehmann of the International Missionary Council in Kitwe wrote that "quite a few Europeans are attracted to Capricorn."[25] Lehmann pointed out that "The African side is rather terrorized by a few Congress leaders who wrote to the press that they were going to blacklist all who attended Capricorn meetings and that threat was published."[26] These threats, coupled with the image Africans held of Capricorn as not only profederation but its association with vampire-men stories, militated against recruitment of any significant numbers of Africans.

Although the Capricorn Africa Society was already "known" in colonial Zambia, no effective organization existed there until after the Salima Convention. Delegates to the convention returned to their home countries with a commitment to find a vehicle through which the Capricorn Contract could be fought for in the political arena. To meet this challenge the Central Africa branch of the Society was dissolved in August 1956 to pave the way for regional branches which were to be established in both Southern and colonial Zambia.

NORTHERN RHODESIA BRANCHES OF THE SOCIETY

Preparations for the establishment of Northern Rhodesian branches had already started as early as 1955. The first meeting to that effect was held in Luanshya. Dr. Charles Fisher was provisionally elected chairperson and was also given the task of establishing another branch in Lusaka.[27] Few Africans attended the first meeting. It was hoped that more talks would draw more Africans to join Capricorn.[28] Dr. Fisher felt that it would be wrong to identify the Society too specifically with Godwin Lewanika "for the same reason that it would be a mistake to give Savanhu or Hove too prominent a position in the Society in Southern Rhodesia."[29] Lewanika had lost credibility among African nationalist leaders because of his moderate views about federation. Despite his favorable views about the Society, nothing was done to bring him into it.[30]

Efforts to establish Capricorn branches in colonial Zambia were undermined by the formation of the United Northern Rhodesia Association (UNRA.) in 1954. As Capricornists were contemplating the establishment of Capricorn branches in the territory, Harry Franklin, nominated member for African interests in the Legco, was developing another scheme. He organized a meeting on 31 July 1954 to discuss the formation of an interracial society to improve race relations in the territory.[31] The UNRA was finally formed in September.

According to the constitution of the UNRA, Northern Rhodesia's prosperity depended on the "development of such harmonious race relations that its people may go forward in mutual confidence."[32] Like Capricorn, the UNRA was "nonpolitical" and its membership was open to all races in the country. Its object was to further cooperation and understanding among the races.[33] The UNRA sought to provide a common meeting ground for the free exchange and discussion of ideas. However, unlike Capricorn, which always had a political agenda in which members of both black and white communities were expected to participate as equals, the UNRA saw itself as a purely social organization. This image made the UNRA acceptable to some nationalists.[34]

The formation of the Association was welcomed by the Rhodesia Selection Trust which donated a building on a five-acre piece of land in Kabulonga (Lusaka).[35] The headquarters of the Association was officially opened by Governor Sir Arthur Benson in May 1955.[36] Northern Rhodesian "liberals", especially those in Lusaka, were more favorably disposed to the Association than to Capricorn.

Yet, as Dr. Charles Fisher pointed out with specific reference to the 1950s Club in Luanshya, "the blacks would come because they were glad to have a few whites whom they could harangue about the evils of their ways".[37] Consequently Europeans began to stay away and the 1950s Club died. This was also true of the UNRA where the admission of Nkumbula and his associates precipitated resignations of some European members from the Association.[38]

Formation of Capricorn branches in colonial Zambia and the growth of the Capricorn movement demanded that liberal elements in the country must be won over. The division of liberal elements coupled with the growing intensity of nationalist politicking made that task particularly difficult. A former colonial Zambia resident magistrate wrote to Jonathan Lewis, Capricorn's executive officer in London, offering to be employed by Capricorn and help in organizing the Society because he wanted to help in the easing of racial tensions in the territory.[39] Colonial Zambia Capricornists now took practical steps to follow up the Contract and widen the scope of Capricorn political activity in colonial Zambia.

First, they arranged for the appointment of an executive officer. A sum of £1,000 was found for that purpose. Appointment of an executive officer was considered a vital step in the establishment of a Capricorn branch in the region. The Executive Officer, like his counterpart in the south, was to be responsible for running the Society's affairs. P.C. Jackson was subsequently appointed as the executive officer for Capricorn's Northern Rhodesia branch.[40] Second, Copperbelt Capricornists undertook to build interracial clubs at all public centers. This was considered most urgent because the Society had no open meeting places. They felt that it was undesirable that they should always use their private houses for Capricorn meetings. The Society therefore appealed for financial assistance from supporters in the United Kingdom to meet this obligation.

There is no clear documentation indicating when exactly the Northern Rhodesia branches began to operate. It appears however, that there was some operating branch for the period 1 January to 31 December 1956 according to the statement of account in Table IV.

It is certain that by the end of 1956 two branches were in operation, one in Lusaka and a second on the Copperbelt at Luanshya. The Lusaka branch was chaired by Reverend Merfyn M. Temple[41] for the period 1956-1957. The Copperbelt branch was chaired by Dr. Charles Fisher, who was also chairperson for the whole of colonial Zambia.

Although the Lusaka branch attracted more African sympathy than the Luanshya branch, it was nonetheless less active. Most of the likely supporters were civil servants whose conditions of service precluded them from active involvement in political and quasipolitical organizations. Capricorn was affected by this civil service regulation. During a tour of Colonial Zambia by the Capricorn executive secretary in mid-1953, John Mwanakatwe,[42] W.S. Matsie and Mswoya, then all teachers at Munali Secondary School, indicated their willingness to participate in Capricorn "as soon as their position as civil servants was clarified."[43] The prohibition of civil servants from political participation, coupled with intense ANC propaganda against Capricorn, already equated to *Amunyama* (vampire-men),[44] made recruitment of African members extremely

Table 4: Receipts and Expenditure: CAS, Northern Rhodesia Branch, 1 January 1956 to 31 December 1956.

Receipts	£ (Pounds)	S (Shillings)	d (Pence)
Donations	105	19	0
Membership	4	5	0
Sales	10	0	0
Salisbury Contributions	1,058	10	0
Undefined	29	14	5
TOTAL	**1,208**	**8**	**5**
Receipts	**£ (Pounds**	**S (Shillings**	**d (Pence)**
To Salisbury	36	10	10
Bank Charges	14	9	0
Refreshments at meetings	27	0	0
Office Equipment	20	10	0
Stationery	21	12	3
Rentals	82	10	0
Car	325	0	0
Petrol and oil	17	5	8
Repairs	28	3	10
Traveling expenses	4	3	6
Cash on hand	33	12	8
Bank Balance	446	12	5
TOTAL	1,206	8	5

Source: CAS Papers, File No. 43, 1957.

difficult. On the Copperbelt, it was largely the fear of ANC that pre-vented many would-be supporters from joining Capricorn.[45]

Thus, attempts to recruit new African members and influence existing political parties to adopt the contract as a platform for political change were unsuccessful. Though membership figures rose by over 100 percent by the end of 1957, judging by the subscription figures, in absolute terms membership remained quite low. In 1956 membership subscription totalled £4 5s, while in 1957 it totalled £8 15s.[46]

Nationalist leaders like Harry Nkumbula chose to join the UNRA. Nkumbula allegedly told Chad Chipunza that although he himself did not believe in Capricorn, he would not regard congressmen who joined Capricorn as traitors at all.[47] Nkumbula appears to have kept his word because there is no record of any public condemnation of Capricorn after this meeting. Before 1956 Nkumbula had been publicly hostile to Capricorn and those associated with it.[48]

The decision to influence political developments from without was obviously unsuccessful and it was later regretted by the Society. Joseph H. Oldham wrote to Jonathan Lewis in 1960 that the crisis began after Salima when the Society withdrew from the political field and chose to concentrate on nonpolitical activities.[49] Consequently, its philosophy was never integrated into the political institutions of the time.

Capricorn's only impact was made on the Luanshya branch of the Federal Party, which borrowed liberally from the contract and changed some phraseology to suit the local political scene of colonial Zambia.[50] The Federal Party, however, rejected the Society's multiple voting system. It substituted for it an electoral system based on the right of all who had attained the statutory qualifications to elect members of the legislature, registered on one common roll.[51] The Federal Party maintained that the vote was not a natural right but a responsibility to be exercised for the common good by those who had attained the necessary qualifications.[52]

FORMATION OF A NEW PARTY: THE CONSTITUTION PARTY

Although the Federal Party's political stand hardly differed from that of the Society, Capricornists decided in mid-1957 to form a multiracial party—the Constitution Party. Its mandate was to seek a political adoption of the contract in its entirety. This decision scattered the liberal elements in colonial Zambia. In late 1957, a planning meeting was accordingly called in Luanshya. According to Robert Rotberg: "By mid-1957 ... those among the liberals who had, like Gore-Browne, stood apart from Capricorn, as well as those who had joined, began rethinking the need for a multi-racial party."[53] Consequently, "liberals" led by Dr. Alexander Scott,[54] joined by David Stirling, Dr. Fisher, the Reverend Merfyn Temple, the Reverend Colin Morris, Gabriel Musumbulwa, Gore-Browne and Harry Franklin, convened a meeting which led to the birth of the Constitution Party.[55] They declared the United Federal Party reactionary and promised to seek a more liberal franchise for Africans. The initial constitution resolved to establish a society "free from racial discrimination with a system of law based on a solemn contract between our peoples to acknowledge our human unity under God and our unity in one loyalty to the Crown."[56]

In conformity with the new Capricorn policy, the draft policy statement of the new party declared that colonial Zambia and Nyasaland were entitled to secede from the federation if the policy of the federal government was not in line with the fundamental principles and the preamble set out in the federal constitution by the time territorial self-government was achieved.[57] Colin Leys, however, expressed surprise at this declaration, which was not only a tactical move to attract African participation, but a demonstration of realism by the Constitution Party. The Society was genuinely concerned with the futility of insisting on maintaining the federation amid vociferous African opposition to it. Capricorn now realized that the success of federation depended on the willingness of Africans to participate in it. The argument that the reality of federation would temper African opposition had been proved wrong.

However, in conformity with Capricorn practices and political ideals, the new party's constitution resolved that the vote was not "a natural right, but a responsibility to be exercised for the common good."[58] The Constitution Party therefore advocated a qualitative franchise rather than universal adult suffrage. The Party adopted a "middle of the road" stance and rejected extremism, either on the right or the left. It was assumed that the right represented white supremacy and that the left stood for black supremacy. As Sir Ronald L. Prain put it a few years earlier, they were trying to create something that was different from the rest of Africa. They were "trying to avoid failures of the Union of South Africa with its emphasis on white supremacy, and to avoid the experience of West Africa with its emphasis on black supremacy."[59] Reaching and sustaining that "middle of the road" position was the main preoccupation of both Capricorn and the Constitution Party.

Lawrence C. Katilungu, president of the African Mineworkers' Union, Norman Hunt, a local architect, and C.L. Patel, an Asian businessman, took up party positions on the Copperbelt as chairperson, secretary and treasurer respectively. Others were Henry Makulu, a Congregational Church minister, Dr. Charles Fisher, Gabriel Musumbulwa,[60] I.R. Menzies, J.C. Mandona, A.J. Adamson and Dean Acheson of the Rhodesian Selection Trust. The Lusaka committee consisted of the Reverend Merfyn Temple, Safeli H. Chileshe, a Capricorn sympathizer and African member of Legco, and Dr. Alexander Scott. According to Robert Rotberg the Reverend Colin Morris of Chingola, Wittington K. Sikalumbi, a member of the African National Congress, and Frank Burton, a Lusaka journalist, also gave support to the newly formed party.[61]

The Constitution Party held its first public meeting at the Palace, a multiracial cinema hall in Lusaka, in the last week of November. Close to 300 people attended the meeting, which was described as "a resounding success ... for pathetic Lusaka."[62] The meeting, chaired by Reverend Merfyn Temple, was addressed by Dr. Scott, Safeli Chileshe and Henry Thorncroft.[63] The new party announced that it would fight the United Federal Party in the federal field and in Northern Rhodesia, but it would not oppose Garfield Todd in Southern Rhodesia.

Katilungu agreed to serve as chairperson of the Copperbelt Regional Interim Committee, which surprised even veteran Capricorn members. On 28 October Dr. Fisher wrote:

> To my surprise Katilungu agreed to serve as Chairman of this [the Constitution Party's Copperbelt Divisional Executive] Committee; a courageous step because he is already under heavy fire from the Congress and for him to associate himself with Europeans and Asians in a political party is a very big thing.[64]

It required much courage for an African to be associated with white liberals, let alone to head one of the liberal organizations.[65] Robin Short wrote that "for the nationalist, it is the liberal that is the danger."[66] The liberal, especially if he was African, became the perfect target for "a calculated hysterical campaign of hatred."[67] However, Katilungu was unable to withstand the barrage that was poured upon him by the Congress. Consequently, he suddenly resigned from the Constitution Party early in December 1957.[68] This was obviously a blow to the newly founded multiracial party.

Lawrence C. Katilungu's flirtations with the Constitution Party were very instructive regarding his stance against the African National Congress. He kept trade union activities of the miners away from the ANC and even persuaded the mining companies to ban ANC meetings in workers' townships.[69] Katilungu's association with the mining industry on the Copperbelt and the history of the trade union movement were synonymous. From the time that he took over union leadership from Godwin Mbikusita Lewanika, Katilungu became an important leader among Africans. He was a moderate man, but kept union matters separate from politics even though he symphathized with ANC. It was for this reason that Katilungu was considered a valuable ally by white liberals and founders of the Constitution Party. However, he did not live long enough. He died in a road accident in November 1961.

Africans had very little choice in joining any of the existing political parties. Some non-Europeans who had voting rights were attracted to the United Federal Party (UFP). Musumbulwa joined the UFP because it supported partnership and quality leadership.[70] The Dominion Party was openly opposed to equality between Africans and Europeans. In the end, the only political party available to Africans was the African National Congress. ANC never sought European backing and particularly opposed any association with Capricorn. The few Africans who disliked racism in any form turned to Capricorn. Capricorn and ANC therefore competed for the Africans' allegiance.

The Constitution Party mounted a campaign aimed at increasing African membership, describing itself as "not just a European Party but ... African in a non-racial sense."[71] Africans were told that the aims of Capricorn and ANC were not very different.[72] The Constitution Party began to emphasize similarities between itself on the one hand, and ANC on the other. When Harry Mwaanga Nkumbula, president of ANC, suggested that Europeans were not to rule colonial Zambia, the Constitution Party leaders responded that "if by this he means that no race as a race can claim to rule the country, this is our fight too."[73]

Similarities did exist. Both ANC and the Constitution Party wanted to see an end to federation, and were opposed to a rapid move toward independence. Both parties wanted to see an end to racial policies then in existence. Yet the two groups never joined forces. The moderate approach adopted by Nkumbula quickly became a minority stand within ANC. Other ANC officials became militant and increasingly opposed any association with liberal Europeans.[74] This cleavage between the moderate Nkumbula and the militant wing of the party not only inhibited cooperation between ANC and the Constitution Party, but also precipitated a split within the ANC itself.

However, the Constitution Party's association with Capricorn proved to be the major obstacle to its success. Despite an early statement that the Constitution Party and Capricorn would be kept apart, the link proved very hard to break and was to haunt the Constitution Party for the rest of its brief life.

The Capricorn stigma prevented the party from making progress in the political arena. Not all "liberals" were attracted into the ranks of the Constitution Party. In spite of his good words about the new party and especially the decision to keep Capricorn out of politics, Lewanika chose to join the United Federal Party. So did Gabriel Musumbulwa.[75] K.S. Chiwama, a known Congress member, wondered whether the Constitution Party was not just a change of name since Capricorn had failed to attract African membership.[76] Another correspondent suggested that the Constitution Party, like Capricorn, was for the middle class and therefore not for ordinary people.[77] These charges prompted David Hamilton, the

Capricorn executive officer, to respond that the two were independent organizations with different objectives.[78]

In early 1958 the Reverend Colin Morris, who was heading the "Church into Politics" movement and was associated with the Constitution Party, came out in defense of the party. He felt that "the existence of the racial party of either extreme was coming to a close."[79] He, nevertheless, was concerned that justly or unjustly any suspicion of a tie-up between the two organizations was a "kiss of death" where African opinion was concerned. Morris pointed out that the problem was simply that some of the ablest leaders were very well known Capricorn officials. Both the Constitution Party and Capricorn were faced with the same dilemma: how to remove the stigma without repudiating the people concerned.[80] In fact, *Equinox*, a Capricorn magazine, had already reported that the formation of the Constitution Party represented a further development of Capricorn.[81] There appeared to be only one solution, the dissolution of Capricorn.[82]

THE DECLINE OF THE CAPRICORN SOCIETY

The Annual General Meeting of the Lusaka branch of Capricorn held in February 1958 "felt that since the formation of the Constitution Party, much of the work previously undertaken by the group, which was of a quasipolitical nature, would now be more correctly handled by the party."[83] It was therefore imperative that Capricorn reexamine its position in colonial Zambia. There were several reasons for this turn of events. The intensity of African nationalist activity during the late 1950s contributed a major part. Capricorn as a nonpolitical organization could not cope with the rapid political changes that were taking place in the country.

Then there were the constitutional developments that since 1954 were aimed at establishing and consolidating multiracial politics. A significant move in this direction were the 1954 Moffat Resolutions.[84] It is plausible to suggest that these resolutions, coupled with Capricorn efforts, contributed to the birth of the multiracial Constitution Party. Yet by 1958, all indications suggest that multiracial party politics were unpopular among both Africans and Europeans. Liberalism was interpreted as weakness by both sides.

The Constitution Party participated in only one election—the federal election of 12 November 1958—with very unimpressive results.[85] None of its candidates came close to winning a seat. By the end of 1958 both Capricorn and the Constitution Party had accepted the fact that African nationalist activities were too strong to permit any significant numbers of

Africans to participate in liberal politics. Meanwhile, racial polarization intensified. A few white Capricornists however, joined African national-ist parties.[86]

There was evidently very little Capricorn or Constitution Party activ-ity in 1959. Meanwhile, liberal leaders of the United Rhodesia Party in Southern Rhodesia with Sir John Moffat from colonial Zambia, with leaders of the Constitution Party, held private meetings in February 1959 and later announced the formation of a new party, the Central Africa Party (CAP).[87] The Central Africa Party was a breakaway group that split under Garfield Todd's leadership. It split from the United Federal Party, with which the United Rhodesia Party had just amalgamated. The CAP was a left liberal party with a very weak base. Most members had sup-ported Whitehead when he took over the UFP leadership from Todd, who was dismissed in 1958.

The General Council acknowledged this decline and admitted that Capricorn had been overtaken by events. Sir John Slessor wrote:

> However true it may be that we detected the *wind of change when it was a faint breeze* and that 90% of whatever we have consistently advocated has now become pretty well the minimum that we can get away with in Africa, the fact is I am afraid that Capricorn in anything like its old form is as dead as the dodo.[88]

Leopold Takawira pointed out in early 1960, after his tour of colonial Zambia (from 27 March to 10 April 1960) that the "existence of the Society as such was now impossible."[89] He wondered whether it would not be reasonable for those who shared the Society's principles on racial matters to be persuaded to cling to the idea and implement it through other organizations, new or old, instead of simply insisting on the per-petuation of the name Capricorn, a word that immediately called for shame and spelled political doom in colonial Zambia.[90]

In response, the General Council sent Jonathan Lewis, secretary of the council, on an assessment tour of the Society's branches in East and Central Africa. The report confirmed Takawira's earlier concerns about the future viability of the Society in Africa. Lewis noted that "member-ship had fallen away catastrophically since Salima."[91] The Society was no longer regarded as a serious force. Perhaps the most disturbing revelation in the report was the serious divisions in the Capricorn leadership. Lewis pointed out that members were leaving the Society and joining national-ist parties. Despite efforts to change the image of Capricorn since federa-tion, the Society continued to suffer from the "handicap of a bad name."[92]

Lewis added that there was hardly any evidence that the Society was taken seriously by Africans any more.

The report suggested, therefore, that there was no point in trying to sell non-racialism to Africans without doing something effective to tackle their basic problem—broadening the franchise. The report concluded that the Capricorn philosophy was meaningless in the contemporary scene because it was too remote from the day-to-day struggle for existence and for advancement by the ordinary semiliterate Africans.[93]

By 1961 it had dawned on the Capricornists that the Society could not be resurrected in the territory. Dr. Fisher, I.R. Menzies and Father Sillot made it clear to Reverend Fred Rea, chairperson of the reconstituted Central Africa branch, that "the Society could not provide a meeting point with Northern Rhodesia Africans."[94] In fact, Capricorn's kind of work was already being done through the Copperbelt Council of Churches.

Consequently, a circular letter was sent to all known Capricorn members in the territory, informing them of the decision to close down the Society in colonial Zambia.[95] Since no objection was raised, the Society proceeded to close down formally. First, it obtained permission from the Autolot[96] to dispose of its gift to the Society as the Society wished, and use the money for interracial purposes. Then it closed its bank account with Barclays Bank in Luanshya, following the distribution of its total asserts of £437 13s 6d as follows:

check to London Office (Zebra House)	£128 16s 9d
check to Salisbury Office	£128 16s 9d
check to Salisbury Office, to assist a student on scholarship to the USA	£180 0s 0d
TOTAL	**£437 13s 6d**

Finally, the Society informed the District Commissioner of the Society's wish to be crossed off the list of registered societies in Colonial Zambia.[97]

IMPACT OF LIBERAL IDEOLOGY ON CONGRESS

The Capricorn Africa Society was a genuine agent for the propagation of multiracial party politics in Colonial Zambia. In spite of the negative response it received, it influenced some Africans toward liberal activism. As early as August 1954 some Congress supporters had begun to value liberal ideas, but they were not able to advocate them outside the Congress. They therefore sought to advance the liberal cause from within the Congress. While this may explain, to a point, the moderate nature of the Congress, it did not lead to any wider expansion of liberal activism.

On 6 August 1954 B.L. Zulu wrote to the general secretary of the African National Congress seeking permission to form a new political party that was to be called the Conventional Peoples Party (CPP). The Congress ignored the letter and others that followed.[98] In October Zulu sent another letter, this time to the president general, informing him that the CPP was formed within the Congress constitution, not to crush ANC but to show difference of policies toward the struggle for independence and that:

> The party is formed by liberal minded Africans of this country who have foreseen that in few years to come we must rule this country on party politics.... The party will carry the opposition within the Congress.... I think we have reached at the time we should have party politics in this country so that we can abolish ARC and all other government institutions which elect African representatives in this country.[99]

There is an obvious paradox in Zulu's letter. How ready were they for party politics if they still sought permission from the Congress to form an opposition party? Axon Jasper Soko[100] charged that they were disillusioned with the way the ANC was conducting its affairs, but added that although they had formed a new party they would continue to give Congress their "due respect for its seniority and superiority."[101]

The attitude of Soko and Zulu reflect the notion of the national leader [father] or the "fanatical faith in the leader principle."[102] From the days that Harry M. Nkumbula became leader of the Congress he was widely regarded as the "father" of Northern Rhodesian African nationalism.[103] His leadership was not to be challenged. The leader and the nationalist struggle were viewed as two sides of the same coin by the vast majority of the Africans in the country. To oppose the leader or to form an independent opposition party was taken to be antinationalist. Worse still, one risked being called a Capricornist, which to many Africans was a term of abuse. Therefore, it was this wish to appear loyal to the leader and committed to the nationalist struggle that characterized Zulu's and Soko's approach to the ANC on the question of forming an opposition party. Kenneth D. Kaunda put it more vividly in his correspondence with Colin Morris when he said the "person of the leader provides a special intense focus of loyalty."[104] Apparently, in colonial Zambian politics, loyalty to the leader was an important factor holding the struggle together.

Most nationalists lacked a sense of true patriotism (love of the country) because their loyalty was to the leader much more than to the country. Many nationalists could not imagine a nationalist struggle that did not have Nkumbula's blessing. There was a general tendency to equate the person of the leader with the country.

Under these circumstances not many Africans were willing to join liberal multiracial parties and organizations. The Convention Peoples Party suffered a similar fate. Its multiracial approach was highly resented. Liberalism, rightly or wrongly, was interpreted by Africans as designed to perpetuate the colonial rule and the imperial connections. Because liberal parties and organizations (Capricorn included) were usually directed by Europeans, these fears appeared to confirmed. Furthermore, those Africans who were prepared to discuss liberalism to have a better understanding of its principles were silenced by vocal nationalists.

Besides, as Leopold Takawira, once Capricorn executive secretary, put it when explaining why many Africans did not join the multiracial Central African Party:

> The CAP caters for the voters and as such cannot speak for the blacks with that natural and native emotion which can only be arrived at from personal suffering and humiliation which Africans encounter day in day out. European friends might be sympathizers, but not physical co-sufferers.[105]

Undoubtedly, Takawira was being propelled by what Ali Mazrui calls the search for "pigmentational self-determination,"[106] after his resignation as executive secretary of Capricorn. This about-turn in Takawira's political career earned him a place among the nationalist heroes in the ZANU/PF. Terence Ranger writes that "Takawira Day was celebrated inside Mozambique during the war of the 1970s, so that his Capricorn connections were plainly not fatal to him."[107] Ranger believes that normally Capricorn connections would have been fatal in colonial Zambia.[108]

Colonial Zambian Africans were more extreme than Southern Rhodesian Africans in their negative attitude toward liberalism. Most Africans saw no meeting point between themselves and Europeans. As Kaunda said, "the multiracial bus" was not going their way.[109] The multiracial parties emphasized economic development before political progress and many members from the business class were "obsessed with the maintenance of political stability." Africans on the other hand wanted political power first and then "all else would follow."[110] This was largely because the African political elite in colonial Zambia came from the white collar-working class and not from the business class. As such, they were more concerned with establishing their hold on the state than on economic development and on exploiting state revenue to propel themselves into a ruling elite.

These conflicting political philosophies made liberalism less attractive to the African nationalists as an ideology for the transfer of political power from European hands to a local multiracial ruling elite. The prospect of an entirely African government was far more attractive than a multiracial government. Consequently petite bourgeoisie members of the aspiring middle class polarized. The aspiring bureaucratic bourgeoisie that controlled UNIP clashed with bluecollar workingclass members, especially trade unionists like Lawrence Katilungu.[111]

Nevertheless, there were a few Africans who came to believe that liberalism could and should be the basis for political development in the territory. William Nkanza and L.H. Ng'andu, both independent members of the Legislative Council, decided to join the Liberal Party in 1961 because it "fought for Northern Rhodesia and was the only party that could ensure unity in the country."[112] Yet these kinds of political shifts were always short lived. Eventually Africans returned to the Congress or United National Independence Party.[113]

LIBERAL IDEOLOGY AND THE AFRICAN REPRESENTATIVE COUNCIL

On 24 November 1945 Governor Sir John Waddington announced the creation of the African Representative Council (ARC) in the Legislative Council.[114] The ARC grew out of the Provincial Councils that had been in existence for some time in the territory. When the Provincial Councils were first established, it was made clear that they were not to interfere with the Native Authorities. They were meant to be organizations for the ventilation of public opinion. Their role was that of advising provincial commissioners who were expected to consult them on many issues relating to Native affairs. Finally, they were also to advise the Legislative Council through the members nominated to represent Native interests.[115]

On 19 August 1946 the ARC constitution was approved. It specified the function of the ARCl as that of advising "the governor on matters *directly* affecting the African population of the territory."[116] Besides this advisory capacity, the ARC acted as an electoral college for the election of two of its members for appointment by the governor to the Legislative

Council. The ARC was not parallel to or in substitution for the Legislative Council or indeed an alternative method of representation open to Africans. It was envisaged as a training ground for future African political leaders in the territory.[117]

The ARC held its first session in November 1946, at which time the acting governor reiterated the role of the ARC in the territory's politics. He emphasized that while the ARC advised the governor, it was not its role to make laws for the land—that was to be done by the Legislative Council. He also pointed out that ARC was not expected to administer the laws of the land, for that was the responsibility of the various government departments through the chiefs and their councils and the Native courts.[118]

The agenda for ARC meetings was decided by the government through the office of the secretary for Native affairs who also presided over its meetings. Members of the ARC were elected by Provincial Councils, except in Barotse Province where they were nominated by the Litunga.[119] Most of the members were initially very moderate in their political views, especially those about race relations. Moses Mubitana's address to the First Session of the ARC is a good example of friendly expression toward whites:

> On behalf of this Council and the Africans of Northern Rhodesia, I wish to take this opportunity of assuring the Europeans in this country that there is no desire on the part of all well-informed Africans to drive the Europeans south across the Zambezi. On the contrary, it is their ardent wish that they stay and continue the good work they have begun. Africans realise that their interests are interdependent with those of Europeans. Today white and black are members of one body (Northern Rhodesia) and each part of the body, even the simplest, has a little contribution to give for the prosperity of the whole body.[120]

For a while the ARC remained essentially a moderate body. The government put in place a system that kept out those individuals who were perceived to be somewhat radical. In 1953 the government rejected a proposal to elect ARC members from a communal roll because it was felt that Congress would easily take control of such a system and would put its own nominees in the ARC.[121]

Consequently, the ARC was criticized by the Congress as a group of stooges unfit to elect African representatives to the Legislative Council and the Federal Assembly. Nonetheless, the ARC elected Mateyo

Kakumbi (10 votes) and Dauti Yamba (9 votes) as Northern Rhodesia's members of Parliament for African interests in the Federal Assembly. Meanwhile the ARC was planning to form a subcommittee that would have formed the nucleus from which to develop an opposition party on strictly moderate lines to oppose the African National Congress. John Moffat, author of the Moffat Resolutions, and one of the European Legco members representing African interests, was asked to advise on the formation of this moderate party.[122] The plan was aborted because it would have antagonized African nationalists.

In the end, the colonial state's intention, in conjunction with the Colonial Office, to train moderate African politicians failed because of Congress activities that pictured moderate Africans as the worst enemy of the nationalist struggle. With time most moderate Africans in the ARC were replaced by militants. The process began at the leadership level. Moderate Godwin M. Lewanika was replaced by Harry M. Nkumbula in 1953 because of his alleged "failure to take a staunch anti-federal stand."[123] In 1951 the ARC had "dropped moderate Legislative Council Members Nelson Nalumango and Reverend Henry Kasokolo and replaced them with "nationalistic" Congress men Dauti Yamba and Pascale Sokota."[124]

Since the political process in Colonial Zambia was entangled with the closer association issue, the liberal wing of the settler community approached the problem of effecting the Federation of Rhodesia and Nyasaland and the problem of African political advancement in colonial Zambia not by seeking to suppress the Congress but by trying to influence it in the right direction. As early as 1949 Sir Stewart Gore-Browne began to impress upon the government the need to come to terms with the aspirations of "radical" Africans.[125] In 1950 he again urged the government to take heed of the "vocal and influential section of the African population" and criticized the African Representative Council as an ineffective government-sponsored and -controlled organ.[126] This criticism of the ARC by Sir Stewart Gore-Browne fueled the African National Congress' own apprehension of the ARC, which increasingly came to be seen as serving the interests of the colonial state and those of the imperial authority. To protect themselves from these insinuations, most liberal-minded ARC members shied away from openly embracing liberalism or Capricorn ideas.

From the mid-1950s ARC members were seen by Congress officials as "collaborators, weak-kneed ... yes-men."[127] This criticism did not, however, preclude Congress participation in the political machinery of which the ARC formed but a part. There was always an overlap between

ANC and the ARC during much of the life of the latter. Despite ANC's vicious condemnation of the ARC, the two bodies worked in cooperation. Congress officials, including Kenneth Kaunda, Harry Nkumbula and Simon Mwansa Kapwepwe, were members of Urban Advisory Councils that elected some of their members to the ARC. Much of the criticism had to do with the fact that Congress wanted more political influence than was possible under the conditions of the time.

Ultimately, on 3 October 1958 the ARC was abolished. Constitutional changes that were being effected had made the ARC irrelevant—particularly the provisions of what became known as the Benson Constitution that, for the first time, made a start toward replacing racial representation with a system under which all members of the Legislative Council were to be elected by a "common machinery providing for direct representation of all qualified voters in a geographical constituency."[128] The ARC held its last meeting on 20 October, marking the end of the official experiment in nurturing liberal politics.

The negative propaganda against Capricorn made it difficult for the Society to gain valuable support from some of the moderate ARC members. Congress militancy proved more influential than the Society's liberal ideology. The presence of Congress elements on the ARC kept Capricorn at a distance. By 1958, when the ARC was dissolved, most its members belonged to Congress and openly criticized Capricorn. The moderate element had been systematically replaced by militants. Capricorn found, not allies, but adversaries in the ARC.

Notes

1. NAZ, HM 53/6 Kenneth D. Kaunda to E.G. Nightingale, member of the Legco nominated to represent African interests, 18 February 1954 (Italics added).

2. See Chapter Two for a detailed discussion of Capricorn original ideas and policies.

3. CAS Papers File No. 10, Letter from David Stirling to Roy Welensky, 16 September 1953.

4. *Rhodesia Herald*, 26 February 1954, p. 5.

5. Tafataona Pasipaipa Mahoso, "Between Two Nationalisms: A Study in Liberal Activism and Western Domination, Zimbabwe 1920 to 1980," PhD Thesis, Temple University, 1987, p. 191.

6. See Appendix I for details of the Salisbury Declarations.

7. *The Capricorn Africa Society Handbook for Speakers*, Salisbury, 1955, A 10. Capricorn further stated that the main difference between the Capricorn

Declarations published by the Society in December 1952 during the early stages of negotiations for Central African Federation, and the manifesto published in February 1954, was that the former was an interim statement, whereas the manifesto laid down the working principles adopted by the Society as the basis of its doctrine.

8. *Rhodesia Herald*, 26 February 1954, p. 5.

9. Ian R. Hancock, "The Capricorn Africa Society in Southern Rhodesia," *Rhodesian History*, 9 (1978), p. 48.

10. NAZ, NR/ARC, *The Proceedings of the First Session of the Council*, November 1946.

11. NAZ, HM 53/1/63/2 Godwin Mbikusita Lewanika to Reverend E.G. Nightingale, 8 January, 1950. It is interesting to note that the Africa National Congress chose an Afrikaans word—"Eendrag"—for its motto.

12. Clyde Sanger, *Central African Emergency* (London: Oxford University Press, 1960), p. 100. Sanger added that "in 1950 David Stirling was co-author of the pamphlet "A Native Policy for Africa" with N.H. Wilson, who later became secretary of the Dominion Party and then resigned even from that reactionary body in protest at what he considered its "middle-of-the-road" views. The sentiments expressed in the pamphlet could hardly be called liberal: it urged the Southern Rhodesian Government to *raise* its franchise qualifications, and applauded its ' two-pyramid' policy of separate development. Stirling once favoured a federation of all six territories of East and Central Africa, but later became one of the most energetic advocates of the present federation, exercising particular influence, it is said, on Attlee's thinking. Finally, seeing the strength of African opposition, he switched his views again and came out against compulsory federation for Africans."

13. *The CAS Handbook*, A 10, Extract from the manifesto.

14. *The CAS Handbook*, Capricorn defined civilization in terms of European norms and values that Africans were expected to acquire through education.

15. CAS Papers, File No. 69, cited from *The Times*, 4 March 1954.

16. For details of the Draft Statement on Partnership, see Appendix II, and compare with the African Representative Council Draft Statement on Principles of Interracial Policy in Appendix III.

17. CAS Papers. File No. 69, cited from the *Rhodesia Herald*, 12 March 1954.

18. CAS Papers File No. 69, David Stirling to F.S. Joelson, 22 March 1954. Stirling enclosed a summary of extracts from statements made by various political leaders in East and Central Africa, as well as the exchange of letters between N.H. Wilson and Capricorn in the *Rhodesia Herald*.

19. *Rhodesia Herald*, 27 February 1954, p. 4.

20. CAS Papers, File No. 12/73 David Stirling to Jack A Couldry, 5 April 1954.

21. CAS Papers, File No. 51, David Stirling to Arthur Stokes, 28 September 1953.

22. For details of the Capricorn Contract, see Appendix IV

23. Hancock, "The Capricorn Africa Society," p. 49.

24. *The Northern News*, 1 January 1957.

25. Zimbabwe National Archives (Zimb. N. A.), S/EQ 84, Dorothy Lehmann to Gibson, 25 March 1956.

26. Zimb. N. A., S/EQ 84 Dorothy Lehmann to Gibson, 25 March 1956.

27. CAS Papers, File No. 48/40 I.R. Menzies to David Stirling, 24 November 1955.

28. CAS Papers, File No. 48/40, Menzies to Stirling.

29. CAS Papers, File No. 13, Stirling to Peter MacKay, 28 March 1955. According to Hardwicke Holderness, "accepting any role in white dominated institutions could imply an acceptance of the status quo and, particularly if there were any elements of patronage in it, turn out to be the kiss of death. Already it looked as if that was what was happening to Jasper Savanhu and Mike Hove, the two who had accepted nomination by the Federal Party for the African seats in the Federal Parliament, and on the fringe of politics, to someone like Chad Chipunza who had become a full time employee of the Capricorn Africa Society (Hardwicke Holderness, *Lost Chance: Southern Rhodesia, 1945-1958*, [Harare: Zimbabwe Publishing House, 1985], p.170.)

30. See NAZ, SEC 5/185/19/1 Godwin A.M. Lewanika, Address to the Central African Sub-Group of the Conservative Commonwealth Council, 1 August 1956.

31. NAZ, HM 53/1 Harry Franklin to E.G. Nightingale, 23 July 1954.

32. NAZ, HM 47, Constitution of the United Northern Rhodesia Association, 1954, p. 1.

33. While it is not clear whether Kaunda joined the Association, evidence suggests that he patronized the association's Kabulonga Club in the 1950s (see *New African*, October 1984, p. 63).

34. Harry Mwaanga Nkumbula, then president of the African National Congress, joined the UNRA in 1956.

35. The reader may be interested to note that the RST was also financially supporting Capricorn.

36. *The Northern News*, Friday, 30 May 1955.

37. Dr. Charles Fisher, Interview with Jane Parpart, 21 August 1976. I am greatly indebted to Jane Parpart for giving me a copy of the transcript of the interview. The 1950 Club, like the '48 Club of Lusaka, was formed as a meeting place for Europeans and educated Africans. The declared motive

was to establish a common ground and better understanding between the races.

38. Wittington K. Sikalumbi, *Before UNIP: A History*, (Lusaka: Neczam, 1977), p. 83.

39. CAS Papers, File No. 30, Letter to Jonathan Lewis, 19 September 1956. The author of the letter did not write his name, only identified himself as a former resident magistrate in Ndola. It is not at all clear from the records available whether he was offered the job.

40. *Zebra*, No. 11 (1956).

41. Reverend Merfyn M. Temple was secretary of the United Society for Christian Literature, president of the Christian Council of Northern Rhodesia, and leader of the multiracial study group appointed by the World Council of Churches to study Christian responsibilities in areas of rapid social change.

42. John Mwanakatwe was an education officer and later became the first African secondary school principal in Northern Rhodesia. In June 1961 he was appointed an assistant commissioner for Northern Rhodesia in London. He was also UNIP's most respected official among Europeans. In 1962 he was appointed Minister of Labour and Mines in the country's first African government. At independence he became Minister of Education and rose to the post of Minister of Finance until he resigned from the government to go into private business in 1986. Mwanakatwe was an able leader, whose moderate political views were clearly noted even then. He had been a member of the multiracial '48 Club, which he joined on 16 September 1952 (NAZ, HM 11, The '48 Club, Minutes of a committee meeting of 16 September 1952). The '48 Club was superseded by the United Northern Rhodesia Association. (See The Record of the last General Meeting of The '48 Club, held in Reverend Nightingale's office on 24 November 1953).

43. CAS Papers, File No. 43, Executive Secretary's Report of the Tour of Northern Rhodesia, 24 June to 9 July 1953.

44. On Capricorn as an agent of vampire-men see Mwelwa C. Musambachime, "The Impact of Rumour: The Case of the Banyama (vampire-men) Scare in Northern Rhodesia, 1939-1964," *The International Journal of African Historical Studies*, 21, 2 (1988), pp. 201-215.

45. CAS Papers, File No. 43, Executive Secretary's Report of the Tour of Northern Rhodesia, 24 June to 9 July 1953.

46. CAS Papers, File No. 119, CAS-N.R. Financial Statement for the month ending 30 June 1957. Since the membership fee was 5s, it meant the numbers of paid-up members rose from 17 to 35. These figures are somewhat misleading because there were people who sympathized with Capricorn ideas who did not actually become paid-up members. In fact evidence suggests that the Luanshya branch alone had up to 70 active members. (*The Northern News*, 25 September and 2 October 1957, and 16 May 1958).

47. CAS Papers, File No. 48/126, Chad Chipunza to David Stirling, 24 March, 1956. Chipunza further informed Stirling that "we should NEVER make it known that we have appealed to Harry. Even his Executive does not know anything about this." A year later Chipunza resigned as the Society's executive officer in order to concentrate on politics. He was replaced by Leopold Takawira on 28 August 1957.

48. NAZ, SEC 5/112/167, Record of a meeting between Clement Attlee and African National Congress delegation, Lusaka, 20 August 1952; PA, ANC 7/83 Harry Mwaanga Nkumbula's letter to various ANC members, 21 November, 1952.

49. CAS Papers, File No. 12/19, Joseph H. Oldham to Jonathan Lewis, 7 October 1960.

50. Eileen Haddon Papers, University of Zambia Library, Special Collections. Federal Party, Luanshya Branch Memorandum to the Proposed Charter (Policy), 1956. At the time I was given permission to go through the papers, they were not yet catalogued by the Library.

51. Eileen Haddon Papers, Memorandum to the Proposed Charter, Clause 6.

52. Eileen Haddon Papers, Memorandum to the Proposed Charter.

53. Robert I. Rotberg, *Black Heart: Gore-Browne and the Politics of Multiracial Zambia* (Berkeley: University of California Press, 1977), p. 303.

54. Dr. Alexander Scott was initially a railway doctor and had since branched out and became a large shareholder in a Lusaka newspaper and a building society.

55. According to Clyde Sanger, the genesis of the Constitution Party "was as much a reaction against Congress violence in the boycott of beer halls in Northern Rhodesia as against the unprogressiveness of the Federal Party" (Clyde Sanger, *Central African Emergency*, p. 104).

56. Cited from Rotberg, *Black Heart*, p. 304.

57. Colin Leys, *European Politics in Southern Rhodesia* (London: Oxford University Press, 1959), p. 124.

58. *The Northern News*, 25 September, 1957.

59. Sir Ronald L. Prain, "The Problem of African Advancement on the Copperbelt of Northern Rhodesia," *African Affairs* 53, 211 (April 1954), p. 92. Prain's comparison with the situation in West Africa is absurd because there was no settled white population there at all. West African nationalists never thought of self-rule as "black supremacy" because racial minority safeguards were never an issue there.

60. Although Musumbulwa participated in the inaugural meeting, he denied having been a member of the Constitution Party. Interview at Luanshya, 15 May, 1989.

61. Rotberg, *Black Heart*, p. 304.

62. CAS Papers, File No. 4, Weekly Summaries #42/57, 6 December 1957.

63. CAS Papers, File No. 4, Weekly Summaries #42/57, 6 December 1957. Henry Thorncroft was the leader of the colored community in Northern Rhodesia.

64. CAS Papers, File No. 30, Letter from Dr. Fisher cited in a letter from Jonathan Lewis to the Earl of March, 3 December 1957.

65. See Chapter Three on the challenges faced by "liberal" Africans in Northern Rhodesia.

66. Robin Short, *African Sunset* (London: Johnson, 1973). p. 193.

67. Short, *African Sunset*, p. 193.

68. *The Northern News*, 3 December 1957.

69. *The Central African Examiner*, 21 December 1957, p.13.

70. Interview with Author, 15 May 1989 at Luanshya.

71. *Northern News*, 28 September 1957, p. 5.

72. *Northern News*, 28 September 1957, p. 5.

73. *Northern News*, 28 September 1957, p. 5.

74. Sikalumbi, *Before UNIP*, p. 59

75. *Northern News*, 5 November 1957.

76. *Northern News*, 9 October 1957.

77. Anonymous, *Northern News*, 9 October 1957.

78. *Rhodesia Herald*, 13 December 1957.

79. *Northern News*, 15 February 1958.

80. *Northern News*, 15 February 1958.

81. "News from Northern Rhodesia," *Equinox*, November 1957, p. 12.

82. CAS Papers File No. 6, *Equinox*, December 1957. It suggested that the founding of the Constitution Party was a step further in the development of CAS.

83. "News from Northern Rhodesia," *Equinox*, June 1958, p. 11.

84. NAZ, SEC 5/270, The Moffat Resolutions, Legislative Council Debates, 29 July 1954. Sir John Moffat, the author of the resolutions, served in the Northern Rhodesia Provincial Administration for twebty years. In 1951 he was appointed to represent African interests on the Legco. In 1955 he was nominated to represent African interests in the federal Assembly and was chairman of the African Affairs Board, a position he resigned before founding the Central African Party (CAP). On the impact of the Moffat Resolutions on Northern Rhodesia's constitutional changes, see David C. Mulford, *Zambia: The Politics of Independence, 1957-1964* (London: Oxford University Press, 1967), pp. 56-57.

85. Most Africans boycotted the 1958 federal elections. It is hard to relate this boycott to the poor performance of the Constitution Party for the simple reason that the boycott was precipitated by African rejection of the electoral system. In a racially polarized political environment it is doubtful if Africans would have supported the multiracial Constitution Party.

86. Reverend Merfyn M. Temple joined the United National Independence Party in 1960. He was appointed deputy director of National Youth Service in April 1964.

87. Joan Lorraine Watson, "The Capricorn Africa Society and Its Impact on Rhodesian Politics," PhD Thesis, St John's University, New York 1981, p. 113. See Chapter Five on the CAP's involvement in Northern Rhodesian politics, and its subsequent change of name to the Liberal Party in 1961.

88. CAS Papers, File No. 19, Sir John Slessor to Jonathan Lewis, 7 October 1959.

89. CAS Papers, File No. 22, Extract from the Report of the Executive Officer's Tour of Northern Rhodesia, 1960.

90. CAS Papers, File No. 22, Extract from the Report of the executive officer's Tour of Northern Rhodesia, 1960.

91. CAS Papers, File No. 93, Confidential Report, October 1960.

92. CAS Papers, File No. 93, Confidential Report, October 1960.

93. CAS Papers, File No. 93, Confidential Report, October 1960.

94. CAS Papers, File No. 43, A Verbatim Report of CAS General Council Meeting Held at St. Julian's Limuru, Kenya, 21-22 January 1961; also File No. 134, Minutes of the General Council, 22 January 1961. The General Council acknowledged the decline of the Society in Africa and its pending dissolution, but resolved that the London office should continue its work.

95. CAS Papers, File No. 131, Memorandum on the closing of Capricorn Africa Society in Northern Rhodesia, 1961.

96. Autolot was a company that had donated a motor vehicle to Capricorn in Northern Rhodesia.

97. CAS Papers, File No. 131, Memorandum, 1961.

98. PA, ANC 5/11, B.L. Zulu, organizing secretary, CPP to the general secretary, ANC, 11 August 1954. It should be pointed out that it was the same Zulu who in 1952 had vehemently denied any involvement with CAS and had said he did not want to discuss liberalism.

99. PA, ANC 5/11, B.L. Zulu to president general, ANC, 14 October 1954.

100. He was among those who later broke away from ANC in 1958, and was consequently appointed Zambia African National Congress' secretary for the Western Province, which then included the Copperbelt region.

101. PA, ANC 5/11, Axon J. Soko to secretary general, ANC, 24 October 1954.

102. Anonymous, *Northern News*, Tuesday 27 January 1953.

103. He was usually addressed as "father" by most of the ANC members. Letters to Nkumbula from ANC members usually addressed him as such. See for example Munukayumbu Sipalo's letter to Nkumbula, 11 November, 1957, PA, ANC 7/63. Indeed, even letters between ANC members also referred to Nkumbula as "father." See, for example, J.K. Chivunga's

letter to Chiyesu, 18 October 1957. Chivunga was then provincial general secretary of ANC. The same spirit was implied in Sikota Wina's letter to Nkumbula when he said, "summon together the United National Independence Party and the African National Congress and declare that you are moving higher in the African leadership hierarchy and that you are prepared to declare unity of all Africans under one banner, that of ANC of Northern Rhodesia. And that because of your pre-occupation with Legco matters you will take the post of *National Guardian*, leaving the entire administration into the hands of a president to be elected by both organizations." PA, ANC 7/63, 10 December,1959 (Emphasis added).

104. Kenneth Kaunda and Colin M. Morris, *A Humanist in Africa: Letters to Colin Morris from Kenneth D. Kaunda, President of Zambia* (London: Longmans, 1966), p. 84.

105. Cited in Philip Mason, *Year of Decision: Rhodesia and Nyasaland in 1960* (London: Oxford University Press, 1960), p. 229.

106. Ali Mazrui, "Pluralism and National Integration," in Leo Kuper and M.G. Smith (eds.) *Pluralism in Africa* (Berkeley: University of California Press, 1969)

107. Letter from Terence Ranger to author, 3 January 1989 (erroneously dated 1988). Ranger writes: "I was briefly a member of Capricorn in Southern Rhodesia at the request of the late Leopold Takawira, who received a salary and travelling expenses as the Secretary of the Society, which he was using to organise for the National Democratic Party. Sceptical though I was about the Society I agreed to join so as to provide him with cover."

108. This is not quite correct. Known former white Capricornists were appointed to various government positions by the UNIP government. Curiously, however, while UNIP was ready to work with former white Capricornists, it was reluctant to work with former black Capricornists. Ranger's assumption is therefore applicable to Africans but not to Europeans.

109. Kenneth D. Kaunda and Colin Morris *Black Government? A Discussion Between Colin Morris and Kenneth Kaunda* (Lusaka: United Society for Christian Literature 1960) p. 93.

110. Mulford, *Zambia*, p. 49.

111. For a detailed analysis of this, see Robert H. Bates, *Unions, Parties and Political Development: A Study of Mineworkers in Zambia*,(New Haven, CT, Yale University Press, 1977).

112. *Northern News*, 17 August, 1961.

113. On the birth of the United National Independence Party, see Chapter Five.

114 On the origins and functions of the African Representative Council, see J. W. Davidson, *The Northern Rhodesia Legislative Council* (London, 1948), pp. 31-34; and Dot L. Keet, "The African Representative Council, 1946-

1958: A Focus on African Political Leadership And the Politics of Northern Rhodesia", MA Thesis, University of Zambia, Lusaka 1975.

115. NAZ, SEC 5/44, Notes on African Representative Council, 1949-1951.

116. NAZ, NR/ARC, Address by Acting Governor, *Proceedings of the First Session of the Council*, November,1946 (emphasis in original).

117. Interview with Gabriel Musumbulwa at Luanshya, 15 May1989.

118. NAZ, NR/ARC No. 1, *The Proceedings of the First Session of the Council*, held at the Jeans School, Chalimbana, November 1946.

119. Litunga was the royal title of the Lozi king in Barotseland.

120. NAZ, NR/ARC No. 1, *The Proceedings of the First Session of the Council* November 1946.

121. NAZ, SEC 5/45/275, Extract from Minutes of Executive Council, 10-11 March 1953.

122. NAZ, SEC 5/43, W.F. Stubbs to J.E. Marnharm, 17 December 1953.

123. Robert I. Rotberg, *The Rise of Nationalism in Central Africa: The Making of Malawi and Zambia, 1873-1964* (Cambridge, MA: Harvard University Press, 1967), p. 234, fn. 43.

124. Sikalumbi, *Before UNIP*, p. 9. Note that two years later Yamba was accused of being a stooge and not fit to represent African interests in the Federal Assembly. According to Mulford, Yamba's position as one of Northern Rhodesia's African Federal M.P.s "fatally damaged his political career" (Mulford, *Zambia*, p. 22).

125. Keet, "The African Representative Council," p. 17.

126. Keet, "The African Representative Council," p. 17.

127. Munukayumbu Sipalo, cited in Keet, "The African Representative Council," p. 144.

128. Cmd. 530, *Northern Rhodesia Proposals for Constitutional Change*, September, 1958, p. 20, cited in Mulford, *Zambia*, p. 57.

Chapter 4

TOWARD INDEPENDENCE: LIBERALISM AND THE TRIUMPH OF AFRICAN POPU-LIST NATIONALISM, 1954-1964

Analyses of Zambia's "march to political freedom"[1] are far from lacking. These studies range from what Fanuel K.M. Sumaili describes as *confessional* writings[2] to works by professional historians, political scientists and interested political commentators.[3] If there is any point of convergence between these works, it is in their handling of the nationalist movement, which is portrayed as a struggle against the unjust political system then in place. Kenneth David Kaunda appropriately put it thus:

> What is it that we are fighting and sacrificing for? One, we want to get rid of foreign domination. Two, we are determined that the present bogus constitution must go. Three, that the majority must rule. Four, that there never can be any other safe repository of the ultimate powers of society but the people themselves, which in fact means that you will never be respected unless and until you yourselves control the reins of power.

> Our problem is practical not ideological. *After all, there are 3,000,000 of us and only 72,000 whites.*[4]

This brief extract from Kaunda's speech in 1960 expressed the core of the ideology of African "populist" nationalism—"Africanism"—that is the need for African nationalists to be in control of the political system. The slogan "Seek ye first the political Kingdom"[5] found wide appeal among Northern Rhodesia's militant nationalists.

From 1924 to 1954 the constitutional arrangements had almost completely consolidated political power in the hands of white settlers. The Colonial Office had meanwhile satisfied itself that political stability would be maintained so long as the political aspirations of the settler community were fulfilled. After all, Africans were yet to prove that they were fit to share in the administration of the country. Although the 1935 and 1940 Copperbelt strikes had sent messages of African discontent, the colonial state in colonial Zambia interpreted the strikes as labor, not political problems.[6]

The federation question quickened and intensified African nationalist activism, which began to influence the constitutional process in a different direction. Contrary to pro-federation propaganda, the reality of federation after 1953 did not lead to the end of African opposition. African nationalists (in the north especially) pointed to federation as a clear example of the strengthening of white domination. There is no doubt that federation was an effective propaganda subject for the nationalists. They were not willing to cooperate with the federal government that represented settler triumph and Colonial Office betrayal of African nationalist trust. Meanwhile the Colonial Office was increasingly anxious to secure that cooperation without undermining the authority of the federal government. How was this to be accomplished?

Colonial authorities in colonial Zambia, with the Colonial Office, diagnosed the problem to be the absence of nonracial politics in the territory. Africans and Europeans were constantly divided on racial lines. Having diagnosed the problem, Northern Rhodesia Governor Sir Arthur E.T. Benson was asked to come up with a solution.[7]

BENSON'S CONSTITUTIONAL CHANGES

Benson's answer to the problem was that in the future all constitutional changes should aim at encouraging the development of nonracial politics. The final objective would be parity in the legislature. There was to be a gradual moving away from the system of racial representation to a constitutional stage when members of the Legislative Council (MLCs) were elected by and represented members of a geographical constituency rather than members of a particular racial group.[8] In part, therefore, Benson's approach sought to adjust the representative estates of the colonial state to strengthen it.

Governor Benson's proposals for constitutional changes were inspired by Sir John Moffat's 1954 Resolutions, which he hoped would guide future policy in the country. The four resolutions adopted in the Legislative Council (Legco) on 29 July 1954 read:

> 1. The objective of policy in Northern Rhodesia must be to remove from each race the fear that the other race might dominate for its own racial benefit and to move forward from

the present system of racial representation in the territorial legislature towards a franchise with no separate representation for the races.

2. Until that objective can be fully achieved a period of transition will remain during which special arrangements in the Legislative and Executive Councils must continue to be made so as to ensure that no race can use either the preponderance of its numbers or its more advanced stage of development to dominate the other for its own racial benefit.

3. During this period of transition, special legislation must be in force to protect, to the extent that may be necessary, in the interests of either race. Meanwhile this Council notes and agrees with the statement of the Secretary of State that it is the duty of Her Majesty's Government to ensure that on contentious issues the balance is fairly held.

4. Every lawful inhabitant of Northern Rhodesia has the right to progress according to his character, qualification, training, ability, and industry, without distinction of race, colour or creed.[9]

The Resolutions were well received both in colonial Zambia and the United Kingdom. On 20 July Sir Thomas Lloyd minuted the colonial secretary that the resolutions should be accepted as a basis for future constitutional development in the country.[10]

However, Governor Benson informed the colonial secretary that the Moffat Resolutions introduced no new principle into the policy followed by the United Kingdom government since 1924. The essence of the resolutions, he noted, was that they set the principles on which government policy was based and confirmed that the special arrangements and the special legislation already established were essential. The acceptance and adoption of the resolutions was an "act of confirmation" of government policy, he concluded.[11]

Africans, no less than Europeans initially responded to the resolutions with excitement. The ANC's "New Look" policy was as much a reflection of the party's acceptance of the resolutions as it was a reflection of the influence of Harry Franklin on the Congress leader.[12] The "New Look" policy was based on the assumption that what Africans required was not so much a rapid advance in the political field, but a gradual well-grounded political advancement preceded by economic development. These ideas conformed to the Capricorn philosophy, which nationalists consistently rejected. Nkumbula insisted that Congress should abandon extremism and adopt moderate policies instead.[13] This position squarely placed Nkumbula outside "populist" political activism favored by most militant nationalists.

Wittington K. Sikalumbi records that Nkumbula's insistence on the "New Look" policy led to the resignation of Job Mayanda, the treasurer general, and Titus Mukupo, the clerk of council, from the Executive Council of the party.[14] Nkumbula was unmoved by these resignations. After the Executive Council meeting Nkumbula, Kaunda, Justin Chimba and Sikalumbi went to the Government Secretariat Building where they met European members of the legislature in the Legislative Council lobby room. During the meeting Nkumbula gave a statement of the Congress "New Look" policy to John Roberts, leader of the unofficials.[15] The statement read:

> There are many things that Congress must do which would take a little time. We must control our members and our branches better. We must control and educate on better lines our extremists. On both sides, both Africans and Europeans, there is room for better understanding.
>
> By this statement, by bringing the Congress onto constitutional practice, and by assuring Africans of this country that the Government of Northern Rhodesia is impartial and genuinely interested in improving the conditions under which Africans live, I am quite confident that race relations will improve to the satisfaction of every decent person in this country.
>
> We will do our best to work for the development of Northern Rhodesia and all its people, but for this we need the help and sympathy of all liberal minded Europeans.[16]

Clearly, the "New Look" policy sought to reform the Congress and prepare it for participation in the multiracial politics that were then the subject of proposed constitutional changes.

Before long, however, nationalists began to despair and question the significance of the Resolutions. Kaunda, then secretary general of the Congress, wrote:

> After the announcement was made about the Moffat Resolutions, which support the abolition of the practice of nominated Europeans to represent African interests in the Legislative Council and the African Representative Council which now operates as the electoral college for African candidates to the Legislative Council and Federal Parliament, an impression was

> created upon the people of Northern Rhodesia that the Reso-
> lutions would form a basis for constitutional talks. The people
> are at a loss as to whether the undefined exotic constitutional
> changes were the same as the Moffat Resolutions.[17]

There was a genuine concern about what was being done (or not done) to put the resolutions into effect. A month later, Francis Mwaba, a Congress member, stated that if Europeans wanted to avoid "Mau Mau" they should accept the Moffat Resolutions.[18]

Meanwhile, the ANC continued to press the imperial government to enfranchise British Protected Persons and to lower income and property qualifications to £50 and £100 respectively. The Congress asked for a single common roll for blacks and whites and a House of Representatives with a total of thirty seats. Its members were to be entirely elected. The Congress also asked for a cabinet of ten ministers distributed equally between the two races.[19] The government rejected these demands as they implied an immediate African majority in the Legco. The rejection suggests the extent to which multiracialism was acceptable. Imperial authorities were not ready to have parity in the Legco yet. Parity in the Legco would eventually have forced a cabinet of equal representation for both races to work together. This did not stop African nationalists from making further demands for constitutional changes.

VOTING QUALIFICATIONS

In June 1956 Francis Chembe moved a motion in the African Representative Council[20] that the government should give British Protected Persons the right to vote on a common roll based on the following qualifications:

(1) twenty-one years of age;
(2) residential period of three years for immigrants;
(3) ability to read and write in the vernacular;
(4) either property of not less than £50; or
(5) an income of not less than £5 a month.[21]

Although these proposals were not calling for one man one vote, the government rejected them along with those put forward earlier by the ANC. It argued that lower income and property qualifications would enfranchise thousands of Africans, especially on the Copperbelt and the railroad line. Inevitably, the African vote would have swamped the

European vote, making it necessary to transfer political power to a largely "ill-prepared" electorate. This was a political scenario the colonial government and the Colonial Office had been trying to avoid all along. Yet had the education, income and property qualifications been applied rigidly, the outcome would have been parity.

Governor Benson had a four-pronged formula with which to respond to the problem: (1) that there should be qualitative democracy; (2) that Europeans should never be swamped by Africans; (3) that British Protected Persons should be admitted to the franchise; and (4) that the system to be adopted should break away from racialism.[22] In other words, he wanted politics in Colonial Zambia to develop along multiracial party lines and avoid racial confrontation.

Consequently, the White Paper[23] published in September 1958 was based on that principle. It envisaged moving away from racial representation to a system by which all members would be elected to the ARC by a common electoral process. The suggested system provided for direct representation of qualified voters in a geographical constituency. Most important, the 1958 constitutional proposals aimed at placing the government "in the hands of responsible men—men with the understanding and of sufficient education and experience of affairs to be able to reason and to exercise judgment between alternative courses of action."[24]

The Benson Constitution, as the proposals became known, was heavily influenced by the liberal ideas in favor at the time. The fundamental principle was to establish an electoral machinery designed to encourage the return of moderate politicians from both sections of the community.[25] The Benson Constitution acknowledged that the gap between Africans and Europeans was too wide for multiracial politics to be achieved within a short period. It was hoped, however, that because only those who positively contributed to the wealth and welfare of the country would be enfranchised, the problem of one race (African) swamping the other (European) would be minimized.[26]

The need for a liberal political instrument committed to multiracial politics and the encouragement of multiracial parties as opposed to racial politics inevitably resulted in the most complicated constitution that was ever introduced by Britain in colonial Zambia or perhaps any other colony. The Constitution also brought about a split in the Congress between those who wanted to give the new constitution a chance and those who were adamantly opposed to its adoption.[27]

The 1958 government proposals aimed at broadening the franchise so as "to do justice both to individuals and to the African race as a whole."[28] The proposals were designed to give a political voice only to those who had achieved a certain European standard, while avoiding leaving the African race feeling underrepresented and ignored. The Northern Rhodesia government believed that these considerations could be satisfied by introducing a second lower set of temporary qualifications that would enable some Africans to qualify at once. It gave the vote to all those who were approaching the threshold of European standards while excluding others who had not yet reached that point.[29] Both sets of qualifications were initially to follow those set for the federal elections—an arrangement that made African nationalists particularly unhappy. The proposed qualifications were as follows:

Ordinary Voters
(a) £720 per annum (or ownership, including leasehold, of property valued at £1,500); or
(b) £480 per annum (or ownership, including leasehold, of property valued at £1,000), plus primary education; or
(c) £300 per annum (or ownership, including leasehold, of property valued at £500), plus four years secondary education; or
(d) Ministers of Religion who have undergone certain stipulated courses of training and periods of service in the Ministry and who follow no other profession or gainful occupation; or
(e) Paramount Chiefs and other Chiefs recognized by the Governor; or those certified by the Resident Commissioner in the Barotseland Protectorate to be of equivalent status.

Special Voters
(a) £150 per annum (or ownership, including leasehold, of property valued at £500); or
(b) £120 per annum plus two years secondary education; or
(c) In addition persons described in paragraph 33 would also be enfranchised for territorial elections.[ad]

The following qualifications were required for all voters:
(i) Simple literacy: applicants must be able to complete in English without assistance the application to be registered as a voter.
(ii) Age: Minimum age 21.

(iii)Nationality: British Subjects, citizen of Rhodesia and Nyasaland, or British Protected Persons by virtual of connection with Northern Rhodesia.

(iv) Residence: Two years in the territory and three months in the constituency.[31]

The government proposals also provided for a Legislative Council composed of a speaker and thirty members constituted as follows: 22 elected members, 6 Official members and 2 nominated members. The twenty-two directly-elected members were to be secured as follows: 12 members to be elected in 12 "Ordinary" constituencies; 6 members to be elected in 6 "special" constituencies; 2 Europeans to be elected in seats specifically reserved for Europeans; and 2 Africans elected to be in seats specifically reserved for Africans. Candidates for the ordinary constituencies were to be elected by voters of every race and each would accordingly represent all racial groups.[32]

THE BENSON CONSTITUTION

For all its shortcomings and complicated electoral processes, the Benson Constitution of 1959 was the first to break away from past practice. This constitution paved the way for the enfranchisement of approximately 24,648 Africans compared to 13,382 Europeans and 1,254 Asians, and provided for eight African seats in the twenty-six-member Legislative Council. This was a significant constitutional development, considering there had been only eleven enfranchised Africans on the 1957 voters' roll[33] and only four African Legco members, elected through an electoral college system culminating in the African Representative Council.

The Benson Constitution initiated a process of change in the composition of the power base of the colonial state. Arguably, it laid (or at least it intended to lay) the foundations of liberal democracy in colonial Zambia. Yet the response it received was reminiscent of Hegel's comment on Spain:

> Napoleon wished to give Spaniards a constitution *a priori* but the project turned out badly enough. A constitution is not just something manufactured; it is the work of centuries, it is the Idea, the consciousness of rationality so far as that consciousness is developed in a particular nation. No constitution therefore, is just the creation of its subjects. What Napoleon gave to the Spaniards was more rational than what they had

before, and yet they recoiled from it as from something alien, *because they were not yet educated up to its level.*[34]

This comment has a good deal of bearing on the colonial Zambian situation. Although the Benson constitution was more rational for colonial Zambia, the people were *"not yet educated up to its level."*

While militant African nationalists felt the constitution did not go far enough to meet their expectations, the European community, for different reasons, believed the pace of change was too fast. Even the most liberal whites believed Africans were not yet ready for democracy. Speaking in the Federal Assembly in June 1961, Sir John Moffat said:

> I would suggest now that the existing system cannot be permitted to continue, but the European population should demand its alteration.
>
> There is a mathematical certainty that within a period, which can be calculated with sufficient accuracy for all practical purposes, the African people, under our present electoral laws, will be in a majority on the voters' roll. Once that happened, it was doubtful whether democracy would be maintained.[35]

It is ironic that Sir John Moffat, author of the 1954 Resolutions, should have made this statement in the Federal Assembly, when the Benson Constitution had already given Africans a majority on Northern Rhodesia's voters' roll. In colonial Zambia he saw the role of the Liberal Party as transitory for a period lasting not more than five years.[36] His assessment of the colonial Zambian situation was based on the same mathematical formula he was now advising federal MPs to watch carefully. Nonetheless, his views reflected the thinking of most Europeans, both on the right and on the left, though for different reasons. For Moffat, the African majority needed time to learn the basics of liberal democracy and the art of governance before they took over the government.

The Benson Constitution sought to introduce multiracial party politics in the country.[37] Nkumbula felt that the constitution should be given a fair trial. Yet the party's militants, led by Simon Mwansa Kapwepwe, were dissatisfied and became apprehensive about the prospects of nationalist success with such a conciliatory policy. The conflict between moderate Nkumbula and militants like Kapwepwe was over timing and the rate of change. The Benson Constitution did not rule out African majority in the Legco but it set a slower pace toward that objective. This was essentially the Capricorn view of the democratization process. Militant nationalists sought an immediate majority in the Legco and therefore, opposed gradualism implied by the Benson Constitution.

FORMATION OF ZANC

Attempts to replace Nkumbula as leader of the party failed. Although Kaunda had by 1957 risen to prominence in the Congress, he was not able to replace Nkumbula as leader. Throughout 1957 and part of 1958 the young militants unsuccessfully tried to replace Nkumbula. Finally on the night of 24 October 1958, Kapwepwe, Kamanga and others, followed by Kaunda an hour later, broke away and formed the Zambia African National Congress (ZANC).[38] Nkumbula's fall from grace was no doubt assisted by his drinking and self-indulgence, but his moderate political stance was the main cause for complaint among the radical nationalists who deserted him.

Kapasa Makasa also cites ethnic conflicts as contributing to the eventual split of the ANC:

> Nkumbula was a good strategist. Having realised that all was not well with him in the party, he summoned an emergency meeting of the executive committee in October 1958 for the purpose of giving the president general wider powers.... To ensure that there would a majority for him in the committee when it came to voting on the amendments, Nkumbula had brought into the committee a contingent of his supporters from Southern Province, his home area, who were neither members of the central committee nor the party, contrary to the party constitution. This was one of the reasons that led to our walking out of the meeting.[39]

It is therefore evident that ethnicity was a factor in the split, and may have played an even bigger role than has until now been admitted.

The birth of ZANC signaled both a rejection of the conciliatory policy adopted by the ANC and the development of race-conscious nationalism driven by the ideology of "pigmentational selfdetermination." ZANC also represented the first real attempt to adopt a "populist" philosophy in the nationalist struggle in colonial Zambia. Although ZANC was short lived, it tried to appear to be championing the interests of the common people.

ZANC's adoption of the "populist" approach reflected imperial policy, which required that before any transfer of power could be sanctioned, the people concerned must prove they were ready to receive power. One requirement was widespread support. This policy encouraged first ZANC and later the United National Independence Party (UNIP) [an] to create the image of "populist" nationalist parties. Yet, it is common knowledge that both ZANC and UNIP, its successor, did not rise out of mass discontent. The elite created the image of UNIP as a mass-based party, ready to articulate the aspirations of the common people. As Peter Harries-Jones noted, "UNIP's success involved far more than the creation of a political band-wagon [but] abjured the elitist type of political organisation characteristic of the African National Congress."[41]

However, this does not negate the fact that those who jumped on the UNIP band-wagon had real grievances against the colonial government. Nationalist leaders hijacked the process and therefore gave the impression that they were leading the struggle.[42] This was not difficult in those days when the villain was identified as the white ruling class. Between 1958 and 1961 there were serious disturbances that affected rural people.[43]

The "populist" ideology, with its search for "pigmentational selfdetermination," was based on the idea that the black person had suffered enough at the hands of white people and that the only way to redress this situation was to secure the removal of white people from the realm of political power and to replace them with black people. "Populist" ideology particularly opposed liberal ideology with its commitment to multiracial politics as an alternative process for transferring political power from the white ruling elite to a multiracial local ruling elite. Kaunda's nationalist "unity ... in the color of our skin"[44] rejected multiracialism and he further argued that no multiracial party in Africa had yet obtained independence for Africans, and that no multiracial party in colonial Zambia was prepared to commit itself to breaking up the federation and fighting for colonial Zambia's independence. He concluded that "since the multi-racial bus is not going our direction, we would be foolish to climb on it."[45]

Nonetheless, Kaunda continued to seek the support of liberal Europeans like Colin Morris. To preserve the dynamism of the populist ideology of his party, however, he outwardly opposed multiracialism as an alternative approach to the politics of decolonization. Consequently, when the ANC announced that it would participate in the coming elections organized under the new constitution, ZANC decided to boycott the elections and began a vigorous campaign to dissuade Africans from registering as voters. The campaign, which involved haranguing, intimidation and harassment of opponents, resulted in only 6,846 Africans being registered from the potential figure of 24,648.[46] ZANC also hoped to persuade those who had registered to stay away during the voting days.

The violence that followed led to the introduction of *The Safeguard of Elections and Public Safety Regulations (1959)* and the proscribing of ZANC and the detention of its leaders. Though the elections were held without serious incident, African participation and performance were below expectations. ANC managed only to return its president, Nkumbula in one of the "special" constituencies. The United Federal Party won thirteen of the twenty-two elected seats, eleven "Ordinary" and both African reserve seats. The multiracial liberal Central Africa Party (CAP),[47] led by Sir John Moffat, obtained both European reserve seats and one "special" seat. The Dominion Party, which stood for white supremacy, won one of the "ordinary" seats. African Independent candidates won two of the four remaining "special" seats, leaving two seats vacant because no qualified candidates were nominated for them.[48]

THE IMPACT OF FEDERAL POLITICS ON COLONIAL ZAMBIA

The nationalist struggle in colonial Zambia was closely connected with the politics of the Federation of Rhodesia and Nyasaland—first to prevent its creation and later to secure its dissolution. Thus the decolonization process in colonial Zambia had a federal dimension. While neither the imperial government nor the colonial state in colonial Zambia was interested in holding back political advancement of the African population permanently, they were continually accused of this. The Benson Constitution was perceived by militant nationalists as a constitution designed to serve the interests of federalists.

Consequently, the British government responded to the crisis with an announcement in July 1959 that it intended to appoint an Advisory Commission "to advise the five Governments, in preparing for the 1960 (Federal) Review, on the constitutional programme and framework best suited to the achievement of the objects contained in the constitution of 1953, including the Preamble."[49] The result of this commitment was the appointment of the Monckton Commission, which was to start gathering evidence by September 1959.

This commission, however, was surrounded by controversy. There were disagreements over membership, terms of reference, and its impartiality.[50] The commission was criticized because its terms of reference were too general and it included very few Africans, some of whom were thought to be too moderate to represent African interests.[51] In colonial Zambia, both ANC and UNIP consequently boycotted the proceedings of the Commission because it was not authorized to consider breaking up the Federation. In Britain the Labour Party refused to join the Commission because secession was not explicitly included among its terms of reference.

Despite these objections, the commission went ahead hearing views, written and oral, from individuals and institutions in the Federation. In colonial Zambia, former chairperson of the Lusaka branch of Capricorn, the Reverend Merfyn M. Temple, submitted a written statement to the commission in which he said:

> I have seen the work of the CAS in Northern Rhodesia founder on the single fact that it failed to obtain any African members because of its support of Federation.
>
> I have seen the first truly multi-racial political party in Northern Rhodesia, the Constitution Party, break up because it maintained against the opinion of its African members a belief in Federation.
>
> I do not believe that the Federal Government will ever be able to win the confidence and trust of the African people while it boasts of its material achievements and bullies the under-privileged.[52]

The chairperson of the colonial Zambia division of the Central Africa Party, a protégé of Capricorn, also submitted a memorandum to the Monckton Commission in which he pointed out that Federation was failing because both Africans and Europeans in colonial Zambia were disillusioned, particularly over the Kariba Dam issue.[53] Franklin concluded that the Federation was hated and could not remain intact without undergoing serious changes. He also pointed out that "as usual, we have given too little, too late and it may be too late to give even too much."[54]

Almost without exception, the evidence overwhelmingly opposed the continued existence of the Federation. When the Review Commission's Report was finally published in October, it emphasized Africans' dislike of the Federation. One of its recommendations, therefore, was that the territories should have the right to secede. Concerning colonial Zambia, the commission recommended that "there should be an African majority in the Legislative Council and an unofficial majority in the Executive Council so constituted as to reflect the composition of the Legislative Council."[55] The commission's report, therefore, marked the start of intensive constitutional negotiations that concluded with the granting of the 1962 constitution.

CONSTITUTIONAL CHANGES, 1960-1964

The 1962 constitution evolved in three stages: the December 1960 London constitutional conference which ended with the colonial secretary's proposals of February 1961; the February-June 1961 phase, which included the governor's consultations with the territory's various political groups in Lusaka and resulted in the colonial secretary's presentation of the June proposals; and finally, the July 1961-March 1962 phase, which followed serious political disturbances in the country. These disturbances led to a reconsideration of the June proposals and the subsequent announcement of further changes on 1 March 1962.

The Northern Rhodesia constitutional conference, which opened on 19 December 1960, ended on 17 February 1961 without reaching an agreement on the future constitutional arrangement for the country. Consequently, Ian Macleod, the colonial secretary, followed the example of his predecessors and issued his proposals in a White Paper[56] whose aim was nonracialism. The Macleod proposals of February 1961 followed previous constitutional changes. According to Mulford: "Macleod claimed that in seeking a middle course the British Government's chief objective was to secure a substantial increase in African representation in Northern Rhodesia's Legislative Council, while still maintaining the principle of "non-racial" politics by requiring political parties to seek support from both races."[57] The Macleod proposals therefore rejected the Monckton Commission's recommendations for a clear African majority, which was to be based on a purely racial approach to colonial Zambia's political development.[58]

The Macleod proposals represented an attempt to reconcile two profoundly opposed racially polarized political groups. Consequently, as Mulford argues, "ambiguities flourished at the expense of both clarity and certainty."[59]

The emphasis on multiracial politics and gradual advance toward universal suffrage made African nationalists believe that "eventually they would be denied majority rule."[60] On the other hand, Europeans were equally unhappy with the Macleod's proposals because in them they saw a very real possibility of an African majority in colonial Zambia. This was going to have broad consequences on federal politics. Thus, as Federal Prime Minister Sir Roy Welensky led the attack on the proposals in Salisbury, in Lusaka John Roberts led his ministers in resigning from the Northern Rhodesia government.[61] Consequently, the February proposals ended in a political stalemate.

Following the deadlock, on 26 June 1961 Ian Macleod issued new constitutional proposals in a second White Paper,[62] which was largely based on the recommendations of the Northern Rhodesia governor.[63] The June proposals did not significantly depart from the course already chartered by earlier constitutional proposals. The principal objective remained the attainment of "nonracial" political development, but with significantly altered arrangements for electing national members. To avoid one race dominating national seats, it was decided that "four of the seven double-member national constituencies proposed were to return one European and one African member. The fifth national seat was to be reserved for Asian and Colored voters, who would vote together in a special national constituency extending over the whole country."[64] The proposals also introduced an additional qualification that required national candidates to secure 20 percent of the votes cast on one or other of the two rolls. The arrangement required candidates to have substantial support at least from one section of the community.

A third and final change concerned the minimum percentage arrangement. According to Governor Evelyn Hone, the February proposals required a national candidate to obtain far more votes from the predominantly African lower roll to be duly elected. In his view, this placed European candidates at a disadvantage. He thus devised qualifying arrangements that would not only place candidates of both races in a more equal position, but safeguarded the spirit of the constitution.[65] Now the minimum support required by a candidate was expressed as 12 percent or 400 votes (whichever was the less) of the votes cast by each race in the election.

According to Governor Evelyn Hone, the complicated formula aimed at giving "practical effect to the principle that National members should be obliged to seek support from voters of both races."[66] The June proposals received qualified acceptance from Sir Roy Welensky and the federal government, but African parties rejected them. In protest, UNIP launched a civil disobedience campaign that led to serious disorder lasting until October. The ANC on the other hand, though opposed to the proposals, issued a statement in September strongly condemning UNIP's campaign of violence.[67] The June proposals were immediately subjected to revision. The revision focused, however, on two technical electoral changes. The first change was about the percentage vote that a candidate was required to obtain to qualify for a national seat. Now a candidate for a national seat was required to obtain 10 percent of the vote cast by both Africans and Europeans instead of the 12.5 percent as provided in the June White Paper. The second change involved the dropping of the numerical alternative of 400 votes. The changes were introduced by Reginald Maudling the new colonial secretary.[68]

Having made these changes, an electoral machinery based on the principle that politics should develop on nonracial lines was set out in the Northern Rhodesia (Electoral Provisions) Order in Council, 1962. The Order in Council provided two separate classes of voters: those qualified and registered under higher franchise; and those qualified and registered under lower franchise. There were, however, four general qualifications that applied to all voters irrespective of their franchise class, namely:

(1) Citizenship of the Federation or of the United Kingdom and the colonies or the status of British Protected Person by virtue of his connection with Northern Rhodesia;
(2) Twenty-one years of age;
(3) Two years continuous residence in the Federation;
(4) Literacy in English (except those exempted under the additional qualifications for the lower roll voters as described below).

All those who satisfied these universal requirements qualified under one of the "Additional Qualifications" for either upper or lower roll voters contained in the schedule to the Order.[69]

With the electoral machinery in place and as the country prepared for the general elections, it was evident that Africans and Europeans were as divided as they had always been. Though the United Federal Party and the United National Independence Party had emerged as the two dominant political parties, they had failed miserably to attract members of the other race. The UFP had remained predominantly white while UNIP had remained predominantly black. Not much was achieved by UFP's Build-a-Nation campaign of mid-October.[70]

The multiracial Liberal Party, which should have attracted most liberally minded and moderate politicians, continued to be marginalized as politics increasingly became racially polarized. The African National Congress, having lost its strong hold on the African people, entered a secret political alliance with the UFP in the hope of defeating UNIP in the coming elections.[71] The ANC-UFP alliance was merely an alliance of convenience. Apart from the two parties' need to defeat UNIP, they had nothing else in common—their policies and traditions remained diametrically opposed, inevitably weakening the alliance.

Worse still, in the racially polarized political circumstances of colonial Zambia at the time, the ANC-UFP alliance played into the hands of UNIP when it became public. Nkumbula was accused of selling out to Europeans. UNIP exploited the alliance to the maximum, increasingly appearing "populist" and truly concerned with the interests and aspirations of the masses. Within the ANC some leaders opposed any cooperation with Europeans. When it became public knowledge that Nkumbula had entered an alliance with the UFP, they tendered their resignations.[72] Nkumbula himself began to waver and accused the UFP of cheating and putting unfair pressure on him.[73]

Nevertheless, the two parties observed the alliance quietly. They put up candidates, for both upper and lower roll seats, in such a way as not to undermine each other but to defeat the UNIP candidate. The arrangement was more successful in some constituencies than in others.[74] After the nominations on 9 October, 144 candidates were nominated for the forty-five seats. UNIP fielded forty candidates and was committed to support three European independent candidates and one for the Asian seat, while ANC put up thirty candidates and supported one for the Asian seat. The UFP and the Liberal Party fielded twenty-eight and twenty-seven candidates each respectively, while the Rhodesian Republican Party (RRP) had five candidates and the Barotse National Party (BNP) three candidates.[75]

Ironically,[76] the campaign was marked by frequent outbreaks of violence between rival ANC and UNIP supporters. The most serious incidents took place in Ndola and in Fort Jameson on 21-22 April where it was reported that at least eight Africans were beaten to death and more were injured during the ANC-UNIP confrontations.[77] There were no reported incidents involving Europeans, at least during this time.

The General Election of 30 October 1962 marked a turning point in the constitutional and political history of colonial Zambia. Though the election results almost confirmed the expected, they marked the decline of the colonial state. The UFP won thirteen of the fourteen upper roll seats[78] while UNIP and ANC split the lower seats between them—twelve to three respectively. Table V shows both the racial composition of the Legislative Council's elected members and the state of the parties after the general election.

Table 5: Legislative Council 1962: Racial and Party Composition of Elected Members Following the General Election

	UNIP	UFP	ANC	TOTAL
Europeans	-	13	1	14
Africans	12	2	4	18
Euro-Africans	1	-	-	1
Asians	1	-	-	1
State of Parties	14	15	5	3

Source: Mulford, *The Northern Rhodesia Election*, p. 147.

These results show that the racial factor was still important for the colonial Zambian electorate despite attempts to develop multiracial politics. While the constitution required that national candidates should obtain a specified percentage of votes cast by both races, party allegiance remained predominantly racial. Liberalism, with its commitment to multiracial politics, suffered a crushing defeat. All Liberal Party candidates, including the leader Sir John Moffat, were defeated.[79] The election results convincingly proved the dominance of UFP and UNIP among European and African voters respectively.

Consequently, the Liberal Party, which came to power following the resignation of the UFP in February 1961, tendered its resignation on 2 November. Later the same day, the governor, Sir Evelyn Hone, announced that a caretaker government of colonial civil servants had been appointed and would be in office until after the by-elections, because no single party had so far obtained a majority of elected members in the Legislative Assembly.

Following its complete electoral defeat, the Liberal Party announced its disbandment on 5 November and recommended that its followers support UNIP, which it said commanded the "support of four out of five African voters."[80] The Liberal Party noted that the aims of both the British government and the Liberal Party were unattainable as Liberals could no longer control the transfer of power to African nationalists.

Though the ANC had obviously been marginalized as a political force, the election results placed it in an important bargaining position.[81] Both the UFP and UNIP began making approaches to the ANC to form a coalition government because that was the only form of government that could emerge even after the by-election. Nkumbula held the balance—he could either move toward multiracial politics by entering into coalition with the UFP, or join forces with UNIP and close the door on multiracial politics. Nkumbula refused to commit himself until after the by-election, which was set for 10 December 1962.

The by-election results improved ANC's bargaining position. While the UFP candidate J. Macmillan easily won the Livingstone upper roll seat, ANC won two additional seats in the National Constituencies. Table VI summarizes the final party and racial composition of the Legislative Council after the December by-election.

Table 6: Legislative Council December 1962: Racial and Party Composition of Elected Members

	UNIP	UFP	ANC	TOTAL
Europeans	-	14	2	17
Africans	12	2	5	18
Asians	1	-	-	1
Euro-Africans	1	-	-	1
State of Parties	14	16	7	37

Source: Mulford, *The Northern Rhodesia Election*, p.176.

After the announcement of the election results, the UFP and UNIP increased their pressure on Nkumbula. The Congress called a National Assembly meeting on 12 December to debate the next step to be taken. Delegates from the Copperbelt opposed the idea of cooperating with UNIP. Meanwhile, Africans, including traditional chiefs, called upon Nkumbula to show his "statesmanship" by joining hands with UNIP to end colonialism.

Finally, when Nkumbula went to the Congress meeting accompanied by Kaunda, it was evident that he had been persuaded to enter into coalition with UNIP. In what Mulford described as Nkumbula's "political agility," Nkumbula "posed three questions in rapid succession: how many favor African Government; how many want African Government now; how many are behind me?"[82] A show of hands decided the fate of the country, and immediately Nkumbula and Kaunda left the meeting for Government House to meet the governor. The search for "pigmentational self-determination" or commitment to "Africanism" had finally prevailed, thereby closing the door on liberalism, and its commitment to multi-racial politics, once and forever.

According to Nkumbula's biographer "Congress agreed to a coalition on several conditions—it demanded three of the six ministerial portfolios, that there should be friendly relations with Katanga government and that a programme of moderate legislation be drawn up giving due regard to Europeans who had confidence in Congress."[83] Yet, as Sumaili observed, this does not explain Nkumbula's motives for entering into a coalition with UNIP rather than the UFP. The demands were so general that even the UFP could have given Nkumbula "a favourable response."[84] The only plausible explanation seems to be that, despite Nkumbula's moderate political views and consistent association with European liberals, deep down he firmly believed in "Africanism."[85] More important, Nkumbula may have believed he would lose any chance as a mass leader if he chose the UFP—he would be labeled as a sell out.

Although Nkumbula and Kaunda had rushed from the meeting to Government House, it soon became apparent that they had not reached agreement between themselves. The governor accordingly advised them to go back and return to Government House after they reached a settlement regarding the coalition. A long meeting at Nkumbula's house through the night was followed by two meetings with the governor the next day.

In spite of having only seven against the fourteen UNIP's Legco seats, the ANC demanded half the six ministries. The constitutional requirement that at least two members of the Executive Council must be Europeans strengthened ANC's case. Between the two parties, the ANC had the only two Europeans, C.E. Cousins and F.N. Stubbs. However, Nkumbula still had a problem on his hands. Stubbs was reluctant to cooperate with UNIP. He had demonstrated his anti-UNIP stand during the period leading up to the by-election, a stand that had ensured him sufficient UFP European support. After consultations with his electorate in his Mufulira constituency, Stubbs "decided to serve the interests of the country" and agreed to be included in the coalition government. On 15 December Governor Sir Evelyn Hone announced colonial Zambia's first African-dominated government that was composed of the following:

Ministers

K.D. Kaunda (UNIP)	Local Government and Social Welfare
H.M. Nkumbula (ANC)	African Education
S.M. Kapwepwe (UNIP)	African Agriculture
R.C. Kamanga (UNIP)	Labour and Mines
F.N. Stubbs (ANC)	Transport and Works
C.E. Cousins (ANC)	Land and Natural Resources

Parliamentary Secretaries

A.G. Zulu (UNIP)	Local Government and Social Welfare
C.J.A. Banda (ANC)	African Education
E.K. Mudenda (UNIP)	African Agriculture
J.M. Mwanakatwe (UNIP)	Labour and Mines
F.B. Chembe (ANC)	Transport and Works
J.E.M. Michello (ANC)	Land and Natural Resources
A.N.L. Wina (ANC)	Finance

Chief Whip

Sikota Wina (UNIP)

Officials

Chief Secretary	R.E. Luyt
Finance	T.G. Gardner
Native Affairs	F.M. Thomas
Justice	B.A. Doyle.[86]

The new government took office on 16 December 1962, marking the end of European political dominance, if not quite the end of the colonial state. The birth of "black government" took place amid calls by UNIP officials for a new constitution based on universal franchise and the granting of independence to colonial Zambia outside the federation.[87] Although UNIP had participated in the election, it had consistently emphasized its unqualified rejection of both the 1962 constitution and its underlying principles.

Within two months the Northern Rhodesia Legco approved on 13 and 14 February 1963 respectively two motions. The first one, moved by the two African coalition parties, "rejected and condemned the Federation," which had been "imposed against the will of the people" and called on the British government to grant the territory immediate secession from the federation.[88] The second motion, moved by Kaunda, condemned the 1962 constitution as "undemocratic and unacceptable." He called on the British government to secure a new constitution that would provide for a legislature of sixty-five members, a prime minister and fifteen ministers. The motion also called for a constitutional provision for general elections every four or five years and the enfranchisement of all adult British Protected Persons or British subjects domiciled in the territory for more than five years preceding registration.[89] Both motions were approved by twenty-one votes to fourteen (UFP).[90]

UFP amendments respectively supporting the continuation of the federation and accepting a constitution based on a qualitative, rather than universal, adult suffrage, as serving the best interests of the people were rejected by twenty-one votes to fourteen. The six officials took no part in the debate, which lasted six days, or in the voting that followed. F.M. Thomas, the acting chief secretary, later explained that officials refrained from taking part in the debate because no matter how carefully articulated their views would have been taken to reflect the view of the British government.[91] This is curious considering that officials were expected to hold the balance on contentious issues. Why did they choose to be spectators this time?

It is arguable that the various constitutional changes, especially the 1961 and 1962 constitutions, had weakened the influence of officials within the colonial state. They were no longer the mediators because the new African government, which came to power in December 1962, for all purposes and intents had changed the power base of the state. Officials were therefore rendered powerless as mediators.

However, the embryo African state that resulted from the "unholy matrimony" of the ANC-UNIP coalition was bedeviled by constant threats of being aborted.[92] Though Nkumbula had formed a coalition with UNIP, he still maintained private contacts with some members of the UFP. A rebel group had been formed by members of the UFP with the intention of befriending and gaining information from ANC's Stubbs, who had been ostracized by whites on the Copperbelt since becoming a minister in the coalition government. The group appointed Norman Coates, MP for Kalulushi, to make the contact.

Nkumbula's continued flirtations with UFP gave UNIP ammunition to declare him a sell-out to the African cause.[93] ANC's position was further weakened by internal dissensions, led by Job Michello and Bellings Lombe who had opposed coalition with UNIP, preferring to cooperate with the UFP instead. It was only a matter of time before the coalition broke up. The federal question again forced the pace of constitutional change and the fate of the coalition in colonial Zambia.

On 19 December 1962, R.A. Butler, minister of the newly formed Ministry of Central African Affairs, announced his intention to visit Central Africa and hold talks with federal and territorial leaders. Accordingly, Butler visited the Federation from 16 January to 3 February 1963. He arrived in colonial Zambia on 24 January. The next day he held talks with leaders of the coalition government who made three demands: (1) that the British government should declare colonial Zambia's right to secede from the Federation; (2) that a conference should be held in London in March in order to "dig the grave of the Federation" and to draw up a new constitution for colonial Zambia; and (3) that a commission should be appointed to study institutions established after the inception of the Federation and to prepare for territorial services taken over by the Federation in 1953 to revert to colonial Zambia.[94]

The Northern Rhodesian nationalist demand for the territory's right to secede was strengthened by the British announcement earlier that Nyasaland should be allowed to secede. Finally, Butler announced colonial Zambia's right to secede on 29 March 1963, and said:

> HMG [Her Majesty Government] consider that the objective of any constructive policy in Central Africa must be to evolve an effective relationship between the Territories which is acceptable to each of them. They recognise that the present situation cannot continue unchanged, and they have therefore sought in the recent discussions with the governments concerned to evolve a basis for a conference at which a new relationship could be worked out. These discussions have been very helpful in clarifying the broad views of the governments concerned. In the light of these views, HMG have had to consider what is the best course to pursue in the interest of all concerned. They accept that none of the Territories can be kept in the Federation against its will and they therefore accept the principle that any Territory which so wishes must be allowed to secede.[95]

This announcement precipitated another series of talks for a new constitution that would provide self-government for colonial Zambia. The government also announced on 23 August that elections would be held based on a new constitution in the second half of January 1964. Preliminary talks to prepare for the new constitution took place in Lusaka from 11 July to 4 September 1963, and involved Nkumbula (ANC), Kaunda (UNIP) and John Roberts National Progress Party (NPP)[96] and the governor.

The provisions of the new constitution were contained in an Order-in-Council made on 20 December 1963 and laid before parliament on 1 January 1964. The provisions included: the governor and his deputy; a Legislative Assembly of seventy-five members (sixty-five of whom were to be elected in the main roll constituencies and ten in reserved constituencies) with an elected speaker who was a minister or parliamentary secretary but was not necessarily a member of the assembly; and an executive consisting of a prime minister with a cabinet of thirteen other ministers who were collectively responsible to the Legislative Assembly.[97] The prime minister was expected to be a member of the assembly whom the governor thought was best able to command the support of the majority of the members of the assembly.

BAROTSELAND'S ENTRY INTO NATIONALIST POLITICS

Barotseland had always occupied a special position within the colonial Zambian political system. It was a protectorate within a protectorate—a status it earned and helped to develop from the days of the BSA Company rule through to Colonial Office administration. This special status was explicitly recognized in article 41 of Northern Rhodesia Order-in-Council, 1924. Barotseland's special status had been further consolidated in 1936 through the Barotse Native Authority Ordinance and the Barotse Native Courts Ordinance, which granted the Barotse Native government wider powers and a greater degree of local autonomy than the other Native authorities in the territory.

As colonial Zambia was approaching independence, the *Litunga* (Paramount chief of the Lozi) of Barotseland began to press for secession. When the British Government intimated that it would abandon the protectorate and let it face the consequences of isolation, the Northern Rhodesia government proceeded to reform the Barotse National Council. It now included twenty-five elected members. For the first time, the Barotse National Council was open to nationalist politics. UNIP candidates won all twenty-five seats in the August 1963 Barotse National Council elections. The reform brought Barotseland into the mainstream of colonial Zambian politics.

JANUARY 1964 ELECTIONS

Registration of voters for the new Legislative Assembly scheduled for 20-21 January 1964 began on 23 September 1963. All persons over the age of twenty-one who fulfilled certain residential qualifications were entitled to register. More than 1,000,000 Africans registered for the sixty-five main roll constituencies and 24,000 Europeans registered for the ten reserved constituencies. Asian and Colored voters were given the option to vote either in the main roll or reserved roll. The registration methods were criticized by ANC and NPP.[98] Roberts protested against the absence of postal registration and voting facilities that he alleged, would deprive up to 30 percent of the Europeans of the vote. He also questioned the methods for the registration of African voters. Nkumbula, on the other hand, complained of the methods used to identify voters seeking registration, alleging that the process was laying the elections "wide open to abuse."[99]

The elections were again preceded by a period of violence, not between white and black, but between rival ANC and UNIP youth movements in which the unemployed were alleged to have played a prominent role.[100] The preelection clashes placed a great strain on the coalition government. Nkumbula repeatedly threatened to resign as minister and end the coalition. He accused UNIP officials of deliberately encouraging their followers to commit acts of violence against ANC members.

A commission of inquiry instituted later to investigate the cause of the interparty strife attributed the strife to "political frustration due to the Nationalist parties' victory and to a sense of anti-climax and loss of direction owing to the virtual attainment of the principal political objectives, thus contributing to a psychological restiveness which in certain cases has exploded into violence."[101] The report added that a contributory factor was the disappointment felt by many that the coming to power of the nationalists had not resulted in immediate and widespread benefits to the masses of the people. On the contrary, however, this assessment fails to place the ideology of violence between ANC and UNIP youth wingers in its proper perspective during the nationalist era.

Violence was used by African nationalists in colonial Zambia as a political weapon to deal with those who were seen as selling out to Europeans. Before the split of the ANC in 1958, violence was usually directed at individuals or organizations identified as serving interests other than those of the African nationalists. The Chief Musokotwane case,[102] the Kabalata Affair[103] and the Chizuma-Kaluwa case,[104] all demonstrate the use of violence by nationalists against those believed not to be in the mainstream of the struggle.[105] The use of violence against political opponents has its origins in the Action Group of the ANC.[106] It is therefore doubtful that the ANC-UNIP clashes in the period preceding the January 1964 elections was a reflection of disillusionment with the nationalist government that had come to power following the 1962 elections. For how else would one explain the clashes just before the 1962 elections?

The emphasis on the unemployed youths as the group responsible for the violence is equally misleading. While the urban unemployed could easily be blamed for the violence, the same cannot be said of the clashes in the rural areas. Besides, as Musumbulwa pointed out, some of the most respected nationalists were quite violent when it came to dealing with people who associated with Europeans.[107] The perpetrators were therefore not always the "unemployed youths" or frustrated masses—they were generally political activists from all walks of life who engaged in violence rather than political debate. Seventy years of colonial rule had not demonstrated the power of political debate. There was no tradition of liberal democracy. Larry Diamond "concluded that—whatever their intentions—even the British and French colonial regimes did more to defeat democracy than to develop it."[108] Instead, Africans had grown accustomed to the idea that change came through violence and militancy. For most Zambians politics was like war in which the mightier army carried the day. Musumbulwa pointed out that the saddest aspect of the nationalist era was the reluctance among UNIP leaders to engage in dialogue with moderate Africans.[109] They had no time for ideological debate—besides, many of them had very superficial knowledge of what it was that made the parties different.

Nevertheless, the leaders of the two "warring" parties issued a joint declaration in mid-November appealing to their followers to stop the violence and prepare to "share in the nation's pride in its first free elections" based on the principle of "one man one vote." The election was important because it would lead to self-government for colonial Zambia.

Three parties contested the elections that resulted in an overwhelming victory for UNIP which won fifty-five of the sixty-five main roll seats. ANC won the remaining ten, while the NPP won all the reserved ten seats. On 23 January 1964 an all African UNIP cabinet was announced consisting of the following:

Kenneth Kaunda	Prime Minister
Simon Kapwepw	Home Affairs
Arthur Wina	Finance
Elijah Mudenda	Agriculture
Solomon Kalulu	Land and Works
Mainza Chona	Justice
Alexander Grey Zulu	Commerce and Industry
John M. Mwanakatwe	Education
Reuben C. Kamanga	Transport and Communications
Munukayumbu Sipalo	Natural Resources
Hyden D. Banda	Housing and Social Welfare
Nalumino Mundia	Local Government
Justin Chimba	Labour and Mines
Sikota Wina	Health

The UNIP government called for immediate constitutional talks, which were held in London from 5-19 May 1964, during which time it was agreed to grant independence to colonial Zambia on 24 October. The independence constitution agreed upon introducing a republican form of government. It was also agreed that Barotseland would be part of the new independent state.[110] Meanwhile the leader of the National Progress Party, John Roberts, pledged that his party would play its part in trying to mold the best form of government for the new state. He pointed out that the NPP was not going to be an opposition party in the legislature, but would seek to help develop democratic processes in the country.

CONCLUSION

The triumph of UNIP following the January 1964 general elections and the subsequent formation of an all UNIP government demonstrated a clear rejection of multi-racial politics. It was indeed the fulfilment of an African dream. More important, it presents a paradox of decolonization. Up to this point imperial authorities continued to argue that Africans were not ready to rule themselves and little was being done to make them ready. Yet within months of handing over power to Africans, independence was granted—telescoping "administrative, economic, educational, political and psychological preparations for independence."[111] However, as Ranger argued, "African leaders were playing not the politics of prosperity but the politics of dignity."[112] Kaunda pointed out that the African could not have dignity until he was ruling himself.[113] The election results therefore indicate that in the minds of Africans, leaders and followers alike, nationalism actually meant "Africanism."

Thus, in the terminal stages of colonial rule, the "march to political freedom" was basically a struggle to restore a sense of dignity in the African—dignity allegedly lost during the process of colonization and colonial rule. The liberal ideology was unacceptable because by advocating multiracialism (or nonracial politics), and by insisting on material and educational progress as the criteria for political advancement, it put itself at odds with the prime motivation of African nationalism—"dignity ... rather than the achievement of economic advancement."[114] For an African nationalist leader, success was determined by how much he articulated the principle of "Africanism." No wonder Kaunda argued that "our problem is practical not ideological. After all, there are 3,000,000 of us and only 72,000 whites."[115]

Kaunda was not the only one who felt that Africans should rule themselves. Even his long-time political adversary, Nkumbula, felt the same when he said:

> I must say one thing that I have always avoided, I cannot help thinking and convincing myself that after my experience ... in political life I have come to the conclusion that the best government for black people is a government run by black people of Africa. That is true of any race.[116]

Indeed, as Sumaili speculates, this probably explains Nkumbula's decision to form a coalition government with UNIP rather than with the UFP in 1962.[117]

Interestingly, liberalism as an ideology for the transfer of power in colonial Zambia—articulated constitutionally as multiracial or nonracial politics—was the main objective of both Colonial Office officials in London and Northern Rhodesia government officials. Constitutional changes, starting with the Benson proposals of 1958 up to the 1962 proposals, all attest to that. It is arguable, therefore, that African nationalists objected to these constitutions and the changes they were supposed to bring because they checked the speedy attainment of "Africanism." Nonetheless, contrary to expectations, the electoral machinery put in place after 1958 led rapidly to the eventual triumph of the principle of "Africanism."

Gradualism with its emphasis on economic advance was no match for African nationalist drive for political freedom and the recapture of African dignity. This was largely because there were not many liberals, either white or black, to balance extreme tendencies effectively. The violent attack on African moderates effectively checked the spread of moderate ideas among Africans. In fact, the stronger African nationalism grew, the more racial it also became, thereby alienating European moderates who were prepared to cooperate with Africans. Calls by some UNIP officials to "hate anything white on two legs," though directed at Europeans, were effectively applied to Africans who associated with liberal Europeans and articulated liberal ideas. Africans were therefore warned to "suspect anybody who says he is a holy or a liberal."[118]

In the end therefore, liberalism as a process through which change could be effected in colonial Zambia was swept aside by forces of "Africanism." The nationalist movement that had begun as a reformist movement, seeking only to reform the political system and acquire some limited power sharing and basic rights for the emergent African elite, was completely transformed into a populist movement claiming to champion the cause of the African masses. Power sharing ceased to be the objective. Those nationalists who cherished liberal ideas and were prepared to give gradualism a chance became, in the eyes of militant nationalists, traitors, or sell-outs or worse still, *Acapricorn*.

Although liberalism as a political process through which change was initiated and finally brought about has generally been seen as of no consequence, one cannot help but notice that "black government" was born out of constitutions whose principal objectives were inspired by the very ideas African nationalists were constantly attacking. Colonial Zambia's independence was evolutionary rather than revolutionary because the process was carried out through liberally inspired constitutional discussions.

It is arguable, therefore, that in colonial Zambia, liberalism played an important role in the political process, a role until now unacknowledged because of the general tendency among "nationalist" historians and other Africanists to attribute the achievement of independence to the power and strength of nationalist parties. The evidence presented in this chapter suggests that the attainment of political independence in 1964 was a combined effort of the various forces then at play in the territory. Liberalism and the triumph of populist African nationalism in the period 1954-1964 were essentially two faces of the same political process. This is why in 1962 the multi-racial Liberal Party recommended that its followers support UNIP and not the white-dominated National Progress Party.

Notes

1. The phrase is borrowed from the title of Kapasa Makasa's book, *Zambia's March To Political Freedom* (Nairobi: Heinemann, 1985).

2. Fanuel K. M. Sumaili, "The Self and Biographical Writings in Zambia," *Zango*, 3, 1 (1988), p. 72.

3. For works in the first category, see Kenneth Kaunda, *Zambia Shall Be Free* (London: Heinemann, 1962); Wittington K. Sikalumbi, *Before UNIP: A History* (Lusaka: Neczam, 1979); Makasa, *Zambia's March to Political Freedom*; Sikota Wina, *A Night Without a President* (Lusaka: Multimedia Publications, 1985); and Goodwin Mwangilwa, *Harry Mwaanga Nkumbula A Biography of the "Old Lion" of Zambia*, (Lusaka, Multimedia Publications, 1982). Sumaili refers to these works as *confessional* writings "because each one of them is a kind of manifesto of the inner world, a turning away from the mechanical and public to the beauties and dangers of the inner soul; they are an attempt to explore nakedly and without apology the unchartered territory of the man himself." (Sumaili, "The Self," p.72). Works in the second category include Richard Hall, *Zambia* (New York: Praeger, 1965); Andrew Roberts, *A History of Zambia 1973-1964* (New York: Africana, 1976); Robert I. Rotberg, *The Rise of Nationalism in Central Africa: The Making of Malawi and Zambia* (Cambridge MA: Harvard University Press, 1965); David C. Mulford, *Zambia: The Politics of Independence, 1957-1964* (London: Oxford University Press, 1967); Fergus MacPherson, *Kenneth Kaunda of Zambia: The Times and the Man* (Lusaka: Oxford University Press, 1974); Cherry Gertzel, Carolyn Baylies and Morris Szeftel (eds.), *The Dynamics of the One-Party State in Zambia* (Manchester,: Manchester University Press, 1984); and William Tordoff (ed.), *Politics in Zambia* (Manchester: Manchester University Press, 1974).

4. Cited from Richard Hall, *Kaunda: Founder of Zambia* (London: Longmans, 1964), p. 80 (italics added). The last remark confirms de Winton's

suggestion that "a much more likely source of common motive was the spirit of "Africanism," that is, an understandable desire to get rid of the control of white men" (M. G. de Winton, "Decolonization and the Westminster Model," in A.H.M. Kirk-Greene (ed.), *The Transfer of Power: The Colonial Administration in the Age of Decolonization* (Kidlington Oxford: Oxford University Press, 1979) p. 184).

5. The slogan was popularized by Kwame Nkrumah, but was one that Sir Stewert Gore-Browne frequently used to counteract Capricorn "liberal" argument that what Africans needed most was economic advancement first before they began to aspire for political advancement. Gore-Browne was a "liberal" himself, but was opposed to the idea of economic progress as a determinant for political advancement, which formed part of the Capricorn philosophy.

6. Although political implications of the strikes were beginning to emerge, especially in the 1940 strike, the problem was perceived as largely to do with the Copperbelt and not national. In response therefore, the Forster Commission recommended the setting up of some quasipolitical bodies through which Africans in the mining towns could express their political views. The result was the creation of the African Urban Advisory Councils on the Copperbelt in 1938.

7. PRO, DO 35/4636/282, Brief for Secretary of State's visit to the Federation of Rhodesia and Nyasaland, December 1956 to January 1957, p. 1, para. 2.

8. PRO, DO 35/4636/282, Brief for Secretary of State's visit, para. 4. See also PRO, DO 35/4636/333, Constitutional Change in Northern Rhodesia, p. 8, para. 18.

9. NAZ, SEC 5/270, The Moffat Resolutions, Legco Debates, 29 July 1954.

10. PRO, CO 1015/1016, Minute by Sir Thomas Lloyd, 20 July 1954.

11. PRO, CO 1015/1016/19, Governor Benson to Secretary of State for the Colonies, 1 October 1954.

12. Sikalumbi, *Before UNIP*, p. 88.

13. Sikalumbi, *Before UNIP*, p. 88.

14. Sikalumbi, *Before UNIP*, p. 88.

15. John Roberts was at the time leader of Northern Rhodesia division of the United Federal Party, which was headed by Sir Roy Welensky at the federal level.

16. Cited in Sikalumbi, *Before UNIP*, p. 90.

17. PA, ANC 7/108, Kenneth Kaunda, Secretary General, ANC to Secretary of State for the Colonies, 7 March 1955. There is no record that this letter was responded to. There are two possible explanations: (1) records in the Party Archives are not properly kept; (2) colonial officials did not respond to all letters from nationalists, even though they sometimes discussed them.

18. NAZ, SEC 5/270, Francis Mwaba, 6 April 1955.

19. PA, ANC 7/108, Kenneth Kaunda to Secretary of State for the Colonies, 7 March 1955.

20. Francis Chembe was also a federal MP. The African Representative Council was a government instituted body through which Africans were expected to air their political views. .

21. NAZ African Representative Council Proceedings, 14-16 June 1956.

22. PRO, DO 35/4636/382, Brief for Secretary of State's visit to the Federation of Rhodesia and Nyasaland, December 1956 to January 1957, p. 2, para. 4.

23. Cmd. 530, *Northern Rhodesia: Proposals for Constitutional Change*, 1958.

24. PRO, DO 35/4636/333, Draft White Paper, February 1958, p. 8, para. 19.

25. The proposals added that "the electoral system must encourage the return of men and women who were prepared and indeed disposed to consider and balance the interests of all racial groups, and who are prompted primarily by a spirit of public service to the whole community; it must discourage the return of extremists who look to sectional interests alone." (PRO, DO 35/4636/333, Draft White Paper, p. 8 para. 19).

26. PRO, DO 35/4636/333, Draft White Paper, p. 9, para. 20 and 22.

27. For a detailed discussion of the split of ANC, see Mulford, *Zambia*, pp. 73-81.

28. PRO, DO 35/4636/333, Draft White Paper, p. 15, para. 31.

29. PRO, DO 35/4636/333, Draft white Paper, p. 15, para. 31.

30. Paragraph 33 read: "The Government have welcomed the decision of the Federal Government to award the vote to Chiefs in their own right, without regard to the means of qualification, and propose that Chiefs should be similarly enfranchised as ordinary voters on the territorial roll. The Government also propose in the territorial franchise to exempt from the means qualifications, though not of course from the other general qualifications, applicants within the following additional groups for registration as special voters:

(i) persons who are and have been for the past two years Headmen or hereditary Councillors, who are recognized as such by their Chiefs, and who are recommended by their Chiefs, and are performing unpaid service in such office to the community;

(ii) persons who are in receipt of a monthly or annual pension earned after 20 years service with one employer.

31. PRO, DO 35/4636/333, Draft White Paper, p. 15. para. 31.

32. PRO, DO 35/4636/333, Draft White Paper, p. 19, para. 47.

33. PRO, DO 35/4636/282, Brief for secretary of state's visit to the Federation of Rhodesia and Nyasaland, December 1956-January 1957, p. 1, para.

1 (3). The same voters' roll had 13,382 Europeans and 1,254 Asians. Most Northern Rhodesian Africans were British Protected Persons, and were thereby excluded from the voters' roll.

34. Cited in Denis Austin, "What Happened to the Colonial State?" *The Round Table*, 295 (1985), p. 210 (italics added).

35. Cited in *Northern News*, 23 June 1961.

36. John Moffat, "The Role of the Liberal in Rhodesian Politics," *Central African Examiner*, 24 September 1960, p. 13.

37. For a detailed discussion of the franchise arrangement it introduced, see David C. Mulford, *The Northern Rhodesia General Election 1962* (London: Oxford University Press, 1964), pp. 11-12.

38. Wina, *A Night Without a President*, p. 43. The decision to name the new party Zambia African National Congress was taken deliberately to replace the ANC. According to Makasa, "the people were used to the name 'African National Congress,' which had been in use for eight years, it would be unwise for us to come out with a completely different name which would not be easy for them to pick up quickly. Our task was therefore, to find a name which should be as near as possible but at the same time without creating confusion among our supporters" (Makasa, *Zambia's March to Political Freedom*, p. 97). This was short of calling the new party ANC2.

39. Makasa, *Zambia's March to Political Freedom*, p. 94.

40. United National Independence Party was formed on 1 August 1959 following the merging of the African National Independence Party (ANIP) and the United National Freedom Party (UNFP), which had recently been formed after the banning of ZANC, by those ZANC elements who had managed to evade detention.

41. Peter Harries-Jones, *Freedom and Labour: Mobilization and Political Control on the Zambian Copperbelt* (Oxford: Basil Blackwell), 1975, p. 117.

42. Thomas Rasmussen has demonstrated that nationalist leaders were not always successful in directing rural protests against the colonial government and that they were at times embarrassed at the extent of rural protest. For details, see Thomas Rasmussen, "The Popular Basis of Anti-Colonial Protest," in William Tordoff (ed.), *Politics in Zambia* (Manchester: Manchester University Press, 1974), pp. 40-61.

43. For details see, Rasmussen, "The Popular Basis of Anti-Colonial Protest," pp. 42-43.

44. Kenneth Kaunda and Colin Morris, *Black Government? A Discussion Between Colin Morris and Kenneth Kaunda* (Lusaka: United Society for Christian Literature, 1960), p. 93.

45. Kaunda and Morris, *Black Government?*, p. 93.

46. Mulford, *The Northern Rhodesia General Election*, p. 15.

47. The Central Africa Party was the successor to the Constitution Party.

48. Mulford, *The Northern Rhodesia General Election*, p. 16.

49. Hansard, 21 July 1959, cited in Mulford, *The Northern Rhodesia General Election*, p. 17. The Preamble was significant in this case because it was the only place in the federal constitution where the partnership principle was mentioned.

50. For a detailed discussion, see J.R.T. Wood, *The Welensky Papers: A History of the Federation of Rhodesia and Nyasaland* (Durban: Graham Publishing, 1983), pp. 661-727.

51. The appointment of Lawrence Katilungu is a case in point. He was associated with the much-despised Capricorn and the Constitution Party.

52. CAS Papers, File No. 128, Memorandum for submission to the Monckton Commission, prepared by Reverend M. M. Temple, secretary of the United Society for Christian Literature in Northern Rhodesia, 1 February 1960. In 1956-1957 he was chairman of the Lusaka branch of CAS, in 1957-1958 he was Deputy Leader of the Constitution Party.

53. PA, ANC 1/6 Vol. 1, Memorandum to the Monckton Commission from the Northern Rhodesia Division of the Central Africa Party, 11 February 1960, pp. 9-12. A copy of the memorandum was confidentially sent to Harry Nkumbula with the compliments of Harry Franklin. The dam project was initially supposed to be on the Kafue River in Northern Rhodesia. However, when Federation was effected, federal officials decided to have the dam on the Zambezi River, on the Southern Rhodesian side. Settlers in Northern Rhodesia were angered by that decision, which was carried out without much consultation with them.

54. PA, ANC 1/6 Vol. 1, Memorandum to the Monckton Commission, p. 15.

55. Advisory Commission on the Review of the Constitution of the Federation of Rhodesia and Nyasaland, October 1960, p. 43; cited in Mulford, *The Northern Rhodesia General Election*, p. 18; see also Mulford, *Zambia*, p. 175.

56. Cmd. 1294, *Northern Rhodesia: Proposals for Constitutional Change*, 1961. These proposals were also referred to as the Macleod proposals or constitution.

57. Mulford, *Zambia*, p. 185.

58. Godwin Lewanika described the Monckton Commission's recommendation that there should be parity of black and white in the Federal Assembly as "illogical and unrealistic, [as] it would mean racial politics and not party politics and would destroy the concept of the multi-racial state." (Godwin Lewanika, "Debate in the Federal Parliament on Monckton Commission's Report", cited in *Keesing's Contemporary Archives*, vol. 13 [1961-62], p. 17921). It is arguable therefore, that to "liberal" minded Africans like

Godwin Lewanika, Macleod's proposals were acceptable as they sought to provide an opportunity for the development of multiracial politics.

59. Mulford, *Zambia*, p. 185.

60. Mulford, *Zambia*, p. 187.

61. *Rhodesia Herald*, 22 February 1961. It was this resignation that brought Sir John Moffat's Liberal Party to power in Northern Rhodesia until its defeat in the October 1962 general elections. The Liberal Party was the only one, according to Mulford ,that had not rejected Macleod's proposals. The search for a formula to bridge the gap between the races had inevitably resulted in "a middle-of-the-road" situation that favored the Liberal Party. The Liberals therefore took over the Executive Council posts vacated by the United Federal Party (*Northern News*, 7 March 1961).

62. Cmd. 1423, *Northern Rhodesia: Proposals for Constitutional Change*, June 1961.

63. *Keesing's Contemporary Archives*, Vol. 13 (1961-62), p. 18585. During April and May 1961 the governor held several consultative talks with Northern Rhodesia's various political groups separately. The talks involved memoranda that essentially provided a detailed version of Macleod's February proposals. The details covered the delimitation of constituencies, the franchise and arrangements for electing the controversial national members.

64. Cmd. 1423, *Northern Rhodesia: Proposals for Constitutional Change*, June 1961, cols. 33-34, cited in Mulford, *Zambia*, p. 195.

65. Cmd. 1423, *Northern Rhodesia: Proposals for Constitutional Change*, June 1961, p. 6, cited in Mulford, *Zambia*, p. 195.

66. Cmd.1423, *Northern Rhodesia: Proposals for Constitutional Change*, June 1961, p. 6, cited in Mulford, *Zambia*, p. 196.

67. *Keesing's Contemporary Archives*, Vol.13 (1962-62), p. 18594.

68. For a detailed discussion of Maudling's handling of the Northern Rhodesian constitutional crisis during the period October 1961 to March 1962, see Wood, *The Welensky Papers*, pp. 967-1013.

69. Cited from Mulford, *The Northern Rhodesia General Election*, pp. 50-52. Cf The multiple voting system proposed by the Capricorn Africa Society discussed in Chapter Three.

70. Although the campaign was aimed at winning the "support for non-racial politics by attempting to persuade those Africans who qualified for the vote to claim it," when they claimed the vote they generally supported African nationalist parties (quotation from Wood, *The Welensky Papers*, p. 967).

71. Mulford suggests that the UFP entered into the alliance with a view to maintaining European dominance through a UFP-ANC coalition government (Mulford, *Zambia*, p. 240).

72. Mulford, *Zambia*, p. 277. Some supporters wrote angry letters to the press denouncing Nkumbula's secret alliance with the UFP (Letters to the Editor, *Central African Post*, 16 and 23 October 1962).

73. *Northern News*, 15 November, 1962.

74. Mulford, *The Northern Rhodesia General Election*, pp. 104-114.

75. *Keesing's Contemporary Archives*, Vol.13 (1961-62), p. 19109.

76. It is ironic because during this campaign there were no recorded incidents of violence involving black and white, even though the power struggle was motivated by the spirit of "Africanism." Instead, it was Africans who fought fellow Africans, thus confirming Lord Hailey's observation that "Africanism" was not a cohesive force.

77. *Keesing's Contemporary Archives*, Vol. 13, (1961-1962) p. 19109.

78. The Livingstone upper roll seat was not contested because there was no qualified candidate.

79. *Keesing's Contemporary Archives*, Vol. 13 (1961-62), p. 19110. Another major setback in the election was the defeat of the right wing Rhodesia Republic Party. All its five European candidates were defeated.

80. *Keesing's Contemporary Archives*, Vol. 13 (1961-62), p. 19109.

81. Sumaili states that "after the 1962 elections...Nkumbula emerged as the king-maker. He could have chosen to enter into a coalition government with either the white-led UFP and deny the country the birth of black government or he could have chosen to go into partnership with UNIP and be credited with having given birth to the first black government of the country. (Sumaili, "The Self and Bibliographical Writings in Zambia," p. 84).

82. Mulford, *The Northern Rhodesia General Election*, p. 180.

83. Mwangilwa, *Harry Mwaanga Nkumbula*, p. 70.

84. Sumaili, "The Self and Biographical Writings in Zambia," p. 84.

85. On 25 December 1951 he had said, "White settlers cannot be trusted." Address delivered by the general president of the Northern Rhodesia African National Congress at a meeting of the Working Committee held at Kitwe, 25 December 1951. He made a similar statement in 1958, when he said Europeans were not to rule Northern Rhodesia.

86. Mulford, *The Northern Rhodesia General Election*, pp. 181-182.

87. *Northern News*, 6 December 1962.

88. *Keesing's Contemporary Archives*, Vol. 14 (1963-64), p. 19295.

89. *Keesing's Contemporary Archives*, Vol. 14 (1963-64), p. 19295.

90. The content of the motions had earlier been presented to Butler in form of nationalist demands.

91. *Keesing's Contemporary Archives*, Vol. 14 (1963-64), p. 19295.

92. For a detailed discussion of the problems of the coalition government, see Mulford, *Zambia*, pp. 304-312.

93. *Northern News*, 13 March, 1963.

94. *Keesing's Contemporary Archives*, Vol. 14 (1963-64), p. 19295.

95. Cited in *Keesing's Contemporary Archives*, Vol. 14 (1963-64), p. 19375.

96. The National Progress Party, formerly the Northern Rhodesia branch of the UFP emerged following the reorganization of the UFP on 19 April into four separate political organizations.

97. *Keesing's Contemporary Archives*, Vol. 14 (1963-64), p. 19889.

98. Although the NPP announced that it would contest all ten European seats and none of the main roll seats, it made it clear that it did not intend to sit in a formal opposition to government. The NPP declared that its role was not that of a political force in the true sense, and that although it represented the European section of the community, it was in every way dedicated to joining the national effort required to build the country (*Keesing's Contemporary Archives*, Vol. 14 [1963-64], p. 19889).

99. *Keesing's Contemporary Archives*, Vol. 14 (1963-64), p. 19889.

100. *Keesing's Contemporary Archives*, Vol. 14 (1963-64), p. 19890.

101. *Keesing's Contemporary Archives*, Vol. 14 (1963-64), p. 19890.

102. PRO, CO 1015/142/1, A. T. Williams to W. L. Gorell Barnes, 3 September 1952.

103. NAZ, SEC 5/113, The Kabalata Affair, 1952.

104. PA, ANC 7/8, Munenga Congress Branch Chairman and Secretary to District Commissioner, 4 March 1953. The two Congress officials were summoned to the district Commissioner's office to answer charges of threatening Chizuma and Kaluwa, both of whom were Capricorn members.

105. See Chapter Three for details.

106. For a detailed discussion of the origins and functions of the Action Group, see Sikalumbi, *Before UNIP*, p. 15. Kapasa Makasa refers to the Action Council as the "Crack Unit" of the nationalist movement (Makasa, *Zambia's March to Political Freedom*, p. 89).

107. Interview with Gabriel Musumbulwa at Luanshya, 15 May 1989.

108. Larry Diamond, "Introduction: Roots of Failure, Seeds of Hope," in Larry Diamond, Juan J. Linz and Seymour Martin Lipset (eds.), *Democracy in Developing Countries: Africa* (Boulder: Lynne Rienner Publications, 1988), p. 10.

109. Interview with author, 15 May 1989.

110. *Keesing's Contemporary Archives*, Vol. 14, (1963-64), p. 20169.

111. de Winton, "Decolonization and the Westminster Model," p. 187.

112. Terence Ranger, "The Politics of the Irrational in Central Africa," *The Political Quarterly*, 34 (1963), p. 285.

113. Hall, *Kaunda Founder of Zambia*, p. 80.

114. Ranger, "The Politics of the Irrational," p. 286.

115. Hall, *Kaunda: Founder of Zambia*, p. 80.

116. Mwangilwa, *Harry Mwaanga Nkumbula*, p. 72.
117. Sumaili, "The Self and Biographical Writings," p. 85.
118. PA, ANC 7/31, Week-by-Week, 11 March 1961. Liberalism was usually associated with religious beliefs, hence the suggestion that people claiming to be holy should be suspected as well.

Chapter 5

THE FIRST REPUBLIC: FROM LIBERAL DEMOCRACY TO ONE-PARTY STATE, 1964-1972

> African unity is not going to come about just because we are
> all black.... We have to ask ourselves whether it is in our inter-
> est now to discuss an East African Federation, agree upon it,
> plan it and determine the various steps to implement it, or
> wait until after independence— when people will be too busy
> with their own domestic problems to pay attention to it.[1]

Nationalist leaders in Zambia, particularly Kenneth Kaunda, were attracted to Tom Mboya's vision of East African unity through a federation. He was chairperson of the Pan-African Movement for East, Central and Southern Africa (PAFMECSA) in 1963, during which time he considered that the functions of the movement could change to forging economic links by mutual consent.[2] Yet they did not grasp Mboya's perceptive warning that unity would not emerge *ipso facto* "just because we are all black". In a distinctly contrary vein Kenneth Kaunda wrote in 1960 that "*our unity is already there in the colour of our skin and our common suffering.*"[3] The generalization, however, vastly oversimplified political reality. Africans had additional loyalties at more intimate levels. "Tribal" affiliation, rooted in the familiar confidences of vernacular languages and precolonial cultures and histories, and strengthened by social and regional differentiation during the colonial period, profoundly affected political behavior.

As Mehgan Vaughan observed, "political struggles during the First Republic often took a regional or ethnic dimension and this continued to be a lasting feature of Zambian politics."[4] President Kaunda soon realized that Zambians were not united as he previously thought. He found himself addressing "tribalism" by way of ethnic balancing through a policy

Vaughan described as "grabbing for spoils by an emerging ruling class."[5] Two issues, therefore, dominated actions of the UNIP government following independence in October 1964. First, UNIP was preoccupied with the struggle to maintain its political dominance under a constitution designed to guarantee liberal democracy. By liberal democracy is meant "a political system characterised by regular and free elections in which politicians organised into parties compete to form the government, by the right of virtually all adult citizens to vote, and by guarantees of a range of familiar political and civil rights."[6] Since 1959 colonial Zambia had a multiparty political system that "for a while maintained competitive pluralistic institutions—a framework for power contests in the polity."[7]

Second, the drive for political supremacy was entwined with UNIP's search for national unity, seen as the prerequisite for nation-building. The process culminated in the declaration of the one-party state in 1972, marking the beginning of the Second Republic in Zambia's political history. These two issues can be seen as emerging in the very process of decolonisation, which contributed to the failure of liberal democracy and the eventual declaration of a one-party state.

The two issues became ever more closely related as UNIP's search for political dominance was increasingly articulated as a process toward national unity. UNIP leaders noted that while "the spirit of Africanism" had successfully led to independence, a sense of national identity had not simultaneously been developed. Indeed, as M.G. de Winton[8] argued, "the creation of a sense of national identity was one of the problems of nation-building."[9] De Winton's observation paralleled Kaunda's own concern as first president of Zambia. Kaunda pointed out that although nationalism had successfully led to independence, its future was uncertain, because many Africans in the country lacked any notion of national identity—"their loyalties were more restricted and fragmentary."[10] The intraparty and interparty factional and ethnic conflict within UNIP and ANC, on the one hand, and between UNIP and ANC on the other, attest to that. Nationalism had to be transformed into national patriotism. There was however a strong feeling within UNIP that the continued existence of an opposition party ran counter to that objective.

UNIP AND THE SEARCH FOR POLITICAL DOMINANCE

UNIP's search for political dominance predated independence. When the Zambia African National Congress was formed in 1958 by militant African National Congress members who broke away, their decision to name the new party *Zambia African National Congress* was deliberately taken to replace ANC.[11] According to Kapasa Makasa:

> Since the people were used to the name "African National Congress," which had been in use for eight years, it would be unwise for us to come out with a completely different name which would not be easy for them to pick up quickly. Our task was therefore, to find a name which should be as near to African National Congress as possible but at the same time without creating confusion among our supporters.[12]

The founders of ZANC worked from what Thomas Rasmussen called the "snowball" and "bandwagon" model, which assumes that "as one party gains a clear advantage over another, it is able to use that advantage to reinforce its dominance."[13] ZANC's principal objective was to destroy the ANC completely and replace it as the only nationalist party.

However, the proscribing of ZANC and the consequent detention of its leaders temporarily left the ANC as the only legal African nationalist party. In August 1959 ZANC elements who had escaped detention regrouped and formed the UNIP.[14] UNIP's policy of "independence now" and its apparent populist ideology ensured it a position at the top. Once at the top, UNIP successfully formed the first African government with Kaunda serving first as prime minister in January 1964, and then as the first president in October 1964. Until the legislation of the "one-party participatory democracy" in December 1972, UNIP enjoyed a political dominance "co-existing with competition but without trace of alteration."[15] Its dominance continued to dwindle with time. This decline in UNIP's influence precipitated a move away from pluralism to a one-party political system, "and a marked concentration of political power in the hands of the executive and the president."[16]

THE SEARCH FOR NATIONAL UNITY

While UNIP easily emerged as the dominant political party from its formation to the attainment of independence, the search for national unity proved elusive. In realistic terms, "the most important single feature of interparty competition was the allegiance of the political parties' geographical bases of support."[17] This had serious political implications—especially for the question of national unity.

Until the formation of the United Party (UP) in 1966, UNIP was virtually unchallenged in most of the country. Only the rural areas of Southern Province remained outside the domain of the ruling party. The emergence of the UP and the United Progressive Party (UPP) in 1971 posed a serious threat to UNIP's political dominance. UPP was particularly strong on the Copperbelt. The search for national unity became a major preoccupation for UNIP.

However, lack of national unity was itself reflected in a lack of unity within the ruling party.[18] Since its formation in 1959 UNIP had remained essentially a coalition of various interest groups. It was never a truly coherent political party. UNIP was formed as a platform for the campaign to end colonial rule. It therefore attracted Africans with diverse interests. While this populist approach was attractive during the struggle for independence, it was no longer possible to contain the various interests within UNIP after independence. In the end, therefore, UNIP experienced intense and potentially serious intraparty competition. As Cherry Gertzel and others pointed out: "the most important level of political conflict, however, was not between UNIP and the ANC, but within UNIP itself,"[19] because UNIP's success contained "the seeds of its own future problems."[20] It became more difficult to accommodate rival political interests and the threat of defections increased.

The problem was further compounded by the quick transition of UNIP from a nationalist party formed in 1959 to a ruling party in 1964. UNIP came to power when it was still in its formative stages—the various interests within the party had only begun to reach the compromise stage. They were yet to coalesce around various interests.[21] Because the basic materials for a parliamentary system of government remained absent until the terminal stages of colonial rule, and colonialism was essentially "bureaucratic authoritarianism" in which "politics, especially opposition politics, were barely tolerated,"[22] UNIP as a political party was ill-prepared to govern the country. It took over political machinery with which most of its leaders had very little experience. Thus UNIP did not consider political pluralism and conflict as necessary or even desirable aspects of national unity. Thus national politicians aimed at gaining control of the state and structuring the political and economic system to suit their own interests.

Consequently, when disaffection emerged soon after independence, UNIP's response was erratic and sometimes exacerbated the conflict. Sources of conflicts were legion—some individuals who expected rewards for their involvement in the freedom struggle felt left out. UNIP files at the party archives contain several letters from UNIP members seeking employment in government on the basis that they had fought for independence. The frequency of such letters prompted the chief administrative secretary at UNIP headquarters to respond to one such request in the following manner: "We have fought and got our independence, but an employment is not a reward, we are already awarded with independence and what is left over is for us to fight against poverty, disease and ignorance."[23]

Because there were not enough jobs to go around for everyone who believed that they had spent time fighting for independence, some people inevitably felt frustrated. Meanwhile, the nationalization program and the creation of huge parastatal organizations such as the Industrial Development Corporation (INDECO) and the Zambia Industrial and Mining Corporation (ZIMCO) not only enabled the elite to control the most lucrative areas of the economy and accumulate capital for their own ends, but faclitated employment of cadres.

Zambia's experience in the first eight years of independence is a typical example of how most newly independent African countries grappled with the need to create a sense of national identity. While the colonial geographical entity colonial Zambia provided the frontiers for nation-building, the peoples inhabiting that unit lacked the ingredients usually required to form "nations" in the classic sense, such as a common language, culture and religion. "Africanism," which had provided a temporary unity during the independence struggle, ceased to be a unifying factor after independence. "Tribal" and regional cleavages within UNIP again brought to light the reality that nationalist leaders had so far deliberately chosen to ignore—namely that Zambia was not yet a nation.

In fact, "tribal" and regional cleavages predated independence. It has already been shown that "tribalism" and regionalism were contributory factors to the October 1958 split within the ANC when Nkumbula packed the central committee with Southern Province candidates.[24]

The process of nation-building was therefore bedeviled by the continued existence of social cleavage coupled with regional economic inequality. UNIP's popularity in the last days of colonial rule was because it shouted the loudest about its commitment to removing social and economic inequalities created by the colonial government. President Kaunda is on recorded as having promised, on 17 January 1964 at a political rally at Chifubu, that there should be "eggs and milk for every child and for every family in Zambia by 1970."[25] Eventually Kaunda and his colleagues in UNIP realized they could not fulfill these promises.

Worse still, the uneven economic development of the preindependence era increasingly became a major political issue after 1964. UNIP's failure to deal readily with the problem became a major source of conflict within the party.[26] As Bornwell C. Chikulo has argued, UNIP officials viewed "securing positions on the Central Committee ... not only as a necessary means of obtaining political power but also of influencing the allocation of economic resources."[27]

However, side by side with the need to unite the black people of Zambia was the more urgent need to "build a non-racial state from the remains of an unashamedly racial society."[28] The UNIP government had to contend with both sectionalism—a competition for scarce resources between interests which reflected the regional or provincial cleavages—and racial strife. From time to time racial antagonism was used by the UNIP government as a strategy for fostering the ideology of togetherness among black Zambians. This was not always successful. UNIP officials began to propound the ideology of togetherness as a countermeasure against an alleged white conspiracy against the Zambian government. The ideology of togetherness was meant to prevent the imminent coalescing of various interests into contending political parties.

Anyhow, race as a political factor in Zambia had been colonially motivated.[29] Thus, at independence (and beginning with the general elections of 1962), the Zambian National Assembly assumed a unique composition. Although UNIP had fifty-five out of seventy-five elected seats in Parliament, the twenty opposition seats were held by politicians, some of whom had played long and important roles in earlier councils. Among the ten European members representing the reserved seats,[30] two had been members of the Executive Council in the preindependence period and five had been members of various councils since 1959.[31] The other ten seats were held by ANC, which represented the parent nationalist party.

However, as Mainza Chona, then minister of home affairs pointed out:

> I am not very worried about the National Progress Party because as I have already said, I do not think that any of them will remain in the House after the next general election, unless they become members of UNIP ... but it is rather from the ANC that a danger would easily come in ... because they are Africans like myself, and more than that they were elected by people for whom we are fully responsible ...
>
> The imperialists will always believe that they [the ANC] have support and they are quite capable of building up people, even those who have no support.[32]

Indeed, the reserved seats were abolished before the 1968 general elections. In the end, racial antagonism again brought to the fore the fact that black Zambians were motivated by the spirit of "Africanism" in their search for nationhood. UNIP appeared to pay lip service to its declared policy of establishing a nonracial society. UNIP officials always harbored suspicions against whites who had chosen to remain in Zambia after independence. These suspicions were further exacerbated by the Unilateral Declaration of Independence (UDI) by whites in Southern Rhodesia in November 1965. There was a general belief that whites in Zambia sympathized with them. Andrew D. Roberts pointed out that while there were "still a large number of racists in the European community; white Rhodesians and South Africans continue to be indispensable, and not only in the copper industry."[33]

It was, however, the judiciary crisis of 1969, that shattered President Kaunda's claim that he was building a non-racial society through his famous philosophy of humanism. Contrary to his preaching, couched in his philosophy of humanism since 1967, Kaunda remained suspicious of white Zambians. That notwithstanding, at independence some whites who had been sympathetic to UNIP were appointed to senior government posts. One such a person was James John Skinner.[34] He was appointed minister of justice at independence and later became attorney-general and chief justice.

The judiciary crisis had its origins in the nullification of fifteen parliamentary seats by judges when ANC successfully petitioned against the election results in 1968.[35] Although for the first five and half years of the country's independence the judiciary had remained independent of the executive, there was nevertheless an air of uneasiness. This was largely because the Bench was composed only of whites, not all of whom were citizens.[36]

The crisis intensified in 1969 following the arrest and subsequent trial of two Portuguese soldiers who had crossed into Zambia from Angola. On 16 June, William Bruce Lyle, a magistrate, convicted the two of illegally entering Zambia from Angola and sentenced each to a fine of K2,000 (£1,166) or, in default of payment, to two years imprisonment. The two appealed to the High Court and on 3 July, Justice Evans quashed the sentences and commented that the incident was "trivial, and a mere technical breach."[37] On 14 July President Kaunda told a press conference that while he had no quarrel with the quashing of the sentences, he found Justice Evans' comments to have been politically motivated to discredit the government.[38]

President Kaunda further told the press conference that the fact that Justice Evans criticized "Zambian authorities" rather than the police or immigration officials, meant that the criticism was aimed directly at him since he was the "sole authority in Zambia".[39] He therefore asked Chief Justice Skinner to explain whether the judiciary was working for a foreign power.

The following day the chief justice totally rejected President Kaunda's complaint and said he did "not accept that the judgment of Justice Evans was in any sense a political one or motivated in any way by political considerations."[40] President Kaunda said for his part, he was dissatisfied with the explanation. On 16 July demonstrations in Lusaka demanded the removal of Chief Justice Skinner and Justice Evans. Some demonstrators carried posters saying that "white men could never be Zambians" and that "the only good white man was a dead one."[41] After the High Court demonstration, the demonstrators marched to the State House where they were addressed by President Kaunda who promised that he would Zambianize the judiciary shortly. What President Kaunda actually meant was that he would "Africanize" the judiciary. The chief justice was a Zambian by naturalization and so was Justice Evans. The *Times of Zambia* editorial of 18 July 1969 pointed out that:

> Let it be clear that Mr. Skinner is a Zambian; he has been a member of UNIP from the days when he risked isolation from those whose skin is of similar pigmentation to his. To lump him with any other person or to condemn every white person smacked of ultra-racialism which, apart from cutting across our national philosophy of humanism, stands in utter contradiction to our efforts in fighting the racists to the south.[42]

The constitution was subsequently amended to enable relatively inexperienced lawyers to be appointed as judges.[43] Thus, President Kaunda was hardly color-blind on this issue. On 18 July the leader of the opposition African National Congress, Harry Mwaanga Nkumbula, described the demonstrations by supporters of UNIP against the judiciary as "the end of justice in Zambia."[44]

Indeed, as Soremekun observed, "Kaunda was virtually led by the radical group," a radical wing of the party embodied in the UNIP youth wing.[45] He chose to reinforce the ideology of togetherness and temporarily appeared to score a victory by siding with the radical wing. He therefore temporarily evaded the real pressing problem of ethnicity and sectionalism within UNIP. In the end, Justice Skinner left the country on 17 July for London and Justice Evans left for Australia on 25 July. The two never returned to Zambia despite assurances that they could.

The quarrel over the judiciary crystallized around wider issues—"a deep-seated problem in Zambian politics: the widespread confusion about where ultimate authority resides, as to the relationship between the law and the executive, and between the executive and the ruling party."[46] The crisis reflected UNIP's discomfort with an independent judiciary. Because it was composed of white judges, not all of whom were Zambians, provided the excuse. The Constitution Amendment No. 5 of 1969 enabled the government to appoint lawyers who were considered loyal to the ruling party as judges. This change began the abolition of the rule of law and its indispensability to democracy in Zambia.

As if this was not enough, a debate on the Copperbelt developed into another racial crisis. This time the issue surrounded the Africanization of some street names. There was nothing particularly wrong with the process, but the proposed new names were those of four Africans who were hanged in 1961 for murdering Lilian Burton during the heat of political struggle in May 1960.[47] This was one of the few cases of violence during the independence struggle in which a white person was brutally killed by nationalist militants. The four were Edward Gresta Ngebe, James Paikani Phiri, Robin Kangwa Kamima and John Bernard Chanda. The trial of the four took place between 8 November 1960 and 5 April 1961 and all four were found guilty of murder and were executed in Livingstone prison.[48]

The controversy involved Peter Chanda, minister of state for the Copperbelt Province, and other radical UNIP members. They openly called the four men national heroes who deserved to be honored, resurrecting the emotionalism that at the time of the murder, had led the UNIP journal *Voice of UNIP* to idolize the murderers of Lilian Burton as courageous freedom fighters.[49] The idea angered Bob Burton, the husband of the murdered woman. He wrote an open letter to Peter Chanda, saying he "was packing his bags and leaving Zambia shortly ... he could no longer associate himself with a country where murder is a laudable accomplishment."[50]

The following day, President Kaunda intervened and courageously wrote an open letter to Bob Burton, apologizing for Peter Chanda whom he said he knew

> well enough to realise that he is regretting having mixed up this very sad incident.... As humanists we place importance on man as an individual, and I want you to know that I would have written a similar open letter had you by the accident of your birth been yellow, brown or black.... May I end by stating

emphatically that Mrs Burton is buried here and I believe that
it is here that her family belongs now, and I ask you to stay.[51]

Burton decided to stay, but Peter Chanda was moved from the Copperbelt to Southern Province, then to Eastern Province and then back to the Copperbelt. In 1970 he was moved to the office of the president.[52]

The judiciary crisis, and even to some extent the Peter Chanda affair, may have helped to create a sense of unity among Africans inside UNIP. The racial conflict was used as a strategy to draw the attention of UNIP followers away from divisions within the party, and among Africans in general. The party, however, was unable to conceive of opposition as anything other than an obstacle to nation-building that must be removed. Initially UNIP leaders believed that this could be done without legally banning the opposition. Rasmussen comments that "Until March 1968, UNIP relied heavily upon tactics of persuasion and positive inducements to convince ANC voters that their political and economic interests could be best served through UNIP."[53]

The consensual technique was explicitly emphasized by President Kaunda in his speech to the UNIP General Conference in August 1967, when he restated several principles:

1. That we are in favor of a one-party state;
2. That we do not believe in legislating against the opposition;
3. That by being honest to the cause of the common man we would, through effective party and government organization paralyze and wipe out any opposition thereby bringing about the birth of a one-party state;
4. We go further and declare that even when this comes about we would still not legislate against the formation of opposition parties because we might be bottling the feeling of certain people no matter how few.[54]

UNIP's popularity and parliamentary strength at independence and the corresponding unpopularity and parliamentary weakness (in terms of seats) of ANC gave UNIP the feeling that the ANC would die a "natural death."

However, instead the ANC steadily gained in strength. In the successive elections UNIP did not win the necessary support for its stated goal of establishing a one-party state through the ballot box. Furthermore, factionalism within UNIP aided ANC's political resurrection between August 1967 and December 1972. The Southern Province by-elections of March 1968 proved the futility of the strategy of achieving a one-party state through the ballot box. Southern Province remained an ANC stronghold. The by-elections were called because four members of Parliament in Southern Province constituencies had changed their party allegiance from ANC to UNIP.[55] The four ANC candidates were elected in the four by-elections in Choma, Kalomo, Magoye and Gwembe constituencies by substantial majorities. UNIP got only 15 percent of the total votes cast in the four by-elections.[56] The December 1968 general election further reinforced that point. Contrary to UNIP's "assumption that its position of dominance, and particularly its ability to reward its supporters, would result in the atrophy and eventual political death of ANC," the ANC continued to be a real political threat. The ideology of togetherness was obviously failing.

In the first four years of independence, UNIP's belief in the "snowball" and "bandwagon" model proved to be a fallacy in relation to the ANC-UNIP power struggle. Although UNIP remained in power, after the December 1968 general elections, the ANC continued to be forceful in its role as an opposition party. Nkumbula was always a rallying point for the opposition despite efforts to discredit him. Some ANC MPs, including their leader, proved more experienced than some government ministers. Efforts by the government to discredit ANC, and thus get rid of it immediately, failed.

Consequently the UNIP decided to deal with the opposition ruthlessly. Two days before Christmas of 1968, President Kaunda gave what Soremekun described as "one of the most unfortunate speeches in his political career."[57] During the ceremony at which President Kaunda announced the new administration following the December 1968 general election, he promised to implement economic reforms to show that "it pays to belong to UNIP." Issuing a warning to members of the opposition, he said:

> I cannot see how I can continue to pay a police officer or a civil servant who works for Nkumbula.... How dare they bite the hand that feeds them? *They must learn that it pays to belong to UNIP.* Those who want to form a civil service of the opposition must cross the floor and get their pay from Harry Nkumbula.[58]

President Kaunda then announced that he had ordered Justin Chimba, the new minister of Trade, Industry and Mines, "to ensure that none of the eight opposition MPs elected in Barotse Province was granted a new licence to run a business or had his old licence renewed" and warned Chimba that "*if you renew these men's licences you would be sacked your-*

self.[59] The determination to force the ANC out was not the real issue. UNIP was still strong enough to govern. However, as long as the constitution protected and allowed opposition parties to exist legally, and UNIP failed to please the various interests within the party, its dominance would wane. To undercut future defections from UNIP and the emergence of new parties, UNIP decided to legislate against the opposition—not against the ANC *per se.*

These remarks were immediately followed by some local authorities taking punitive measures against known ANC supporters. The Kitwe City Council decided, on 31 December, to grant no further licenses to members of ANC. Hyden Dingiswayo Banda, minister of state for Western Province (now Copperbelt Province) was reported to have banned all ANC meetings in the province "in order to pave the way for the creation of one-party state in Zambia."[60] Banda's announcement was echoed by Fines Bulawayo, one of the district governors in the province on 14 January 1969. Bulawayo said Banda "was ready to expel all opposition party supporters from their jobs and homes."[61]

In the Southern Province "local UNIP leaders turned the Christmas season not into a time to show goodwill toward all men, but into a time to apply ` selective sanctions' against ANC members."[62] Water taps were cut off to ANC areas, and loan applications were canceled. The current slogan became "It Pays to Belong to UNIP."

President Kaunda's decision to use the economic weapon against ANC was not only a breach of the spirit behind the economic reforms announced in April 1968, but also impeded the process of nation-building. Non-UNIP supporters were alienated from the process of national integration. Because of the regional base of political pluralism, Kaunda's decision to use the economic weapon to marginalize ANC exacerbated ethnic divisions in the country.

ECONOMIC REFORMS

On 19 April 1968 President Kaunda unfolded Zambia's economic reforms that were directed at foreign-owned companies. "The Government invited twenty-six key companies to sell 51% of their shares. Second class trading areas where most of the retail trade was conducted by Indians, became proscribed areas to non-Zambians."[63] President Kaunda also announced that from January 1969 no more trade licenses would be issued to non-Zambians. According to Soremekun, this part of the reforms affected nearly 8,000 trading places all over the country.[64] Credit facilities were from now on to be restricted to Zambians only. The government also made a clear-cut decision for the development of the rural areas through the promotion of agricultural cooperatives.[65]

The principle behind the economic reforms was to stimulate indigenous entrepreneurship. Party affiliation was not originally part of the equation of the economic reforms. Thus the introduction of party affiliation into the equation on 23 December meant that non-UNIP members were lumped together with non-Zambians, at least as far as President Kaunda's interpretation of how he intended to see the economic reforms implemented. If he believed that this was a shortcut to nation-building, he only managed to exacerbate the ANC-UNIP rivalry. More important, it made it difficult for ANC members to be patriotic to the nation when they were being treated like foreigners. Kaunda had just worsened his problem of how to transform nationalism into patriotism.[66] He was destroying the nation.

NONRECOGNITION OF THE OPPOSITION

The "economic sanctions" unilaterally imposed on all ANC supporters were soon given a parliamentary twist. On 22 January 1969, the new speaker of the National Assembly, Robinson N. Nabulyato, refused to recognize ANC as the official opposition in the assembly on the grounds that the ANC was too small a minority to constitute an official opposition. He argued that the ANC could "form neither a quorum to execute the business of the House nor a government if UNIP resigned."[67] According to the constitution at the time, a party needed twenty-seven seats to form a government, but ANC had only twenty-three.

The previous speaker of the House, Wesley Nyirenda, commented that the new speaker was within his constitutional rights. He added, however, that while Nkumbula would continue to oppose and lead his party, he would cease to be an important personage in Parliament and would neither receive the salary of leader of the opposition nor have an office in the assembly building. Nkumbula was also deprived of an official residence as leader of the opposition.[68] While Nabulyato was exercising his constitutional rights, the fact that his decision followed President Kaunda's speech in which he publicly stated that he intended to show members of the opposition that "it pays to belong to UNIP," the decision was understood as yet another attempt to clamp down on the ANC.

Ultimately, that decision destroyed the democratic principles that were needed for a smooth operation of political pluralism. The crucial element of liberal democracy—the willingness, without even considering the possibility of an alternative, by the government in office to hand over power to the winners of the next election, and to administer political conditions that allow that opposition to work openly to win over a majority of the electorate in the meantime—was no longer acceptable to the UNIP. The "political society" as defined by A.H. Somjee began to behave in a peculiar way. [bq] According to Somjee:

> A political society occupies a position between social organisation and economic structures on the one hand, and legal and political institutions on the other. *It is an arena where people born to certain ethnic, religious and class groupings make efforts to build or join secular collectives of political parties, unions and interests groups, with a cross-section of people to influence and control public institutions.* It is the product of a continuing interaction between social and cultural conditions, goal directions, mobilisational processes and participatory involvements, and above all a constantly emerging pattern of political behaviour which influences and conditions a part of the subsequent political activity.[70]

Instead of being an arena where politically mobilized individuals joined secular collectivities of party organizations, unions or interest groups to pursue their political goals, the Zambia political society became an arena for domination and for awarding political rewards. The "political society" ceased to be in the center. It became entangled with the legal and political institutions as well as the social and economic structures into which the individuals were born. The political behavior of the Zambian political society reflected the nature of the social realities and divisions within society. These social realities and divisions were in turn reflected in the behavior of party leaders.

Thus the lack of unity within UNIP, as shown during the August 1967 Mulungushi Conference, served only to prove the falsity of "Africanism" as a unifying force. On the last day of the conference party elections were held as scheduled—the first and last open and competitive elections for UNIP leadership. Before the elections it was agreed that certain party posts would correspond to certain cabinet posts. For instance, the candidate elected as the president of the party would automatically become the president of the state. The UNIP national vice president would be the vice president of the state.[71]

When the voting was over, nearly all the candidates from Lozi-speaking Barotseland and Nyanja-speaking Eastern Province were defeated by Tonga-speaking and Bemba-speaking candidates. The party had split along linguistic lines. The Bemba-Tonga alliance headed by Simon

Kapwepwe and the Nyanja-Lozi alliance headed by Reuben Kamanga, became the key entities in the fight for elections.

The electoral results were shattering for a party that boasted of building a nontribal and a nonracial nation under the motto of "ONE ZAMBIA ONE NATION." The political aftermath first surfaced on 20 August when President Kaunda appointed a Commission of Inquiry under Chief Justice Jack Blagden to investigate the election results in light of reports that the number of votes cast had exceeded the total number of people qualified to vote at the conference in four of the seven contests. The Blagden Commission reported on 24 August that there were "substantial errors in the counting of votes at Mulungushi," but never had the number of votes cast exceeded the number of voters, nor did the recount suggest any change in the results of the election.[72]

Ethnic tension mounted as it became apparent that the election of Bemba representatives for five of the eleven posts in the Central Committee, and the defeat of long-time Lozi representatives such as Sipalo and Wina, had upset the careful ethnic balance until now maintained in the party hierarchy. Table VII summarizes the electoral results of the August 1967 party elections.

Table 7: Unip Party Elections, August 1967

Elective Party Office	Candidate	Votes Cast (Mulungushi Count)	Votes Cast (Commission of Inquiry Recount)	Ethnic Background
National President	Kenneth Kaunda	Unopposed	— —	Bemba
National Vice-President	**Simon Kapwepwe**	2,742	2,740	Bemba
	Reuben Kamanga	2,404	2,010	Nyanja
National Secretary	**Mainza Chona**	2,404	2,740	Tonga
	Munu Sipalo	1,911	1,210	Lozi
	Aaron Milner	1,493	1,134	Coloured
Deputy National Secretary	**Justin Chimba**	2,953	2,450	Bemba
	Humphrey Mulemba	2,314	2,259	Kaonde
National Treasurer	**Elijah Mudenda**	2,964	2,962	Tonga
	Arthur Wina	1,800	1,782	Lozi
Deputy National Treasurer	**Lewis Changufu**	2,893	2,888	Bemba
	Wesley Nyirenda	1,919	1,868	Nyanja
Deputy National Chairman	**Grey Zulu**	2,522	2,674	Nyanja
	Peter Matoka	2,390	2,083	Tonga
Director of the Women's Brigade	**Maria Nankolongo**	3,220	3,323	Bemba
	Princess Mukwae Nakatindi	1,436	1,436	Lozi

Source: Robert I. Rotberg, "Tribalism and Politics in Zambia", *Africa Report*, 12 (December 1967), p.32. Fifth column added by author.

President Kaunda expressed concern at the cleavages revealed by the election results:

> What happened in the last elections shows clearly that we have not understood [the dangers of our methods]. We have canvassed so strongly and indeed, viciously, along tribal, racial and provincial lines, that one wonders whether we really have national or tribal or provincial leadership. It is very easy to shout "ONE ZAMBIA ONE NATION." but very difficult to think and act in that way honestly and sincerely.[73]

Things came to a head in February 1968 during the UNIP National Council meeting in Chilenje, Lusaka. The National Council met to endorse the party's new Central Committee, but because of dissension from a large section of the party hierarchy, this was not possible. Incensed by the jubilation of the winning groups, and by the bickering and hostility that resulted from the August 1967 election, President Kaunda resigned his post as UNIP's president and *ipso facto* as Zambia's president on February 4, 1968.[74]

The outcome of President Kaunda's brief resignation is interesting to follow for it provides a focus of his subsequent control of the party. It also accounts for the decline of political pluralism and the consequent declaration of the one-party state in 1972. Alexander Grey Zulu, chairman of the Chilenje meeting, was quoted as having said: "In the name of the 4,500,000 people of Zambia, in the name of the unborn children and our dead ancestors, I must plead with you to withhold your final decision until tomorrow."[75] An impression was therefore created that only Kaunda was able to lead Zambia. Kaunda later said he withdrew his resignation when many people, "some of them with tears in their eyes begged him to stay."[76] One minister of state at the time responded to President Kaunda's brief resignation as follows:

> I left that Hall with one theme in mind—the Republic is finished.... My family was left behind in the Solwezi provincial capital of the North-Western Province. My first thought, following the shock of Ken's resignation, was of the security of my family who were more than six hundred and forty kilometres away from this confusion.... I was therefore going to drive all night to Solwezi, pick up my family, pack a few essential belongings and drive back to Lusaka, and then to Lundazi in the Eastern Province, which is my home. I was going to leave them in the safety of the villagers and return to Lusaka with my shot gun and join in the street fighting.[77]

Nephas Tembo's reaction and thoughts reflect vividly how "tribal" and regionally inspired they were. Although he was a minister of state, for the North-Western Province, his thoughts reflected his belief that he was an Easterner first and Zambian second. Therefore, when President Kaunda briefly resigned his presidency, Tembo was more concerned about the safety of his family in Solwezi among strangers. It is therefore, plausible to suggest that the "Zambian nation" as imagined by Tembo and others in UNIP was yet to be consolidated—a process they imagined untenable without Kaunda, whom they visualized as the epitome of unity. Nephas Tembo, like Grey Zulu, believed that without Kaunda's leadership Zambia as a nation would be in jeopardy. Both equated the existence of the nation with Kaunda's leadership. Several years later, Mwizenge S. Tembo restated this theme when he wrote:

> It had very grave potential implications for the four million people of Zambia at the time. This was a young and fragile country barely four years old. It was surrounded by White Rhodesia, racist South Africa, and white colonial Portuguese Angola and Mozambique. These regimes would have been more than jubilant to see turmoil and bloodshed in independent black Zambia. That would have been ammunition for these regimes' racist colonial campaigns. Obviously cooler heads among the Zambian political leaders at the time prevailed. During that twelve-hour political crisis, Zambia's future hung in the balance. Fortunately, the leaders restrained their selfish political ambitions for the sake of the unity and safety of Zambia and its citizens.[78]

Mwizenge Tembo's interpretation of the February 1968 crisis reflects "nationalist scholarship," which tends to blame the outside world for most problems of the newly independent countries. Here Mwizenge Tembo gives the impression that Zambia needed Kaunda to remain united as a nation and therefore avoid foreign-engineered political instability. This is a refusal to take cognizance of the fact that the Zambian political society was not monolithic and had great potential for political conflict.

However, neither Mwizenge Tembo nor Sikota Wina explain why none of the other candidates who were also returned unopposed at the Mulungushi elections of Central Committee members in 1967 could effectively lead the party.[79] One could argue that, as in 1958 when Kaunda first emerged as leader of the newly founded Zambia African National Congress and similarly in 1968, Kaunda appeared least motivated by the politics of tribalism. In 1958 Simon Kapwepwe, Reuben Kamanga and others had led the breakaway, yet Kaunda, who followed them one hour later, became leader of the new party. Why?

In retrospect, it is plausible to suggest that only Kaunda lacked strong tribal inclinations. Although born among the Bemba, Kaunda's Nyasaland (now Malawi) parentage seems to have been at the back of the minds of those who formed ZANC. Events of 1968, and Kaunda's apparent strong antitribal sentiments, seem to suggest that only he was capable of playing politics above tribal lines.

The manner in which President Kaunda was persuaded to resume the presidency following his twelve-hour resignation (although he did not hand his letter of resignation to the chief justice), created a great psychological impact among UNIP officials. The "Leadership Principle" began to be a reality. President Kaunda emerged stronger than he was before the crisis. It was a political gamble that paid handsome dividends. President Kaunda promised never to resign again.

While President Kaunda emerged strong, UNIP as a party was increasingly weakened. Its grip on political power was no longer a *fait accompli*. In response, President Kaunda began moving toward a one-party state—not so much as a process of nation-building, but as a strategy for maintaining UNIP's political dominance and thereby his own in Zambia. To remain an epitome of unity, Kaunda had to remove all existing and potential sources of challenge to his leadership. Conflict within UNIP gave the United Party a position of political significance that it had never enjoyed since its formation. Because of ethnic polarization in the country, UP's strength grew in Western Province and along the railroad line. The UP was however proscribed in 1968 because of violent clashes with UNIP. After that, UP leaders directed their followers to join ANC. Consequently, between 1968 and 1972 ANC's effectiveness increased substantially and undermined UNIP's hope of achieving a one-party state through the ballot box.

TOWARD THE SECOND REPUBLIC, 1969-1972

Although Zambia became *de jure* a one-party state in December 1972, the country had been a *de facto* one-party state since 1969 following Robinson Nabulyato's decision as speaker of the National Assembly not to recognize the ANC as an official opposition in Parliament. ANC protests could not stop the process toward the creation of a one-party political system in Zambia. Meanwhile, the government continued to deny that it intended to legislate the opposition out of existence. In August 1969 President Kaunda said:

> It is necessary for me to repeat also that if we wanted, we
> would make Zambia a one-party state today. We have all the
> necessary instruments including the will of the majority of the
> people. But we do not want to do so now and we will avoid
> having to do it by legislation, although I must warn that this is
> no licence for trouble makers to force our hand in it.[80]

However, the behavior of UNIP officials in the provinces did not reflect
their leader's sentiments. Punitive measures continued to be carried out
against ANC supporters.

Meanwhile, cleavages within UNIP continued to grow. In August
1969 President Kaunda issued a party presidential decree that dissolved
the Central Committee and abolished the post of party president and
vice president. In their place he created a temporary National Committee
to deal with routine party affairs.[81] He began to call himself secretary-
general of the party. From the point of view of Zambia's constitutional
set-up, President Kaunda had emerged as a virtual dictator.

He then appointed two commissions, one to redraft the UNIP constitution (which he blamed for the lack of stability and efficiency), and
another to work on the question of discipline in the party. The president
also reorganized and changed the relationship between the party and the
government. Henceforth the party was supreme over the government.

Simon Kapwepwe tendered his resignation as vice president of the
party and government the same day, saying:

> Some of my colleagues and fellow leaders have never recog-
> nised me as a properly elected Vice-President and have engaged
> in mud-slinging in the press, at public meetings and in dark
> corners.... The people from the northern part of Zambia—the
> Bemba-speaking people—have suffered physically.... They
> have suffered demotions and suspensions because of my being
> Vice-President. I cannot sacrifice any longer these people.[82]

However, on 27 August 1969 Kapwepwe withdrew his resignation from
the government and said he would stay on until his term expired in August
1970. Meanwhile factionalism continued to dominate UNIP politics.

In August 1971 Kapwepwe resigned from the government as minister of provincial and local government and culture, and became leader
of newly formed United Progressive Party. The UPP epitomized the
tendency for intraparty competition in the guise of regional conflict that
culminated in the secession from UNIP of some skilled politicians. The
defections seriously impaired UNIP's capability for mobilizing votes.[83]

Although UPP was generally a Bemba-dominated party, it attracted those within UNIP who had always emphasized mass participation and popular control as opposed to those who emphasized the importance of unity and control from above as a basis for party organization. The former was usually Bemba dominated while the latter was usually Lozi dominated. This was the ideological basis for the founding of UPP. The new party attracted small businesspeople, middle-level civil servants, local elected councillors and some party militants from UNIP whose services during the anticolonial struggle had seemingly gone unrewarded after 1964. The UPP was strongest on the Copperbelt. It is in this respect that Gertzel, Szeftel and Baylies argue that UPP was "an expression and consequence of competition for limited resources."[84]

Kapwepwe's resignation had a sobering effect on the UNIP leadership. A popular politician outside UNIP represented a real threat. President Kaunda was left with no choice but to go for the one-party state. What he now needed was a justification to make his move. He did not wait very long. Because of the violence that followed, which was blamed on the new party, President Kaunda on 4 February 1972 proscribed UPP and detained Kapwepwe and 123 leading UPP members.[85]

On 25 February President Kaunda announced the cabinet's decision to establish a one-party state in Zambia through constitutional change.[86] A National Commission was set up under the chairmanship of the vice president, Mainza Chona, to recommend necessary changes to the constitution in preparation for the introduction of the one-party state system. The Chona Commission reported in October 1972. Public debate was minimal.

The tenor of the Chona Report "suggested the `liberal' influence of Zambia's new administrators and entrepreneurs, rather than the populist influence of the party."[87] The government therefore rejected most of the Commission's recommendations, which would have made Zambia's "one-party participatory democracy" a reality. The recommendation that the incumbent president be eligible to stand for a second five-year term, after which he or she would not be eligible to stand for office until yet another five-year period had elapsed, was rejected. The government also rejected the proposal for an electoral competition between three presidential candidates. Instead, the government White Paper[88] provided for one presidential candidate who was to be elected by the party's general conference.

In the end, the constitutional changes that ushered in the Second Republic reinforced party control over the presidency, while simultaneously providing for greater presidential control over the party. Contrary to President Kaunda's suggestion in March 1972 that "one-party participatory democracy" would end the politics of patronage, the reverse was true. On 4 December 1972 the UNIP National Council discussed the Chona Report and accepted the government White Paper on it. On 8 December by a vote of seventy-eight to none, the National Assembly approved the second and third reading of the Constitutional Amendment Bill prohibiting all opposition parties. It established the ruling UNIP as the country's sole legal party.[89] President Kaunda signed the Bill on 13 December at a ceremony to mark its enactment.[90]

Under this bill no person was allowed to attempt to form a political party or organization other than UNIP. Further, no one was allowed to "belong to or assemble, associate, express opinion or do anything in sympathy with any such political party or organization."[91] While President Kaunda had in September 1963 openly turned down a proposition that he become life president of UNIP (and *ipso facto* of Zambia),[92] the constitutional changes that ushered in the one-party state made him a *de facto* life president. The current slogan was "ONE ZAMBIA ONE NATION; ONE NATION ONE LEADER, THAT LEADER KAUNDA WAMUYAYA."[93] President Kaunda never objected to the slogan. In fact he always began his political speeches by starting the slogan and letting his audience carry it to its logical conclusion.

Although Zambia was *de jure* a one-party state from 13 December 1972, the ANC continued to be a major political threat. It became necessary therefore to have the Choma Declaration—a document signed at Choma in the Southern Province between President Kaunda for UNIP and Harry Nkumbula for the ANC in June 1973——to dissolve the ANC formally and ask all ANC members and such structures as branches to identify themselves fully with UNIP.[94] Yet while the Choma Declaration resolved the ANC-UNIP power struggle in the Southern Province, it did not resolve all the problems. Nalumino Mundia and Kapwepwe were still not welcome into UNIP. Many national and local UNIP officials adamantly opposed the readmission of former UPP members into UNIP.[95]

Thus Zambia became officially and constitutionally a one-party state. Throughout the developments leading to this outcome, UNIP had argued that the necessities of nation-building dictated each step in the process. Yet there was little to suggest that a unified sense of belonging to a single national community was much stronger, in 1972, than it had been during the struggle to avoid absorption in the Central African Federation.

CONCLUSION

This chapter has demonstrated the inadequacy of the spirit of "Africanism" as a motivating factor in the quest for nation-building. At independence "blackness" ceased to be a unifying factor. Other variables entered the equation. In fact, they were always inherent in the nationalist movements, except that during the struggle against colonial rule these forces were less pronounced and were temporarily suppressed.

However, after October 1964, Zambians came to grips with the fact that Zambia as a nation lacked a strong political society capable of sustaining liberal democracy. The UNIP government was intolerant to opposition and was incapable of administering a political system that protected and even allowed that opposition to grow. For UNIP, nationalism, and the national consciousness—a sense of a shared national identity—which it aroused during the struggle for independence, was assumed to be monolithic. Thus intraparty violence and cleavages posed a serious challenge to UNIP's perceived national unity. Because liberal democracy was a new phenomenon with no established tradition, its continued existence was precarious. Political pluralism was viewed negatively and was associated with lack of a strong sense of national identity—which for UNIP meant speaking with one voice.

In the end UNIP officials decided to take the easy way out by establishing a one-party state. Yet the introduction of the one-party state not only put a brake on the development and nurturing of liberal democracy, it became an obstacle to the process of nation-building. Evidence suggests that UNIP's decision to declare a one-party state was motivated more by threats of intraparty leadership conflicts, which usually led to defections, than by fear of opposition parties. In fact, it was Kapwepwe's resignation in 1972 and his becoming leader of the newly formed United Progressive Party that gave the movement to a one-party state further impetus.

Finally, the experience of Zambia's First Republic from 24 October 1964 to 13 December 1972 suggests very strongly that the brief transition from colonial rule to independence did not provide any experience whatsoever of liberal democracy. The time between the introduction of party politics in the late 1950s and independence was not long enough to determine that elections would be regular and free or whether the government was willing to foster political conditions that guaranteed political pluralism. Rather, Zambian politicians admired the bureaucratic authoritarianism of the colonial era that they believed was essential for nation-building. This helped to focus loyalties on the frontiers of the

former colonial state, which became symbolized in the UNIP slogan—
"One Zambia One Nation."

Thus the eventual declaration of the one-party state, disguised as
"one-party participatory democracy," was in essence a return to the
much-criticized bureaucratic authoritarianism of the preindependence
days. Zambia's experience in the First Republic and UNIP's search for
national unity was essentially a struggle for political control and the
financial rewards that accompanied office-holding. Because the political elite did not emerge from the business class, the state and access to
its resources was the best and easiest way to accumulate capital. It was
therefore economically and financially disastrous for the ruling elite to
relinquish power to an oppositional excluded elite. A successful implementation of political pluralism or liberal democracy—as the antithesis
of bureaucratic authoritarianism—would have prevented UNIP from
using its political dominance to reward its supporters at the expense of
the opposition. UNIP's reluctance to allow the proliferation of opposition parties between 1964 and 1972, disguised as the search for national
unity through the establishment of "one-party participatory democracy,"
was not only the death knell of liberal democracy, but a return to an
authoritarian political system and an impediment to economic growth.

Notes

1. Tom Mboya, cited in Richard Cox, *Pan-Africanism in Practice: An East African Study, PAFMECSA 1958-1964,*(London: Oxford University Press, 1964), p. 3.

2. On PAFMECSA see Cox, *Pan-Africanism in Practice.*

3. Kenneth D. Kaunda and Colin Morris, *Black Government? A Discussion Between Colin Morris and Kenneth Kaunda* (Lusaka: United Society for Christian Literature, 1960), p. 93 (italics added).

4. Megan Vaughan, "Exploitation and Neglect: Rural Producers and the State in Malawi and Zambia", in David Birmingham and Phyllis M. Martin (eds.), *History of Central Africa: The Contemporary Years Since 1960* (London: Longmans, 1998), p.179.

5. Vaughan, "Exploitation and Neglect", p.179.

6. Richard Sandbrook, "Liberal Democracy in Africa: A Socialist-Revision-ist Perspective," *Canadian Journal of African Studies,* 22, 2 (1988), p. 241.

7. Ali A. Mazrui, "Pluralism and National Integration," in Leo Kuper and M.G. Smith (eds.), *Pluralism in Africa* (Berkeley: University of California Press, 1969), p. 333.

8. He was legal advisor in the service of the Nigerian government between 1950 and 1960, and legal advisor and constitutional draftsman in the Colonial Office between 1960 and 1968.

9. M.G. de Winton, "Decolonization and the Westminster Model," in A.H.M. Kirk-Greene (ed.), *The Transfer of Power: The Colonial Administration in the Age of Decolonization* (Kidlington Oxford: Oxford University Press, 1979), p. 184.

10. Kenneth D. Kaunda and Colin M. Morris, *A Humanist in Africa: Letters to Colin Morris from Kenneth D. Kaunda* (London: Longmans, 1966), p. 84.

11. For a detailed discussion of the formation of ZANC and later UNIP, see Chapter Four.

12. Kapasa Makasa, *Zambia's March to Political Freedom* (Nairobi: Heinemann, 1985), p. 97.

13. Thomas Rasmussen, "Political Competition and One-Party Dominance in Zambia," *The Journal of Modern African Studies*, 7, 3 (1963), p. 405.

14. UNIP was an amalgam of the African National Independence Party (ANIP) and the United Freedom Independence Party, both of which had been registered in July. David C. Mulford pointed out that "little is known about UNIP's actual formation" and speculates that perhaps the "ANIP and UNFP leaders regarded this as a first step towards African unity." (David C. Mulford, *Zambia: The Politics of Independence, 1957-1964*, [London, Oxford University Press, 1967], p. 119).

15. W.H. Morris-Jones, "Dominance and Dissent: Their Interrelations in the Indian Party System," *Government and Politics*, 1, 4 (July-September 1966), p. 454.

16. Vaughan, "Exploitation and Neglect," p.180.

17. William Tordoff and Ian Scott, "Political Parties: Structures and Policies," in William Tordoff (ed.), *Politics in Zambia* (Manchester: Manchester University Press, 1974), p. 141.

18. Leadership conflict and crisis was not only confined to UNIP. ANC also experienced internal dissensions. In September 1965, for example, a section of ANC National Council led by Bellings Lombe publicly deposed Harry Nkumbula and asked Edward Mungoni Liso to head the party. But Liso, who was Nkumbula's nephew, refused the invitation and pledged his loyalty to the "deposed" leader (*Times of Zambia*, 27 September 1965). The failure to replace Nkumbula led to the formation of a splinter group led by senior national executive officials and five of the ANC MPs. They formed a new political party called the United Front, which comprised the following:

    | National President | Bellings Lombe |
    | National Secretary | Price S Chanda |
    | Treasurer | Jack Manzies |

Director of Youth   Jairnes Mate
Deputy Director of Youth   Maxwell Sikufweba
Publicity Chief   Patrick Mulandu

(Patrick Wele, *Kaunda and Mushala Rebellion: The Untold Story*, [Lusaka: Multimedia Publications, 1987], p. 29.)

19. Cherry Gertzel, Carolyn Baylies and Morris Szeftel (eds.) *The Dynamics of the One-Party State in Zambia* (Manchester: Manchester University Press, 1984), p. 7.

20. Rasmussen, "One-Party Dominance in Zambia," p. 408.

21. For a detailed discussion on the different stages of political development concerning political integration in a plural society such as that of Zambia, see Mazrui, "Pluralism and National Integration," p. 335.

22. J.S. Coleman, "Economic Growth and Political Reorientation", in Melville J. Herskovits and Mitchell Harwitz (eds.), *Economic Transition in Africa*, (Evanstown: IL: Northwestern University Press, 1964), p. 396.

23. PA, UNIP 6/45, Chief Administrative Secretary, UNIP Headquarters to Alfred Lukonga, 21 January 1967. For more letters from UNIP supporters seeking employment, see File ANC 2/3 Vol. II, Enquiries and Complaints.

24. See Makasa, *Zambia's March to Political Freedom*, pp. 88 and 94, and also Chapter Four.

25. Kenneth Kaunda, Speech at Chifubu (Ndola), 17 January 1964, cited in Fola Soremekun, "The Challenge of Nation-Building: Neo-Humanism and Politics in Zambia, 1967-1969," *Geneva-Africa*, 9, 1 (1970), p. 5.

26. See Robert Molteno, "Cleavage and Conflict in Zambian Politics: A Study in Sectionalism," in William Tordoff (ed.), *Politics in Zambia* (Manchester: Manchester University Press, 1974), pp. 62-106.

27. Bornwell C. Chikulo, "Elections in a One-Party Participatory Democracy," in Ben Turok (ed.), *Development in Zambia: a Reader* (London: Zed Press, 1979), p. 202.

28. John de St. Jorre, "Race Tension on the Copperbelt: Rhodesia Infects Her Northern Neighbour," *The Round Table*, 225 (January 1967), p. 75.

29. See Chapter Two for details.

30. Under the Northern Rhodesia (Constitution) Order-in-Council 1963, which provided for these reserved seats, the United Federal Party reorganized as the National Progress Party, contested the 1964 elections and won all the ten reserved seats. The independence constitution (Cmd. 2365) provided for the continuation of these seats unless the president desired otherwise.

31. Anirudha Gupta, "The Zambian National Assembly: Study of an African Legislature," *Parliamentary Affairs*, 19, 1 (1965-66), p. 50.

32. Parliamentary Debates, January 13, 1965, col. 93, cited in Gupta, "The Zambian National Assembly," p. 52.

33. Andrew D. Roberts, "White Judges Under Attack: Growing Pressure for a One-Party State," *The Round Table*, 236 (October 1966), p. 426.

34. James J. Skinner was a Lusaka lawyer originally from Dublin. He acted as UNIP's legal and campaign advisor. In July 1962 Skinner prepared UNIP's *Election Workers' Handbook* (30 July 1962), an impressive and extensive electioneering guide that was distributed to party officials at all levels. Skinner was also involved in winning over other whites to UNIP.

35. Soremekun, "The Challenge of Nation-Building," p. 22. See also Roberts, "White Judges Under Attack," pp. 423-430.

36. Robert Molteno and William Tordoff, "Conclusion, Independent Zambia: Achievements and Prospects," in Tordoff (ed.), *Politics in Zambia*, p. 368.

37. *Keesing's Contemporary Archives*, Vol. 14 (1969), p. 23533.

38. *Keesing's Contemporary Archives*, Vol. 14 (1969), p. 23533.

39. *Keesing's Contemporary Archives*, Vol. 14 (1969), p. 23533.

40. *Keesing's Contemporary Archives*, Vol. 14 (1969), p. 23533.

41. Soremekun, "The Challenge of Nation-Building," p. 36.

42. *Africa Research Bulletin* (July 1-31, 1969), p. 1381.

43. The Constitution (Amendment) (No. 5), Act, 1969, S. 12, cited in Molteno and Tordoff, "Conclusion," *Politics in Zambia*, p. 368.

44. *Africa Research Bulletin* (July 1-31 1969), p. 1481.

45. Soremekun, "The Challenge of Nation-Building," p. 37.

46. Roberts, "White Judges Under Attack," p. 428.

47. *Northern News*, 9 May, 1960.

48. Nephas Tembo, *The Lilian Burton Killing: The Famous Trials of Zambian Freedom Fighters* (Lusaka: Apple Books, 1986), p.55

49. J.R.T. Wood, *The Welensky Papers: A History of the Federation of Rhodesia and Nyasaland* (Durban: Graham Publishing, 1983), p. 1020.

50. Bob Burton, "An Open Letter to Minister of State Peter Chanda," *Times of Zambia*, 22 October 1968.

51. K.D. Kaunda, "An Open Letter to Bob Burton from His Excellency The President of the Republic of Zambia," *Times of Zambia*, 23 October 1968.

52. It is important to point out that Peter Chanda himself never apologized to Bob Burton, nor did he suffer any political setback. His frequent transfers were not unique—they were a common feature in the UNIP government. It was one way in which President Kaunda kept holders of party and government posts under control by creating uncertainty. Peter Chanda was later appointed Zambia's ambassador to Ethiopia until his subsequent arrest and detention in February 1972 for supporting the United Progressive Party. (*Africa Research Bulletin*, 1-29 February 1972, p. 2377). He was

released from detention together with Simon Kapwepwe on 31 December 1972 (*Africa Research Bulletin*, 1-31 December 1972, p. 2688).

53. Rasmussen, "One-Party Dominance in Zambia," p. 407.

54. Proceedings of the Annual General Conference of UNIP, held at Mulungushi, 14-20 August 1967. Lusaka, Zambia Information Service, 1967, pp. 10-11, cited in Chikulo, "Elections in a One-Party Participatory Democracy," p. 202.

55. According to the Zambian constitution then, an elected member of Parliament ceased to be a member of the house if he or she changed party allegiance. A by-election was therefore mandatory in such cases.

56. Rasmussen, "One-Party Dominance in Zambia," pp. 410-411.

57. Soremekun, "The Challenge to Nation-Building," p. 24.

58. *Keesing's Contemporary Archives*, Vol. 17 (1968-69), p. 23321. (emphasis added).

59. Soremekun, "The Challenge of Nation-Building," p. 25 (emphasis added).

60. *Keesing's Contemporary Archives*, Vol. 17 (1968-69), p. 23321.

61. *Keesing's Contemporary Archives*, Vol. 17 (1968-69), p. 23321.

62. Soremekun, "The Challenge of Nation-Building," p. 26.

63. Soremekun, "The Challenge to Nation-Building," p. 13.

64. Soremekun, "The Challenge of Nation-Building," p. 13.

65. This work does not discuss the failures or successes of the economic reforms as they were unveiled by President Kaunda in 1968.

66. Kaunda and Morris, *A Humanist in Africa*, p. 83.

67. *Keesing's Contemporary Archives*, Vol. 17 (1968-69), p. 23321.

68. *Africa Research Bulletin*, (1-31 January 1969), p. 1296.

69. A. H. Somjee, *The Democratic Process in a Developing Society* (New York: St. Martin's Press 1979), pp. 127-128.

70. Somjee, *The Democratic Process*, p. 128 (emphasis added).

71. Soremekun, "The Challenge of Nation-Building," p. 10.

72. *Africa Report*, 12 (October 1967), p. 35. See Table VII, columns 3 and 4.

73. President Kaunda, Address to the United National Independence Party Council, 29 August 1967, cited in *Africa Report*, 12, 9 (December 1967), p. 33.

74. Soremekun refers to Kaunda's resignation for a few hours in September 1967. This is an error because all evidence suggests that it was in February 1968, not September 1967, that Kaunda staged his dramatic brief resignation. For a detailed account of these events see Sikota Wina, *A Night Without a President*, (Lusaka: Multimedia Publications, 1985). The central thesis of Wina's book is that without Kaunda, Zambia would erupt into violence and all would be lost.

75. Wina, *A Night Without a President*, p. 45.

76. Soremekun, "The Challenge of Nation-Building," p. 11.

77. Nephas Tembo, quoted in Wina, *A Night Without a President*, p. 46.

78. Mwizenge S. Tembo, "Zambia By Zambians," *Canadian Journal of African Studies*, 22, 1 (1988), p. 151.

79. The following were also returned unopposed: chairman, Solomon Kalulu; publicity chief, Sikota Wina; and director of the youth brigade, Dingiswayo Banda.

80. *Africa Confidential*, 17 (22 August 1969), p. 3.

81. *Africa Research Bulletin*, (1-31 August 1969), p. 1494.

82. *Africa Research Bulletin*, (1-31 August 1969), p. 1495. Kapwepwe's claims that the Bemba-speaking people suffered physically because he was Zambia's Vice president do not reflect African political realities. In fact the conflict within UNIP centred around the party leadership that reflected Bemba dominance (see Table VII). Because of the patronage system, Bemba-speaking people were more secure than is acknowledged.

83. Gertzel et al. "Introduction: The Making of the One-Party State," in Gertzel et al (eds.), *The Dynamics of the One-Party State in Zambia* (Manchester: Manchester University Press, 1984), p. 14.

84. Gertzel, et al "Introduction," p. 14.

85. *Africa Research Bulletin*, (February 1-29, 1972), p. 2377.

86. *Africa Research Bulletin*, (1-29 February 1972), p. 2377.

87. Gertzel, et al *The Dynamics of the One-Party State*, p. 18.

88. *Summary of Recommendations Accepted by Government*, Government Paper No. 1 of 1972 (1972).

89. Congress MPs walked out in protest and therefore did not participate in the voting.

90. *Keesing's Contemporary Archives*, Vol. 19 (1972), p. 25676.

91. *Keesing's Contemporary Archives*, Vol. 19 (1973), p. 25676.

92. Colin Legum (ed.), *Zambia: Independence and Beyond, the Speeches of Kenneth Kaunda* (London: Oxford University Press, 1966), pp. 154-155.

93. *Wamuyayaya* means "for ever and ever" in Chinyanja.

94. *Times of Zambia*, 28 June 1973; *Sunday Times* 1 July, 1973.

95. *Times of Zambia*, 23 January, and 13, 23 and 25 September 1973.

Chapter 6

THE SECOND REPUBLIC: THE MYTH AND REALITIES OF ONE-PARTY PARTICIPATORY DEMOCRACY, 1972-1991

Democracy ... can only flourish in a mature and stable society with a stability established by a long tradition.[1]

It is an established fact that in modern political experience, Dictators have been able to rule only if the masses of their people have a fanatical faith in the Leader principle.[2]

Few can deny that in independent Africa the masses (and in some cases, politicians as well) have "a fanatical faith in the Leader principle," and that democracy never flourished nor experienced a long tradition. The "fanatical faith in the Leader principle" emerged during the colonial era, and especially in the last days of colonial rule when nationalist leaders began to challenge the political establishment.[3] Kapasa Makasa noted with respect to Harry Mwaanga Nkumbula, then president of the African National Congress that:

Harry Nkumbula led the African National Congress party almost beyond challenge or question.... This arose from the fact that he was extremely popular with the masses and as a result was carried away by the myth of being a Messiah and the emotional regard in which the majority of the people in the country held him under the slogan "Lead us Kindly H.M. Nkumbula."[4]

Propelled by such popularity, nationalists began to challenge the colonial administration. They argued that colonial rule was undemocratic and that it was designed to perpetually undermine the political progress of the vast majority of the people, who happened to have been Africans.

How did such views and perceptions develop into the myth of one-party participatory democracy?[5]

ORIGINS OF POLITICAL MYTHS

To grasp the mythology of "one-party participatory democracy" in Zambia, it is necessary to establish the origins of political myths and their political and social values. Political myths are narrative visions of the past or the future that have practical value to the groups of people who believe in them. John Day noted that "political myths are not mere intellectual inventions, but are produced in particular historical circumstances to satisfy social needs."[6] The use of the word "myth" in this chapter conforms to Day's definition, which includes fantasies in their generalized forms. More important, it is assumed that people "adopt myths to make coherent what is fundamentally self-contradictory in their beliefs or in their practical life."[7]

Zambia attained political independence in October 1964 under an executive presidency model, "which rested so much power in one man,"[8] but with a constitution that nonetheless allowed political competition.[9] Herein lay the first contradiction that made nationalist leaders uncomfortable. UNIP won an overwhelming majority and formed the first independent government. ANC, which was the first African political party in Zambia, became the opposition. Because of UNIP's strong position at independence, and the weak position of the opposition, UNIP erroneously believed that the ANC would die a natural death. This belief conformed to the myth that UNIP was a party for the masses who saw in UNIP unity and progress. The belief also conformed to the myth that the African nation ought to remain united to deal with the white regimes in the south. The existence of the opposition went against the ideology of togetherness and could not be tolerated.

Since its inception in 1959 UNIP had to contend, first with its inability to replace the ANC, and then from 1964 with increasingly serious internal divisions that occasionally resulted in the formation of splinter political parties—the United Party in 1966 and the United Progress Party in 1971. As Jan Pettman noted, "far from being the main agent for unity, UNIP itself was becoming a threat to the political stability of Zambia."[10] To avoid the painful acknowledgment of factionalism and disunity within UNIP as well as UNIP's inability to eliminate the opposition through the ballot box, UNIP resorted to a convenient myth. The strength of UNIP was diligently constructed in a world of fantasy. The masses were portrayed to be 100 per cent behind UNIP. Leaders of the opposition were described as power hungry without any support from the masses. Speaking during the UNIP Annual General Conference in 1967, President Kaunda reiterated the myth when he said: "As already pointed out, every indication on the political horizon shows that at the next general election UNIP will be returned with an overwhelming majority, if not 100 per cent."[11] Yet all indications were that things were not going well in UNIP.

While the myth of "one-party participatory democracy" was itself a subsequent outcome of earlier myths about political opposition, it is plausible to suggest that it had its origins in the colonial period. Throughout the independence negotiations African nationalists behaved as though they were united and symbolizing the oneness of the will of the people. This was partly in response to Colonial Office decolonization policy, which sought to reconcile, in conference, all the significant interests in Zambia so that they entered upon independence with an agreed system of government. African nationalists went further when they formed a coalition government in 1962. The Colonial Office insisted on some form of unity among Africans before it was ready to relinquish political power. Furthermore, Kenneth Kaunda, reporting to the National Assembly at the end of the Independence Conference, appealed to African traditions when he said: "In accordance with our African way of life we intend that the President should be no mere figure-head and that he will have strong executive powers."[12]

Thus, by appealing to African traditions, Kaunda invoked the masses' fanatical faith in the leader principle and therefore sought to neutralize all forms of political opposition.[13] That this was possible reflects the lack of liberal democracy as a political process during the colonial period. For all practical purposes and intents, colonialism was essentially "bureaucratic authoritarianism" in which "politics, especially opposition politics were barely tolerated."[14] In fact, as colonial Zambia's chief secretary pointed out, the constitution did "not permit of an opposition or the formation of absurd parties."[15] It was only very late that the colonial administration in conjunction with the imperial government in Britain attempted to establish a political system that resembled a liberal democracy. Thus, at independence democracy as a political process was still in its infancy and susceptible to abuse.

As J.J.N. Cloete correctly observed, "political parties are products of the Western democracies" and "were hardly an accepted part of the way of life of the various African societies when they gained political independence."[16] Pettman also eloquently made the point that Zambia inherited a political system of government and administration ill-suited to the tasks of political development imagined by the new leaders.[17] He added that the new leaders, therefore, proceeded to search for a more suitable political system—one that could cope with the needs of independence while providing stability of the state and survival of the government.[18]

Pettman concluded that "the establishment of a one-party state in Zambia, ... by freezing the power situation in an artificial and unrealistic way ... may be a conservative solution to political difficulties," and that if that was the case, "then the government may find itself liable to partial paralysis—perhaps able to maintain its own position against those who would replace it, but unable to translate its ambitious goals into practice".[19] Interestingly Pettman's opening statement conforms to the commonly believed myth that liberal democracy was ill-suited for Africa. Eighteen years of one-party rule in Zambia have shown that "one-party participatory democracy" was autocracy—pure and simple—and failed to achieve national unity or political stability. Hence the contention in this chapter that the idea of a one-party participatory democracy was nothing but a highly glorified political myth in Zambian politics.

THE DEMISE OF DEMOCRACY

For over seventy years Zambians did not experience any form of government remotely resembling democracy in its traditional or European forms. Consequently, at independence democracy as a political process was still in infancy and susceptible to abuse. Small wonder that a few months after independence President Kaunda stated openly that he favored a one-party state, but that the people would have to decide.[20] He considered a multi-party system a luxury the new state could not afford and that a multiparty system unnecessarily divided people. Since nation-building followed decolonization, multiparty liberal democracy was perceived as an obstacle toward that goal.

Africa was largely a continent without nations. While the geographical units created by the colonial powers provided the basis for nation-building, the peoples inhabiting these units lacked the factors usually required to form nations (such as a common language, culture and religion).[21] UNIP's realization of these shortcomings appears to have been one of the leading factors that pushed the UNIP government toward the single-party state system. The other factor was that the educated elite who dominated UNIP proceeded to behave exactly as seventy years of colonialism had taught them. They had not experienced democracy.

They were a product of their history and proceeded to govern exactly as the British before them had.

Since coming to power in 1964 UNIP carefully avoided the crucial element of liberal democracy—the willingness by the government in office to hand over power to the winners of the next election, and to administer political conditions that allow that opposition to openly work to win over a majority of the electorate in the meantime. Rural people presumably were close enough to their distant past to recall traditional accountability of rulers to their people. The urban elite, on the other hand, followed the example of the British. More important perhaps, UNIP adopted a myth already established during the colonial period—that the masses were generally law abiding and contented with government policies. UNIP officials argued that the masses were behind the party. Whenever signs of disaffection toward government policies came out in the open, they were quickly blamed on the opposition—in much the same way that colonial officials portrayed the masses as happy and always blamed nationalists for revolts in rural areas.

Further, this chapter explores the principle of "one-party participatory democracy" in order to provide a focus for an understanding of why the system increasingly came under attack. Finally, this chapter discusses prospects of multipartyism in Zambia. It is suggested that multipartyism has a better chance of flourishing than was the case in the 1960s and early 1970s. This optimism is based on the high level of urbanization, which has a very profound impact on national politics. It is plausible to suggest that Zambia has reached a stage whereby a "political society" capable of sustaining liberal democracy does exist.[22] It is also suggested here that constitutional developments that were initiated during the colonial period, but opposed by African nationalist leaders, formed a base for a successful liberal democratic practice in Zambia. One such constitutional development that started the process were the Benson Constitution proposals of 1958.

THE SECOND REPUBLIC

Under the one-party participatory democracy the party president became the only presidential candidate, and the country's president if elected by at least 51 percent of the total vote cast during the presidential elections. However, in September 1978 Harry Mwaanga Nkumbula, former leader of the African National Congress, Simon Mwansa Kapwepwe, the former vice president and leader of the banned United Progress Party, and Robert Chiluwe, a Lusaka businessman, decided to contest for the country's presidency. But on 10 September, *by a show of hands,* the UNIP general conference held at Mulungushi Rock near Kabwe approved constitutional amendments under which candidates for the presidency had to have been UNIP members for five years, with no criminal record and supported by at least twenty UNIP delegates from each of the country's nine provinces attending the conference. This amendment effectively disqualified the three independent contestants.[23] Kapwepwe and Nkumbula's appeal against their disqualification was turned down by the High Court on 16 November, thereby leaving President Kaunda as the sole presidential candidate. He was subsequently elected having obtained 80.5 percent of the total votes cast in a 66.7 percent voter turnout.[24]

UNIP's reluctance to allow a free and fair contest for the presidency and other top party posts remained the vivid evidence of the lack of democracy within the party machinery. While many top UNIP officials condemned the intentions to challenge Kaunda's leadership, only Alexander Chikwanda spoke openly in support of the concept of free and fair elections for any post in the party by any party member.[25]

The process through which the constitution was amended made a mockery of "one-party participatory democracy" and, consequently, democracy itself, and once again demonstrated the myth of one-party participatory democracy. Since the people who gather for the party's general conference are generally party "faithfuls," and those who in fact fanatically believe in the leader, securing a vote to amend the constitution in order to secure the position of the leader was their greatest service.

For a while, the one-party state was justified because the country needed unity in view of the external enemies in the region. But as the political situation changed in the region, some Zambians began to question the continued existence of the one-party state system.[26] The poor economic performance of the country enhanced the attack on the one-party state system. The political leaders maintained, much against the reality of the situation, that such individuals were nothing but enemies of the state. However, as Bertha Osei-Hwedie pointed out, "both external and internal pressures contributed to the adoption of multiparty politics in ... Zambia."[27] Meanwhile, UNIP tightened its grip on political power by systematically filling the most important positions by sycophants. Those who could challenge the system from within were either fired or resigned, or given diplomatic jobs abroad to keep them out of the way.

"Exiling" potential challengers has been one of the most used methods of dealing with leadership conflicts within the party and the government. Those affected include the late Nalumino Mundia, former prime minister (United States); Mainza Chona, former secretary general (China); Humphrey Mulemba, former secretary general (Canada); and Kebby Musokotwane, former prime minister (Canada).[28] The list is long and includes some individuals from the armed forces. Lieutenant-General Christon Tembo was Zambia's ambassador to West Germany at the time of his arrest on 7 October 1988. He had been replaced as army commander in January 1987 by his deputy, Gary Kalenge.[29] On 1 July 1990 Kalenge was relieved of his command and replaced by his deputy Francis Sibamba following the 30 June coup attempt.

Once avenues for opposition were closed, members of parliament began to use parliament to express their disaffection with the one-party participatory democracy. The government responded by warning the MPs not to use the House as a forum from which to oppose the government. In the end, however, Speaker of the National Assembly Robinson Nabulyato found himself increasingly involved in efforts to prevent UNIP from further restricting MPs.[30] He was not very successful in this. After the 1988 presidential and parliamentary elections, he is reported to have sought no further appointment as Speaker of the National Assembly.

The transformation in the country's demography changed the way political opinions were perceived. As more and more Zambians became permanently urbanized, and as the rural-urban links became weaker, people looked more to the state for survival. Geoffrey J. Williams pointed out that by 1980 Zambia was "the third most urbanised country in main land black Africa, with 41 per cent of its population of 5,661,801 ... residing in towns of more than 5,000 inhabitants."[31] Some 78 percent of the urban population was located in ten largest urban areas situated along the railroad line. This has had profound social, political and economic implications. Economically the government found it extremely difficult to continue subsidizing the urban population. When 70 percent of the population was in rural areas and the economy was in good shape, it was economically possible to implement some very costly politically motivated policies.

However, as the urban population grew, coupled with an ever-declining economy, such costly policies as subsidizing the urban population became impossible. Economic decline created unemployment, which in turn resulted in increased social decadence among the urban poor. All this had very serious political implications. First, UNIP's power base, which was rural based, significantly dwindled. While it had been easier to buy off the rural poor, UNIP found it hard to do the same with the urban poor. Since 1986 food riots became a prominent feature in the urban areas. The food riots that took place in June 1990 culminated in the 30 June coup attempt.

Initially the state was able to meet the needs of the urbanites through the policy of subsidizing food and other societal requisites. However, as the long economic depression that began in the mid-1970s worsened in the 1980s, most urbanites became disillusioned with government performance. While it had been easy to satisfy the rural population, the urbanites were more difficult to buy off. The unemployed youthful urbanites became a source of worry for the Kaunda government. Several schemes were developed but they failed to successfully solve the problem. Because of frustration, the urbanites became easily involved in food riots that rocked the late 1980s. These culminated in the June 1990 food riot that precipitated the Luchembe coup attempt.[32] It was this coup attempt that effectively broke President Kaunda's grip on power and led to the formation of a pressure group, the Movement for Multiparty Democracy (MMD).

Worse still, Western aid donors capitalized on the downfall of the Soviet Union, a model for African one-party states, and withheld aid to the authoritarian government of Zambia. Political liberalization became one of the conditions for donor aid. Undoubtedly, this external pressure assisted civil society within Zambia to advance demands for the establishment of multiparty politics. Thus popular struggles in the 1980s forced the Kaunda regime to initiate political reforms. As Lloyd M. Sachikonye observed, "the popular demands for political and economic change [were] influenced by debates on the relationship between democracy and development, between the state and civil society."[33] The debate itself was informed by the rise of social movements that invigorated civil society and thereby inpinged upon the one-party state itself that had become moribund.

Thus resulting from this popular struggle emerged the MMD, "a loose congeries of various social forces and politicians disillusioned by two decades of one-party state rule." The rise to power of the MMD "represented a new context [in] which the people's role was more representative and decisive therefore making a new level of state organisation and political consciousness."[34] Though by 1992 the MMD seemed to reproduce the structural conflicts and factional intrigues as happened with UNIP, that does not negate the fact that it was the popular struggles that toppled UNIP and the Kaunda regime. Arguably, therefore, the role of civil society and society at large in the demise of autocracy in Zambia cannot be denied.

Faced with these mounting challenges, President Kaunda felt inse-cure, vulnerable and excessively sensitive to criticism. Times had changed. Zambians had also changed their allegiance. They were more supportive of the ideas about the need to remove the one-party state system. MMD political rallies attracted thousands of people. Less and less people openly supported UNIP. Even the notorious uniformed party militants were no longer as forceful as was the case a few months earlier. Most had switched sides and were looking forward to change.

More important perhaps, the collapse of autocracy in Zambia can be better understood when one takes into account the fact that some leading members of the UNIP Central Committee declined to stand for reap-pointment during the 1991 UNIP Mulungushi extraordinary confer-ence. Those who offered to step down include Elijah Mudenda, Reuben Kamanga and Gray Zulu. Obviously, the retirement of these seasoned UNIP politicians from active politics extremely weakened President Kaunda's hold on political power. His efforts to replace them with young inexperienced leaders failed to sustain him in the position of power.

Furthermore, some of the more experienced politicians had already identified themselves with the MMD. People like H. Mulemba, the former UNIP secretary general and then Zambia's high commissioner to Canada, had since 1988 become an MP and increasingly critical of UNIP policies. He was among the first MPs to move over to the MMD and was indeed a founder member of MMD. The MMD also gathered further support from most of those who had suffered humiliation during the one-party state era. Even the recently pardoned coup plotters like Edward Shamwana supported the MMD.

Perhaps the only positive development was the emergence of a strong movement for multiparty democracy. Equally important was the fact that the call for multipartyism could no longer be dismissed as an attempt to revive ethnic politics. The high level of urbanization makes ethnic politics less attractive. This is why perhaps UNIP found it very difficult to resist the demand for change—its power base was no longer there. UNIP could no longer rely on the rural population to maintain the status quo. Michael Bratton has suggested that "there is evidence that rural voters turned to MMD in 1991 because they were equally affected by the urban economic collapse, leading to declining remitances.[35] The MMD, like UNIP before it, came to power by appealing to the dissatis-fied and increasingly impoverished urban population.

The October 1991 multiparty elections were not just decisive in top-pling UNIP and the Kaunda regime by the MMD, but demonstrated the

success of the popular will of the people. Although it was business interests, the intelligentsia, labor leaders and politicians who met at Garden
House Hotel in 1990 to charter the way forward, it was the informal
sector producers, peasants and the lumpen-proletariat who formed the
all-powerful social movements with the objective of ushering in a multiparty political system. The latter constituted the vast majority of the
voters in Zambia, and were also the most affected by the political and
economic decline during the Second Republic. Consequently, proponents of multiparty politics appealed to these social movements to secure
change. They constituted the critical mass and hence played a significant
role in toppling the one-party state in 1991.

Undoubtedly, social movements played a major role in the democratization process in Zambia. They gave life to civil society. It is no small
wonder that the one-party state gave in to pressure that was brought to
bear upon it, resulting in the reintroduction of plural politics in which "the
balance of power shifts from the political party or political institutions, to
the people themselves."[36] The demise of one-party rule in Zambia in 1991
was a classic example of how economic decline resulted in the decline of
the state. This was exemplified by the state's failure to meet people's needs,
in both economic and political arenas as already noted above.

The decline of the state was clearly evident in the failure to provide
medical services and education facilities to the citizenry. Worse still, the
buying power of the kwacha was weakened by auctioning of the US dollar
and other foreign currencies in October 1985. The system was quickly
abandoned, but not before it had induced high levels of inflation. Under
these circumstances, particularly the decline of the state, the civil society
came to occupy an important position in the democratization process in
Zambia.[37] Evidently, as Donald Chanda observed:

> MMD rose to power through the provision of a legitimate
> alternative. People were prepared for change and all the
> MMD had to do was to present itself as the legitimate alliance
> of people who provided that alternative. People had suffered
> severe poverty and political fatigue under UNIP rule and its
> never changing leadership.[38]

It is important to point out that people were not only prepared for change,
but facilitated that change by withdrawing their support from the moribund UNIP. It is arguable to suggest that the rise of the MMD to power
in 1991 "marked a new stage in political state organization where the
people's role is more respected, more representative, more authoritative

thereby marking a new level of state organization and political conscious-ness."[39]

There is no reason to doubt, as do Michael Bratton and Beatrice Liatto-Katundu, the continuing ordinary people's roles as protesters and voters in playing ongoing roles as active and well informed citizens.[40] This optimism is largely because of the role played by NGOs and civil society that are actively involved in civic education. Thus far, we have focused on the internal problems and political situation in the demise of the one-party participatory democracy in Zambia. However, Zambia's involve-ment in the liberation of Southern Africa played a contributing factor to these internal political and economic problems.

ZAMBIA AND THE LIBERATION OF SOUTHERN AFRICA

At independence in October 1964 Zambia was obsessed with the pre-occupation to participate in the liberation of Southern Africa. This obses-sion grew out of several factors that resulted from Zambia's colonial experi-ence and geopolitical situation. Among these factors were: an ideological commitment to eradicate colonial rule in the region, and the elimination of racism and minority rule in the region. Zambian leaders considered that the independence of Zambia was incomplete as long as other countries in the region remained under minority white regimes. Consequently, Zambia did not only oppose the white minority regimes in Southern Africa, but undertook to accommodate refugees and freedom fighters from Angola, Mozambique, Namibia, South Africa and Zimbabwe.

Zambia's geopolitical position meant that it was in the front line of the liberation struggle from the date of its independence. Worse still, when Britain decided that it could not use force to end the Unilateral Declaration of Independence (UDI) in Rhodesia in November 1965, it galvanized Zambia's total commitment to support the African national-ists in that country to free themselves from the Smith regime. Zambia even went to the extent of offering to host British soldiers had Britain chosen to intervene militarily in Rhodesia to end the UDI.[41] However, Zambia received a slap in the face when the British government made it very clear that it was not its intention to impose majority rule in Rhodesia by force, and warned the Zimbabwean nationalists that "Britain would not herself act unconstitutionally whether by armed force or otherwise, to change the constitution."[42]

The British response to UDI clearly demonstrated what African nationalists in Central Africa had always known: that Britain always protected white interests, and hence its support for multiracial liberal schemes and organizations like Capricorn. The British government remained committed to prospects for a multiracial solution in Rhodesia. Undoubtedly, therefore, the British attitude toward Rhodesia strengthened Zambia's resolve to support African nationalists in Rhodesia and other countries in the region. Consequently, between 1966 and 1974 Zambia suffered much more from the economic sanctions imposed on Rhodesia than Rhodesia itself.

Zambia's commitment to the liberation of southern Africa left the country as one of the world's largest per capita recipients of foreign aid. The country is heavily in debt to foreign banks, particularly the International Monetary Fund (IMF) and the World Bank. Since the late 1970s Zambia experienced a steady rise of inflation rates and ever-declining currency value. This made Zambia one of the poorest countries in the region. Yet, throughout Zambia's postcolonial era, the country spent huge amounts of its resources assisting the liberation struggle in the region.

From a political point of view, this commitment to the liberation of Southern Africa served two purposes. For President Kaunda it represented a real challenge for African leaders to champion the cause of Pan-Africanism, which he had supported long before he became Zambia's republican president in the early 1960s. He played an instrumental role in the Pan-African Freedom Movement for East, Central and Southern Africa (PAFMECSA), which was promoting and keeping alive the idea of an East African Federation.[43] In 1963 President Kaunda became the chairman of PAFMECSA. Second, Zambia's commitment to the liberation of Southern Africa was used by the UNIP government to pursue the policy of togetherness, which was later transformed into the one-party state political system.

From 1964 to the early 1990s Zambia was the major base for Zimbabwe nationalists, Namibia's South West Africa Peoples Organization (SWAPO) and South Africa's African National Congress (ANC), all of which had their headquarters in Lusaka. Apart from hosting the leaders of these organizations, Zambia became home to thousands of refugees from these countries. As a result Zambia suffered several bombing raids on its soil. Casualties included Zambians and Zambian infrastructure. While most political analysts blame Zambia's economic decline on poor economic policies of the one-party state era, it is plausible to suggest that Zambia's geopolitical position and its commitment to the liberation of Southern Africa greatly contributed to the poor performance of the Zambian economy.

From colonial times Zambia was linked to the outside world through South Africa. Almost all its industries were maintained by supplies from South African industries or were imported through South Africa. However, when economic sanctions were imposed on Rhodesia and South Africa because of racial policies, Zambia was forced to change routes. It was forced to go into partnership with the Chinese and Tanzanian governments and build the Tanzania-Zambia Railway (TAZARA) in order to reroute its exports and imports. However, TAZARA proved more costly than the traditional routes. The Benguela railway link through Angola could not be used because of the civil war that started in the late 1970s as the Portuguese were withdrawing from Angola.

Despite bombings and raids, President Kaunda remained a persistent and very visible advocate of peaceful change in Southern Africa. In April 1969 Zambia hosted the East and Central Africa Summit Conference, which led to the signing of the Lusaka Manifesto on relations with Portugal, Rhodesia and South Africa on 16 April. In 1995 Zambia hosted peace talks between the Angolan government and the Union for the Total Independence of Angola (UNITA), generally referred to as the Lusaka Protocol. In July 1999, Zambia hosted peace talks between the Democratic Republic of Congo and the rebels, which culminated in the signing of a cease fire agreement between the warring parties.

Although Zambia has spent a lot of time and resources in the attempt to secure peace and security in the region, the country has suffered economically and politically. Zambia's commitment to the liberation of Southern Africa impacted negatively on the economy, resulting in failure to sustain economic growth and capital formation in the country. This condition contributed to political instability, which in turn exacerbated capital formation problems. Throughout Kaunda's rule he countinued to seek solutions to the civil strife in the region.

Internally, Zambia's role in the liberation of Southern Africa and its support for liberation movements was a source of conflict between the government and University of Zambia Students Union (UNZASU). As Randi Balsvik noted, "before the first closure of the University of Zambia in 1971, the Students Union had staged six demonstrations", all of which were engineered by events outside the country.[44] Of the six demonstrations, five were in support of the government's fight against white minority rule in Southern Africa. In 1966 students staged three protests at the British High Commission in Lusaka to protest against the Unilateral Declaration of Independence in Southern Rhodesia (Zimbabwe). Students believed that Britain supported the declaration. While these views were shared by politicians, student protests over the events were viewed with suspicion and politicians usually advised students to "leave politics to the politicians."[45] Because of the attitude of politicians, police tended to brutalize students who participated in the demonstrations.

Between 1966 and 1999, the university experienced several student demonstrations, some of which led to ten closures of the university.[46] The first closure of the university took place on 15 July 1971 following student demonstrations against the French government's decision to sell arms to South Africa.[47] The closure was a culmination of a series of events and incidents.[48] Aaron Milner gave the official version of why the university was closed and blamed the closure on student behavior. Yet while the student demonstration that led to the closure was officially condemned, some politicians supported the student cause and even condemned police brutality against students. For example, Rupia Banda, in an interview over the demonstration, expressed disappointment with police behavior. He supported the students and argued that "if the police knew what they were doing they should be on the side of the students."[49]

The 1971 closure demonstrated that students and government took different approaches to issues they agreed on. However, because students took a militant approach, which was not diplomatically acceptable, the government reacted by closing the institution and used the laws of the land to justify this decision. For example, following the demonstration on 7 July 1971 the government was reported to have had no other option but to close the University because:

(1) the students' demonstration was illegal;
(2) the students' demonstration was not peaceful;
(3) the students' demonstration was out of control and the leadership was not informed;
(4) according to Zambian laws, the procession was illegal, though the intentions were good.[50]

The decision taken by the government set a precedent for dealing with future student demonstrations. It is equally tenable to suggest that the government decision to close the university was influenced by the way other governments in the region had dealt with similar problems in the past. The closure lasted about a month. The university was again closed on 9 February 1976. The first decade of the life of the university was very volatile from the point of view of student politics, because Zambia was still surrounded by white ruled regimes.

On the international scene, university students and the government were moving in opposite directions and supporting or sympathizing with different liberation movements. This was evident on the Angolan situation. Students supported the Movement for the Popular Liberation of Angola (MPLA) while the government supported UNITA. Students urged everyone in Zambia to support the MPLA in its struggle against Portuguese colonial rule because "since its inception in 1956 ... [the MPLA] clearly demonstrated that it was not simply a liberation movement but a truly revolutionary movement."[51] All other liberation movements in Angola, including UNITA, were considered reactionary and puppets of the imperialist forces of the West. The student position was clearly a direct challenge to Zambia's official foreign policy over Angola. Earlier in the year students had authored several circulars expressing open support for the MPLA when the government had clearly stated its support for UNITA.

It was not surprising therefore, that when students organized a demonstration in support of the MPLA in February 1976, the demonstration was stopped by police.[52] Following the abortive demonstration, a British lecturer in political science, Dr. Lionel Cliffe, was arrested and detained for eight weeks on allegation that he was at the center of the demonstration. He was accused of inciting students to demonstrate against the government, and when he was released from detention he was deported from Zambia. Students reacted by boycotting classes because the arrest of Dr. Cliffe was seen as intimidation and an affront to academic freedom. Two other Lecturers, Dr. Kasuka Mutukwa and Professor Eyo Ndem, the dean of the School of Humanities and Social Sciences, were accused by students as "mercenaries in the case of Dr. Cliffe."[53] In the unfolding events, "seventy-two Lecturers, including eighteen Zambians, issued a statement which said Zambia needed an intelligentsia that was free to analyze issues in order to improve the conditions of the country."[54] The statement was a manifestation that these Lecturers agreed with the student condemnation of the government approach to the issue.

Government reaction was condemned by the *Times of Zambia,* which argued that the reaction showed downright ignorance about the role of a university.[55] The university was closed on 9 February, and five expatriate lecturers were deported. Fifteen students, including UNZASU President Munyonzwe Hamalengwa and Secretary-General Samuel Miyanda were detained by police for over six months. Nine students were expelled from the university.[56] The student publication correctly described the expulsions and government reaction to the events that led to the closure of the university as a travesty of academic freedom and social justice. Students had a strong case, and had read the situation correctly. Government was too rigid to admit that students were right. Yet, within months of the closure and reopening of the university, the government recognized the MPLA government in Angola. Relationship between UNZASU and the government remained tense.

From the foregoing, it is no wonder that University of Zambia students have always been part of the equation in the political history of Zambia. They have always been major players in propagating democracy and good governance. It was in the same spirit that in 1996 they were instrumental in organizing interparty dialogue at the University of Zambia between the ruling MMD and opposition parties. As elections were approaching they became part of the Committee for Clean Campaign (CCC), which was involved in civic education.

CONCLUSION

This chapter has demonstrated political developments in Zambia since the end of the colonial period through Second Republic. The rise and then demise of liberal democracy in a newly independent country have been analyzed. The shortcomings of the one-party participatory democracy as reflected in this chapter arose, in part because of the fact that in reality, the one-party system turned out to be a one-party dictatorship. Evidence suggests that there was no democracy within the party itself. In fact, as Soremekun noted, "from the point of view of Zambia's constitutional set-up, Kaunda had emerged as a virtual dictator" by 1969.[57] It was therefore idealistic to expect a nondemocratic party to produce a political machinery at the national level that was democratic.[58]

The supremacy of the party, coupled with the *de facto* life presidency of the incumbent surrounded by sycophants in the Central Committee, militated against the development of democracy. Parliamentary candidates were screened and "adopted" by the party before they could participate in the parliamentary elections. Candidates considered objectionable from the party's point of view were never allowed to stand.[59]

Another aspect that needs highlighting pertains to the development of a "political society" that is strong and large enough to sustain liberal democracy. The general rise in the call for a return to a multiparty system,[60] in Zambia indicated that Zambia was approaching that stage.

Meanwhile, Soremekun's observation that "Kaunda appears to his country men more as the embodiment of the Most High than that of the most humane" again came into play.[61] Playing God, President Kaunda decided, in a typically brilliant tactical maneuver, to release all political prisoners, including Lieutenant-General Christon Tembo and Lieutenant Mwamba Luchembe who announced the coup attempt on 30 June, 1990 and called for reconciliation.[62] At the same time President Kaunda announced the postponement of the referendum on the one-party state from October 1990 to August 1991. He cited as his reason the need to update the electoral roll, which was a key opposition demand.

President Kaunda also pardoned former High Court Commissioner Edward Shamwana and three of his colleagues who were serving life sentences for attempting to overthrow the government in 1980. He told the news conference that "What I have announced today does not come from the point of extreme weakness but from strength."[63] Nevertheless, these concessions resulted from demands made by advocates of multiparty rule who were demanding the lifting of the state of emergency in force since July 1964, the release of all political prisoners, termination of all political trials and the proper registration of voters for the referendum on multiparty rule.

Finally, the rise and demise of liberal democracy in Zambia reflected the nature of politics in a country where for a long time opposition politics were anathematized by those in power—both before and after independence. The will of the people set the agenda. By the late 1980s Zambia was the only country in Southern Africa where political demonstrations "have rallied crowds of similar size to those which gathered in Leipzig and Prague to sweep away one-party states in Eastern Europe."[64] The Zambian government was forced to respect the will of the people and on 28 September 1990 decided to restore a multiparty constitution. The referendum that was originally scheduled for October 1991 was canceled. Instead, the government scheduled presidential and parliamentary elections for the same month, which were conducted under a multiparty constitution drafted by the Mvunga Commission of 1990. The Commission resulted in the drafting and subsequent passing of the 1991 Constitution of the Republic of Zambia.[65] Elections were conducted in October 1991. UNIP and the MMD (which had been transformed into a political party) were to participate.

With this newly found freedom, several other parties emerged. The most important being the MMD and UNIP. During the October 1991 presidential and parliamentary elections, MMD overwhelmingly defeated UNIP. F.T.J. Chiluba was elected president, and on 1 November 1991 he was sworn in as Zambia's second republican president.

Chiluba's accession to the political throne in Zambia's political history marked the end of an era—the end of the long dawn—according to *The*

Economist.[66] The twenty years of autocracy also taught Zambians one major lesson. Zambians will never again surrender their political rights to one individual. Thus the success or failure of liberal democracy today would depend on whether or not Zambians internalized the problems of one-party rule. This chapter has shown that the concentration of political power in President Kaunda's hands was possible only because the people made it possible. The Zambian society hero-worshipped the president so much that with time, they managed to make an autocrat out of an otherwise democrat. With the return to liberal democracy, it is hopped that Zambians will guard against creating another autocrat out of President Chiluba by avoiding hero-worshipping him as they did President Kaunda.

Notes

1. John S. Moffat, Text of the speech given during the presentation of the Moffat Resolutions in the Northern Rhodesia Legislative Council on 29 July 1954.

2. Anonymous, *The Northern News*, Tuesday, 27 January 1953.

3. By political establishment is meant the colonial governmental and non-governmental institutions to which Africans were mostly excluded. The Northern Rhodesia government (civil service) was controlled by whites until after the 1962 general elections which ushered in the first black government.

4. Kapasa Makasa, *Zambia's March to Political Freedom* (Nairobi: Heinemann, 1985), p.88.

5. An earlier version of this chapter was published in *Geneva-Africa*, 29, 2 (1991).

6. John Day, "The Creation of Political Myths: African Nationalism in Southern Rhodesia," *Journal of Southern African Studies*, 2, 1 (1975), p. 52.

7. Day, "The Creation of Political Myths," p. 52.

8. M.G. de Winton, "Decolonization and the Westminster Model," in A.H.M. Kirk-Greene (ed.), *The Transfer of Power: The Colonial Administrator in the Age of Decolonization*, (Kidlington Oxford: Oxford University Press, 1979), p. 189.

9. *Report of the Northern Rhodesia Independence Conference Held in London*, May 1964, p. 4.

10. Jan Pettman, "Zambia's Second Republic: The Establishment of One-Party State" *Journal of Modern African Studies* 12, 2 (1974), p. 233.

11. President Kenneth Kaunda, *Proceedings of the Annual General Conference of the United National Independence Party*, held at Mulungushi 14-20 August 1967, p. 11.

12. De Winton, "Decolonization and the Westminster Model," p. 189.

13. Anonymous, *The Northern Rhodesia News*, 27 January 1953.

14. J.S. Coleman, "Economic Growth and Political Reorientation," in M. J. Herskovits and M. Harwitz (eds.), *Economic Transition in Africa* (Evanston, IL: Northwestern University Press, 1964), p. 396.

15. H.C. Donald C. Mackenzie-Kennedy, Northern Rhodesia Chief Secretary to Stewart Gore-Browne, June 12, 1935, cited in Robert I. Rotberg, *Black Heart: Gore-Browne and the Politics of Multiracial Zambia*, (Berkeley: University of California Press, 1977), p. 168.

16. J.J.N. Cloete, *Emergent Africa: Political and Administrative Trends*, (Pretoria: Africa Institute, 1966), p.11.

17. Pettman, "Zambia's Second Republic" pp. 231-244.

18. Pettman, "Zambia's Second Republic," p. 231.

19. Pettman, "Zambia's Second Republic," p. 243.

20. *Keesing's Contemporary Archives*, Vol. 15 (1965-66), p.21511.

21. Cloete, *Emergent Africa*, p.11.

22. On the discussion of the concept of "political society," see A.H. Somjee, *The Political Society in Developing Countries* (New York: St. Martin's Press, 1984), pp.3-6.

23. *Keesing's Contemporary Archives*, Vol. 25 (February 1979), p. 29450.

24. Carolyn Baylies and Morris Szeftel, "Elections in the One-party State," in Cherry Gerzel et al (eds.), *The Dynamics of the One-Party State in Zambia*, (Manchester: Manchester University Press 1984), p.29.

25. Fanwel K.M. Sumaili, "The Self and Biographical Writings, in Zambia," Zango 3, 1 (1988), p.105. Readers may be interested to note that Chikwanda later left the party and government and went into private business.

26. *Africa Confidential*, 21, 11 (21 May 1980), p.1.

27. Bertha Osei-Hwedie, "The Role of Ethnicity in Multi-Party Politics in Malawi and Zambia," *Journal of Contemporary African Studies*, 16, 2 (1998), p. 227.

28. The countries in parentheses are where the named individuals were "exiled" as either high commissioners or ambassadors.

29. *Keesing's Contemporary Archives*, Vol. 35, 12 (1990), p. 37142.

30. *Africa Confidential*, 22, 24 (25 November 1981), p. 8.

31. Geoffrey J. Williams, "Zambia: Physical and Social Geography," in *Africa South of the Sahara, 1990* (London: Europa Publications, 1990), p. 1980. Current figures are higher than those cited here.

32. See Beatwell Chisala, *Lt Luchembe Coup Attempt* (Lusaka: Multimedia Publications, 1991).

33. Lloyd M. Sachikonye, "Introduction," in Lloyd M. Sachikonye (ed.), *Democracy, Civil Society and the State: Social Movements in Southern Africa* (Harare: SAPES Books, 1995), p. i.

34. Sachikonye, "Introduction," p. viii.

35. Michael Bratton, "Economic Crisis and Political Realignment in Zambia," in J. Widner (ed.) *Economic Change and Political Liberalisation in Sub-Saharan Africa* (Baltimore: John Hopkins University Press, 1994), p. 119.

36. Donald Chanda (ed.), *Democracy in Zambia: Key Speeches of President Chiluba, 1991-92* (Lusaka: Africa Press Trust, 1993), p. 1.

37. For detailed discussion on the role of the civil society in the democratisation process in Zambia, see Julius Ihonvbere, *Economic Crisis, Civil Society and Democratisation in Zambia* (Lawrenceville, NJ: Africa World Press, 1996); Donald Chanda, "The Movement for Multi-Party Democracy in Zambia: Some Lessons in Democratic Transitions," in Lloyd M. Sachikonye (ed.), *Democracy, Civil Society and the State: Social Movements in Southern Africa* (Harare: SAPES Books, 1995).

38. Chanda, "The Movement for Multi-Party Democracy in Zambia," p. 127.

39. Chanda, "The Movement for Multi-Party Democracy in Zambia," p.127.

40. Michael Bratton and Beatrice Liatto-Katundu, "A Focus Group Assessment of Political Attitudes in Zambia," *African Affairs*, 93, 373 (1994), p. 536.

41. Douglas G. Anglin and Timothy M. Shaw, *Zambia's Foreign Policy: Studies in Diplomacy and Dependence* (Boulder, CO: Westview Press, 1979), p. 122.

42. Arthur Bottomley, *House of Commons Debates.*, Vol. 708, 8 March 1965 Column 36, British High Commission, Salisbury, Press Release, 3 March 1965, cited in Anglin and Shaw, *Zambia's Foreign Policy*, p.116.

43. Richard Cox, *Pan-Africanism in Practice: An East African Study, PAFMECSA 1958-1964* (London: Oxford University Press, 1964), p. 1.

44. Randi R. Balsvik, "Student Life at the University of Zambia: Strikes, Closures and Disruption of Learning, 1965-1992," *Zambia Journal of History* No. 8 (1995) p. .8.

45. M. Burawoy, "The Roles of the University Student in the Zambian Social Structure," MA Dissertation, University of Zambia, 1972, p.49.

46. The University of Zambia Council, Interim Report of the Special Committee of Council on the Closures of the University of Zambia, April 1997, p.1.

47. University of Zambia Library, Special Collections, File on UNZA Closure, 1971.

48. The Hon. Aaron Milner MP, secretary general to the government, Address to the National Assembly, "Why the University Was Closed," 20 July 1971.

49. University of Zambia Library, Special Collections, File on 1971 UNZA Closure, 10 September 1971.

50. University of Zambia, Dean of Student Affairs Office, Closures of the University of Zambia Since 1966.

51. *Trunza*, Vol. 12, No. 1, 8 December 1975.

52. *Zambia Daily Mail*, 10 February 1976.

53. University of Zambia Library, Special Collections, UNZASU Statement on the Strike, 10 February 1976.

54. Balsvik, "Student Life," p. 10.

55. *Times of Zambia*, 8 April 1976.

56. *UZ Spokesman*, 2 , 7, 30 November 1976.

57. Fola Soremekun, "The Challenge of Nation-Building: Neo-Humanism and Plotics in Zambia, 1967-1969," *Geneva-Africa*, 98, 1 (1970), p. 39.

58. UNIP held its first and last open and competitive election for the leadership of the party in August 1967. It was this election that precipitated the 1968 resignation of President Kaunda.

59. See Carolyn Baylies, "Luapula Province: Economic Decline and Political Alienation in a Rural UNIP Stronghold," in Gertzel et al., *The Dynamics of the One-Party in Zambia*, p. 196.

60. *New African*, May 1990, p.9.

61. Soremekun, "The Challenge of Nation-Building," p. 39.

62 *Africa Confidential*, 31, 16 (10 August 1990), p.2; and *The Weekly Review* ,Kenya (27 July 1990), p. 45. However, President Kaunda has lost control of the political development. In the past, pardoned political prisoners became ardent supporters of UNIP. This time, those pardoned and released from detention have openly become spokesmen and champions of multi-partyism. In a personal communication to the author, an informant wrote: "Be informed that Lt.-General Christon Tembo is as free as you.... He is in fact a multi-party advocate or today an enemy of UNIP. Lt. Mwamba Luchembe though discharged from the Army without benefits, has joined the Chilubas.... At one of the meetings he attended in the Copperbelt he was lifted shoulder high while people were chanting President Luchembe, President Luchembe. Can you imagine the situation?" (Personal communication to the author, 24 September 1990).

63. Cited from *New African*, September, 1990, p. 17.

64. *Africa Confidential*, 31, 20 (12 October 1990), p. 6.

65. The Constitution of Zambia Act, 1991.

66. *The Economist*, 7 July 1990, p. 15.

Chapter 7

THE MIXED FORTUNES OF MULTIPAR-
TYISM IN THE THIRD REPUBLIC, 1991-
2001: DEMOCRACY OR MOBOCRACY?

> The change of government in our country that took place fol-
> lowing the general elections of 31 October 1991 was not just
> a change of government like in the USA or the UK, where a
> new administration comes in after parliament and Presiden-
> tial elections. No, ours was a transformation of the political
> system, from one based on the supremacy of a political party
> which was espoused by the ruling UNIP in its constitution
> and practice, to a totally new system where the will and
> consent of the people is the basis of power and legitimacy of
> government.[1]

The above quotation clearly demonstrates the excitement that the
democratic revolution experienced in 1991 brought to Zambians.
Undoubtedly, the October 1991 parliamentary and presidential general
elections were as significant as the October 1962 elections held under
the unpopular and complex constitution originally conceived by British
Colonial Secretary Ian MacLeod.[2] John Mwanakatwe observed that
"the process of reintroducing multiparty politics in Zambia was not easy
after eighteen years of single party rule."[3] Although it was clear by the
late 1980s that the political system needed to be reformed, advocates of
multiparty politics met many obstacles.

However, President Kaunda gave in and in October 1991 presidential and parliamentary elections were held. The United National Independence Party was swept out of power by the Movement for Multiparty
Democracy, whose mandate was to ensure that democracy would not be
denied to Zambians again. Yet, within months of the MMD's ascendancy
to power, the MMD was facing serious challenges over its alleged failure

to carry out the political reforms talked about during the run up to the October elections. Although the government had changed, and rhetoric had changed, the basic pattern of Zambian politics was the same. It is arguable to suggest that mobocracy slowly replaced democracy. This was evidently strong during President Frederick T.J. Chiluba's second term.

NEW POLITICAL PARTIES

When Zambia reintroduced multiparty politics in 1991, the country witnessed "a host of strange splinter groups [which] presented their papers so that they [could] campaign in Zambia's forthcoming multiparty elections."[4] By March 1991 at least seven new political parties had lodged their papers with the Registrar of Societies for certification. These included the Movement for Multiparty Democracy, the National Democratic Alliance (NADA), the Multiracial Party (MP), the Theoretical Spiritual Political Party (TSPP), the People's Liberation Party (PLP), the Democratic Party (DP) and the Movement for Democratic Process (MDP).[5] These parties joined UNIP in the race to Manda Hill (as Zambia's Parliament is popularly known). The significance of the multiplicity of parties was that for the first time in many years in the political history of Zambia, Zambians enthusiastically responded to the challenge and spirit of liberal democracy or multipartyism. For all practical purposes, Zambia was truly a multiparty democracy. Yet, in reality, at least then, only UNIP and the MMD, which spearheaded the campaign for multipartyism, were real contenders for the formation of a new government in a multiparty political system. The remaining parties, even at this early period, lacked clear leadership or platform and appeared to represent eccentric elements. They existed only on paper.[6]

While this multiplicity of political parties before the October 1991 general elections was lauded as a symbol of the freedom of association, it was nonetheless an indicator for problems of liberal democracy in a developing country. Soon after the MMD came into power, several other political parties were born. The MMD began to experience similar problems UNIP had experienced as a dominant political party in the First Republic. The MMD was born out of a coalition of many interests that were generally agreed that there was a need to remove the Kaunda regime from power. Once the Kaunda regime and his one-party dictatorship were removed from power, the various interests began to look more toward their own interests as opposed to those of the MMD. Accusations and counteraccusations led to resignations, which in turn led to the birth of new political parties. It was not long before President Chiluba began to face mounting criticism of authoritarianism and corruption. Some MMD members rejoined UNIP while others founded new political groupings. The coalescing of politicians around self-interests at the expense of national or group interests worked against national interests and the spirit of liberal democracy. This process also threatened the growth of a political society in which politicians of various interests and backgrounds are expected to work together for the common good of the nation and to champion the liberal democratic ideals.

Thus, it was the birth of the National Party (NP) in 1993, the Zambia Democratic Congress (ZDC) in 1995, the Liberal Progressive Front (LPF) in 1994, the National Lima Party (NLP) now the Lima Party (LP)) in 1996 and the Agenda for Zambia (AZ) in 1996, that had the greatest impact on the politics of Zambia. The formation of these political parties, all of which broke away from the MMD, signified the mixed fortunes of multipartyism in the Third Republic. Furthermore, by 1996 there were over thirty-seven registered political parties in Zambia. Of these, only UNIP, the NP and the ruling MMD were represented in the 1991-1996 Parliament. In the current parliament only the ruling MMD, NP, AZ, UNIP and the United Party for National Development (UPND) are represented besides several independent members of parliament.

The Third Republic in Zambian politics generated the most heated debate as to the theory and practice of liberal democracy in the political history of Zambia. The political process and practice have been the most criticized in the history of Zambia. Unlike the Second Republic, the Third Republic was relatively open and therefore accommodated divergent views and interests. Consequently, the political leadership and the MMD are openly attacked and criticized in the most crude ways at times.[7] Various issues generate this criticism or support. First, there is the constitution, especially as amended in 1996. The presidential clause and the qualifications for candidature have been the most criticized. In addition to this was the registration of voters under Nikuv Computers (Israel) Limited, which was contracted by government to update and register voters in preparation for the 1996 presidential and parliamentary elections. For some reasons, Nikuv Computers was widely believed to specialize in rigging election results in favor of the ruling political party. Consequently, opposition political parties, led by UNIP, championed a campaign to discredit the government's use of the Nikuv Computers. It was this, among other reasons, that led to UNIP's decision to boycott the 1996 general elections.

Then there was the issue of the economy and its performance. There was a cry, especially between opposition politicians and non governmental organizations (NGOs) that since the MMD came to power in 1991, poverty levels worsened. Yet, A.W. Chanda observed that the MMD had been most successful in the economic field and that these "economic reforms have not been matched with political reform."[8] Nonetheless, the structural reforms of the economy through the privatization of parastals resulted in mass redundances and retrenchments. This in turn caused mass poverty, particularly among the urban population. This increasingly became a source of concern by opposition political parties and the civil society. As the MMD was halfway through its second term, it appeared incapable of dealing with the problem. Instead, the MMD paid more attention to remaining in power and seeking an amendment of the constitution to facilitate President Chiluba's third-term bid. In the process mobocracy slowly gained ground.

As noted above, a few years after the MMD came to power several key politicians resigned from the MMD and formed the NP. It was generally believed by those who quit the MMD and founded the NP that the MMD had lost direction and had abandoned the ideals for which it was founded. The MMD leadership was accused of being undemocratic and that some of them were corrupt and drug traffickers. Thus, the founding of the NP in 1993 was expected to bring down the MMD government. Several ministers and MPs resigned from the MMD.

The move forced by-elections in the affected constituencies. The MMD won back some seats contested, while the remainder of five were won by the NP. While the by-election results served to strengthen the opposition in Parliament, the MMD nonetheless remained firmly in control of the political situation in the country. The MMD further demonstrated that unlike UNIP in the First Republic, it could deal with the intraparty problems differently by allowing those dissatisfied to leave. While UNIP celebrated the departure of these members, it did not directly benefit from the resignations. However, the by-election results that followed demonstrated the fragility of democracy in Zambia. Thus, between 1991 and 1996 three political parties were represented in Parliament. Multipartyism was truly in place, though the ruling MMD was clearly overrepresented in Parliament in much the same way that UNIP was in the First Republic. The Speaker of the National Assembly, Dr. Robinson Nabulyato, decided that in the spirit of democracy UNIP would be recognized as the official opposition party in Parliament, although it did not meet the criteria for that recognition. This recognition was the opposite of his decision on ANC in the First Republic. This situation lasted until 1996, after which there was no official opposition in Parliament.

THE 1996 ELECTIONS

The MMD was again faced with another round of mass resignations by some of its founding members as the first MMD mandate was finishing. The major player being Dean Mung'omba, who was then deputy minister at the National Commission for Development Planning (NCDP). Mung'omba and others founded the ZDC, which emerged as a formidable political party in the country and soon surpassed the NP in popularity. Undoubtedly, Mung'omba projected himself as the next president of Zambia. He rated himself so highly that he believed he would sweep the 1996 presidential elections. His television campaign advertisements were definitely electrifying and persuasive. At the individual level he was perhaps only matched to President Chiluba. In spite of this projection, Mung'omba performed poorly during the elections. He hailed Zambians for turning up in the thousands to cast their votes.[9] He further implored the winners and losers to ensure that peace and stability continued so the democratic process was not derailed. Yet once the results were announced and Mung'omba realized that he had lost to President Chiluba, he refused to recognize the results, claiming that the elections were rigged by the MMD.

A last minute entry in the race to Manda Hill was the Agenda for Zambia which was founded by Akashambatwa Mbikusita Lewanika. The AZ entered the race without much preparation and invited individuals and organizations to join it "to break out of the malaise of the past and betrayal of the present."[10] Another late entry was the National Lima Party, which was also formed by a group that broke away from the MMD. Chama Chakomboka's MDP also managed to enter the presidential race at the last minute. There were five presidential candidates in the 1996 general elections. The MDP did not field any parliamentary candidates. However, UNIP announced in September 1996 that it would boycott the November 1996 presidential and parliamentary general elections. The announcement was received with mixed feelings as anxiety gripped the nation as to the implications of the boycott by the largest and perhaps the only well-organized political party in Zambia at the time. Yet, in retrospect, it would appear that UNIP's decision to boycott the November 1996 elections was informed more by UNIP's failure to mobilize the necessary clout *vis-a-vis* the MMD than by the openly stated reasons. As

Zambia was approaching the 1996 elections, UNIP was suffering a deep, internal split, which was further compounded by former president Kaunda's decision to attempt a comeback and stand as a presidential candidate for UNIP. Evidently since Kaunda took over the leadership from Kebby Musokotwane in 1994, seeds of discontent were sowed within UNIP.

Nonetheless, the 1996 presidential and parliamentary general elections were heavily contested. This was yet another demonstration by Zambians that they had taken liberal democracy seriously. In the end, however, the performance of the opposition was a dismal failure, leading to the MMD returning to power easily. Several reasons can be cited to explain this poor performance by the opposition. Most opposition parties entered the race ill-prepared. As the NP executive secretary in Ndola observed, "the question of finance or lack of it, played a significant role in influencing the last [1996] elections."[11] The NP candidate further observed that "mediocre performance by the opposition parties cannot be attributed solely to malpractice by the MMD as most opposition parties may want us to believe."[12] These views were also expressed by a ZDC losing candidate, who pointed out that while his party spent large sums of money on the presidential campaign, parliamentary ZDC candidates entered the race with no resources at all. The opposition parties were obviously disadvantaged compared to MMD candidates.

The opposition parties also suffered from lack of grassroots support and party structures to spearhead their campaigns. Some opposition parties fielded ill-prepared and inexperienced candidates. The NLP, for example, made an open invitation to anyone willing to be nominated on their party ticket. Party membership, therefore, appeared not to have been a requirement. Evidently, the NLP could not have been considered a serious contender in the competition for power. With UNIP boycotting the elections, the MMD had an easy task of retaining its grip on power. MMD's position was further made easy by the fact that only a minor proportion of the Zambian population was involved in political life. This resulted from apathy developed during the twenty years when UNIP monopolized power and exercised excessive control over all aspects of social life.

The plurality of opposition parties, while demonstrating the existence of multipartyism in Zambia, also helped the MMD to easily win the 1996 elections. Although voices of dissent against the MMD government were legion, because of their divided approach to dealing with the perceived shortcomings of the MMD government, the ruling party easily ran over the opposition. Instead of acknowledging this problem, the opposition parties in Zambia were engaged in some unproductive politicking, like participating in the burning of voters cards. As UNIP, the largest and most experienced political party in Zambia, championed these unproductive and less than democratic methods of seeking redress in a democratic nation like Zambia, its decision to boycott the 1996 Presidential and Parliamentary general elections affected the outcome of the elections. Thus contrary to President Chiluba's claim that his election to office and a majority of MMD candidates to Parliament signified Zambia's achievement of the democratic ideal, the country remained a *de facto* one-party state because of the poor organization of the opposition. The 1996-2001 Parliament did not have an official opposition party because none of the opposition political parties represented in Parliament had sufficient numbers to qualify for recognition as the official opposition party in Parliament. Not even the combined opposition MPs with independent MPs met the requirement to be officially recognized as such. Thus, while Zambia was politically stable in the first ten years of the Third Republic, its democracy remained fragile because the country lacked a credible opposition.

THE PRESIDENTIAL PETITION

The Mwanakatwe Constitutional Review Commission appointed by President Chiluba in 1992 made a most contentious proposal in the history of Zambia. The contentious proposal, which was accepted by government after some modifications, concerned the qualification of a presidential candidate. The Mwanakatwe Commission recommended that presidential candidates must be Zambians and their parents must be Zambian citizens by birth or descent. The commission further recommended that candidates for the presidency must have been resident in Zambia for at least twenty years.[13] The citizenship clause was accepted by the government after amending it to include the requirement that parents of the candidate must be Zambians by birth. The presidential citizenship clause generated criticism and resentment. Some opposition parties and NGOs argued that the clause was targeted at former President Kaunda, whose parents were of Malawian origin. Former President Kaunda took up the challenge and began a campaign aimed at discrediting the MMD government for putting in place such "a discriminatory constitution." His campaign gained support because yet another clause in the same constitution barred anyone who had twice before been president from seeking reelection to the office of state president. In the political history of Zambia only former President Kaunda had such a background. Consequently, it was generally believed by UNIP and other opposition parties that the clause was targeted at former President Kaunda.

The mixed fortunes over the presidential clause were soon to emerge when UNIP and other opposition parties began an intense search for President Chiluba's parents. As it turned out, President Chiluba did not seem to have a clear background about where his father, in particular, hailed. His own book *Democracy: The Challenge of Change*, said that he was born on 30 April 1943 at Wusakili in Kitwe on the Copper-belt, to Titus Chiluba Nkonde and Daina Kaimba of Mwense District. John Mwanakatwe, however, wrote that "He was born in April 1943 in Musangu Village in Mwense District in Luapula Province in Zambia. He was the third born named Frederick Jacob Titus Mpundu in a family of four.... His father was a miner before his retirement from employment with Rokana Mine."[14]

Those in opposition saw an opportunity to test the credibility of the constitution and petitioned the High Court over his nomination for reelection because there were doubts as to the origins of his father, who was believed to have hailed from the Democratic Republic of Congo (former Zaire). Four opposition parties--the AZ, LPF, NP and UNIP, initially filed a petition against President Chiluba's nomination for the presidency.[15] The petition arose from the belief that " the national status of the 2nd respondent (President Chiluba) with respect to the citizenship of his parents ought to be investigated and established so that an alien or a person with uncertain origins is not allowed to stand as a candidate for Presidency in contravention of the Constitution."[16]

The petition was rejected by the Court on the grounds that it was prematurely brought before the Court according to Section 9 (1) (d) (i), which barred the returning officer from questioning the validity of nomi-nation papers presented to him. Thus President Chiluba was allowed to participate in the elections, much to the discontent of the opposition parties. Consequently, after his reelection in November 1996, a fresh petition was filed in the High Court seeking the nullification of his elec-tion on the basis that he did not qualify to be Zambia's state president.

Undoubtedly, therefore, multiparty democracy in Zambia was no longer a dream until 1996. It was a reality and most Zambians believed so. As ZDC treasurer Daunte Saunders correctly observed over the court's rejection of an opposition demand for a DNA test on President Chiluba: "The verdict is neither here nor there. But I believe that if the person holding the highest office of the land can be brought to court, it is a wonderful example of democracy in Zambia. Who would have thought a few years ago that the people of a country would question a president in court?"[17] That Zambians could openly criticize their government and openly question political leaders was a sign of the existence of democracy in Zambia. This was scarcely possible in the Second Republic, which was popularly referred to as "one-party participatory democracy."

The presidential petition highlighted one of the major constitutional crises in the political history of Zambia. Although this is not the first constitutional crisis ever to be experienced by Zambia, it is by far the most contentious. The 1996 Mwanakatwe Constitution caused intense debate in Zambia's political history. Interestingly, the guarantees for freedom of expression and assembly have made this possible. The lack of a consensus on two issues was at the center of this crisis: the method of adopting the new constitution and the citizenship clause in the new constitution.

The Mwanakatwe Constitutional Review Commission recommended that the constitution should be adopted by a more representative body such as a Constituent Assembly. The government rejected this recommendation and instead decided that the National Assembly would effect the amendments to the constitution.[18] The opposition parties' attempt for a judicial review was dismissed by both the High Court and the Supreme Court because the government did not abuse its discretion in using Parliament to amend the constitution.[19] Consequently, the 1996 Constitution of Zambia is widely projected as lacking legitimacy and therefore a source of instability.

THE CHURCH AND POLITICS

Since independence Zambia has been predominantly Christian, although it is a secular nation. The church and politics were kept separate as they played separate roles in the lives of Zambians. Occasionally religious leaders would issue statements on the politics of the country. For example, in 1979 when the government of President Kenneth Kaunda attempted to impose atheistic "Scientific Socialism" on the country, Christian churches strongly opposed the move, forcing the government to abandon the idea. Similarly, in July 1991 Christian churches spearheaded by the Catholic Church brought together MMD and UNIP leaders to dialogue at the Cathedral of the Holy Cross in Lusaka on 24 July 1991.

Evidently, during the process of change from one-party rule to multi-party democratic dispensation, the church did not leave politics to politicians. Church leaders played a major role in initiating political dialogue that effectively contributed to political reform in Zambia. They brought together businesspersons, trade union leaders, students and politicians to persuade President Kaunda to seriously consider political reform. As Mwanakatwe pointed out: "On 19 July 1991, leaders of three national organisations of the Christian Churches in Zambia met with President Kaunda at State House to discuss the political situation with particular emphasis on the disagreement among political parties over the proposal for a new constitution."[20] The church leaders represented the Christian Council of Zambia (CCZ), the Evangelical Fellowship of Zambia (EFZ) and the Zambia Episcopal Conference (ZEC). At the time the church was anxious to ensure that politicians reconciled and that the process of political transformation from one-party rule to multipartyism took place peacefully.

Furthermore, the three mother bodies of the Christian Church formed the Christian Monitoring Group (CMG) to ensure that elections were free and fair. The CMG was later joined by the Law Association of Zambia (LAZ), the Press Association of Zambia (PAZA), the Women's Lobby Group and the University of Zambia Students' Union (UNZASU) and became known as the Zambia Elections Monitoring Coordinating Committee (ZEMCC).[21] ZEMCC was a church-dominated nonpartisan NGO that intended to objectively observe the campaign environment and the entire process during and after elections. Apart from calling upon the citizens to pray for peace and God's guidance, it mounted a vigorous civic education campaign. It urged registered voters to show political maturity by voting responsibly and in accordance with the dictates of their conscience.

It was becoming increasingly clear at this stage that church organizations were putting their full weight behind the MMD.[22] Earlier, on 23 June 1991, "a historic meeting was held in the Anglican Cathedral in Lusaka attended by Kaunda and Chiluba with their senior advisors."[23] This meeting was arranged by the Roman Catholic Church (RCC), the Anglican Church (AC) and other Protestant church organizations. The purpose of the meeting was to discuss the proposed constitution changes by members of the Mvunga Constitutional Review Commission. During this period church leaders saw their role as that of mollifying extreme views of politicians to facilitate dialogue. They spoke on political issues as religious leaders and not as politicians or proponents of political systems. Christian churches saw themselves as partners in development.

Undoubtedly, the influence of church leaders on politics had become considerable and their role in the political arena was taking on new dimensions. Thus after the October 1991 presidential and parliamentary general elections, church leaders, mainly those from the Pentecostal persuasions, met at State House to dedicate the nation to God and declare Zambia a Christian nation. The declaration was not without controversy.

Other denominations were not invited and felt marginalized. The non-Christian religious groups like the Muslim community felt threatened by the declaration. The government on its part assured the nation that the declaration of Zambia as a Christian nation would not result in the banning of other religions. These would continue to conduct their business as before.

Despite these concerns the *Constitution (Amendment) Act* No. 18 of 1996 Section 2 repealed and replaced the Preamble and declared Zambia a Christian nation. Surprisingly, several church groups and organizations opposed the constitutionalization of the declaration.[24] The only group that appeared favorably disposed was the Pentecostal churches. These were the ones that had been in the forefront of the earlier declaration at State House. However, it would be wrong to suggest that the declaration was very unpopular as argued by Chanda.[25] Other non-Pentecostal churches equally embraced the declaration and it is not uncommon in Zambia today to hear church leaders from churches previously thought opposed to the declaration praising the government for the decision.

However, many church leaders are being criticized for behaving like politicians and making pronouncements similar to those made by politicians. While the church is happy with the declaration, Christians would like to see church leaders leave politics to politicians. One church leader who has attracted much criticism in this area is Pastor Nevers Mumba of the Victory Ministries International (VMI). Pastor Mumba was very critical of government failures and especially its religious implementation of the IMF-World Bank-driven structural adjustment program. Pastor Mumba was generally perceived as the spoke'sperson for the poor who are said to be the main victims of the structural adjustment programs. Yet when Pastor Mumba announced the formation of his National Christian Coalition (NCC) on 4 September 1997, both religious leaders and politicians, almost in unison, called upon Pastor Mumba to declare his true intentions.[26] Pastor Mumba pointed out at the launching of the NCC that it was not a political party and that he did not have designs for political office. He nevertheless indicated that the NCC had "an agenda" and that it was "not a sin to participate in politics and in fact it is a sin not to participate in politics."[27]

The reaction to Pastor Mumba's formation of the NCC was mixed. The CCZ general secretary, Reverend Violet Sampa-Bredt, advised Pastor Mumba to resign his position as president of VMI before forming a political body. She added that the move by Pastor Mumba was against Christian norms.[28] At the launching of the NCC Pastor Mumba respond that "A Christian who discourages a fellow Christian not to participate in politics is a traitor to his own country. While we differ in style of our preaching and doctrine, we should never compromise on the Judeo Christian values."[29] While Pastor Mumba was having this verbal exchange with Reverend Sampa-Bredt, both UNIP and MMD separately called upon him to be bold enough and form a political party instead of hiding behind the church. Pastor Mumba claimed that the NCC's role would be to "spearhead a revolution of morality and prosperity" for Zambia.

However, Pastor Mumba was accused of being too judgmental and one politician wondered whether Pastor Mumba was himself morally upright.[30] The Evangelical Fellowship of Zambia (EFZ) also challenged Pastor Mumba to declare whether his movement was a political party. Reverend Thomas Lumpa, executive director of the EFZ added that:

> EFZ through its executive committee has cautiously wel-
> comed the NCC with reservations. If it is a political party,
> EFZ feels that it is an unwise move. And with his new role
> in the NCC it will now be difficult for the EFZ to consider
> him in future delegations as that may send wrong signals to
> the political parties concerned.[31]

Clearly, therefore, Pastor Mumba's NCC was received with mixed blessings and only added to the already precarious mixture of religion and politics in Zambia. While Zambia is a Christian nation, the concept raises serious questions as to its application and implications. Are religious leaders to participate in politics or should they just be observers? If the debate generated by the formation of the NCC is anything to go by, church leaders are not so sure about what their role is in a Christian nation. It is plausible to argue that they are as divided as politicians are on the question of democracy and how best it should be practiced.

Nonetheless, Christian churches still felt duty-bound to work for the strengthening of the institutions and operations of democracy. Resulting from this conviction, the Christian Council of Zambia and the Zambia Episcopal Conference joined hands with other civil groups and NGOs and formed the Foundation for Democratic Process (FODEP). Its main objective was to promote a new political culture of civic responsibility through education about the rights and responsibilities of both leaders and the citizens. Since its inception FODEP has consistently spoken out against human rights violations, corruption and unfair practices in the political arena. Evidently, the church not only played a crucial role in the democratization process, but remains a key player with other NGOs in ensuring that political players observe democratic practices in the political arena.

ECONOMIC REFORMS IN THE THIRD REPUBLIC

Initially, Zambia's Third Republic appeared most successful in the area of economic reform, particularly during the first five years. Even the most critical observers acknowledged that the MMD's religious following of the IMF-World Bank-inspired structural adjustment program (SAP) led to a complete restructuring of the economy.[32] Zambia is fully liberalized. There are no foreign exchange restrictions as in the Second Republic. Import, export and even price controls were removed. The country embarked on a vigorous privatization program and by June 1996 over 120 state-owned companies had been privatized.[33] All this was possible because of the Privatisation Act No. 21 of 1992.

Furthermore, in 1993 Parliament enacted the Zambia Revenue Authority Act No. 28 of 1993, which resulted in improved tax collection and lowering of tax rates. The reform in the tax regime generally assisted the MMD government in addressing other critical areas of the economy. The government also created the National Roads Board, whose responsibility was to rehabilitate the road network that was completely dilapidated at the time the MMD came to power in 1991. The program of rebuilding the road network was financed by funds raised through the fuel levy and by donor support. The National Roads Board collects this levy from every litre of fuel purchased by motorists. For the first time in many years in the history of Zambia, the government put in place a scheme whose benefits were clearly visible. Motorists in Lusaka, for example, breathed a sigh of relief as they did not have to negotiate through countless potholes on the roads in and around the city. It should be pointed out, nonetheless, that there are still several roads in the city that need to be completely redone. The program might be in danger of running aground as funds from the program seem to be misdirected.

The MMD government also put in place several other laws to strengthen the liberalization process. These laws not only ensured the success of economic reforms, but made Zambians less dependent on government. Zambians learned and appreciated the spirit of entrepreneurialship and self-reliance. Zambians no longer looked to the government for handouts. Instead they learned to stand on their feet and fend for themselves. Undoubtedly, Zambia made major strides in this area in first five years of liberal democracy.

The initial misery of the liquidation of loss making state-owned companies turned into success stories. The liquidation of the United Bus Company of Zambia (UBZ) led to the birth of several privately owned bus companies. People no longer waited for a nonavailable state-owned bus. The government's success in this area owes much to the government's decision in 1992 to allow transporters to import buses duty free. The result was most successful as private bus operators were no longer constrained in their operations by a state-owned bus company enjoying an undue advantage over them.

Other areas where the Third Republic scored initial, but only temporary, successes were in the fields of education and health. Both sectors also underwent reform that transformed these sectors to the benefit of the users. Schools were equipped with desks and rehabilitated through a process of cost sharing with the Micro Project Unit (MPU), which encouraged self help. The MPU funded projects only where local participation through the Parent Teacher Association (PTA) was evident. This was very successful and many schools were transformed into better learning institutions.

However, the successes of these programs were short-lived. With the decline of the economy, particularly during the 1996-2001 period, there were clear signs that the education reforms had not achieved the intended results. This prompted the government during 2000 to abolish statutory fees, including examination fees, in all government primary schools to enable children of the poor to remain in school.

The health reforms that required patients to pay user fees, though initially resented, also assisted in the general improvement in the delivery of health services. Yet against this background the MMD faced criticism for insisting that people needed to pay for their health services. With time, Zambians adjusted to these new requirements and appreciated the benefits of the reforms, although there was a marked decline in services provided.

However, it is important to point out that the liberalization process left a trail of redundancies as both the private sector and the public sector were downsizing. The result of these redundancies was that many people were in poverty and unable to sustain their livelihood in the urban areas. As if this was not enough, the weather equally brought misery to many more, especially in the rural areas. Drought and floods brought about untold misery to thousands of people in the countryside. The government on its part did all it could to assist these people through a program of giving relief food to drought and flood victims. Politicians, both in the ruling MMD and the opposition parties, openly supported the government's handling and distribution of relief food under the office of the vice president.

Above all else, it was the poor economic performance by the MMD government that led to Zambians turning against it. By the end of 2000 more Zambians were living in abject poverty than was the case in 1991 when the MMD took over from UNIP. It is in this respect that the state of the economy during the ten-year period that the MMD was in power became one of the major campaign issues during the run-up to the 2001 tripartite elections.

THE OCTOBER 28 "SOLO" COUP ATTEMPT

The second term of the MMD was more problematic than the first.[34] Thus far, it is evident that the Third Republic in Zambia's political history is bedeviled with mixed fortunes. While multiparty democracy was getting rooted in Zambia, there were elements that were seriously working toward ensuring its failure. The main threat to multiparty democracy in Zambia in the Third Republic was the intolerance of those in the ruling party and some members of the opposition. These elements were not prepared to follow democratic principles in addressing their grievances. While civil society was constantly reminding government of its obligations in a multiparty political system, some perpetually issued inflammatory statements bordering on treason.

Former President Kaunda was instrumental in threatening political violence and an uprising by Zambians. On Monday 27 October 1997 he was reported as having said "something big will come and of course MMD will blame UNIP for that.... But it won't be UNIP. It will be the people of Zambia who are going to act."[35] While Kaunda was not ready then to disclose the form of the explosion, the next morning at about 06:00 Hours a Captain Stephen Lungu (alias Captain "Solo") announced on Radio 2 and 4 of the Zambia National Broadcasting Corporation (ZNBC) that the army had taken over the country. Captain Lungu further announced that all army service chiefs had been fired and was appealing to President Chiluba to surrender.[36] He claimed to have been representing the National Redemption Council, a political wing of the army. By 08:30 Hours the attempted coup had been thwarted by soldiers loyal to government and the president addressed the nation to confirm that he was still in control. Two hours later the president addressed the nation again on both radio and television at State House to signify the fact that he was still in State House and in firm control of the situation in the country.

Shooting was heard at both the Mass Media Complex, which housed the ZNBC, and at State House. The ZNBC studios and offices were extensively damaged in the fight to quell the coup. The president was firm and thanked the soldiers who quelled the coup and requested people to go about their normal business as the situation in the country had returned back to normal. The Church of God through its Overseer Bishop John Mambo immediately condemned the coup and requested President Chiluba to hold talks with leaders of the opposition, trade unions and others to discuss problems the nation was facing. The American Ambassador at the United Nations, Mr. Richardson, who was in Kenya, also condemned the coup.

Meanwhile, when President Chiluba came on the radio to address the nation, there was jubilation as people had earlier been saddened by the announcement of a coup. ZNBC reported during its 13:15 News Bulletin that there was jubilation in Kitwe when President Chiluba addressed the nation. Kitwe Mayor William Nyirenda addressed the people who gathered at Kitwe Civic Centre to celebrate the crushing of the coup that they should be calm and orderly. There was a clear absence of jubilation when the announcement of the coup was made earlier in the day. Most people were sad at the development. Several people talked to on the phone hoped the coup would fail. It would appear that the reasons the coup plotters were using to take over a democratically elected government were not shared by the majority of Zambians. Most people saw no justifiable reasons for the army to take over, arguing that in the 1990 Luchembe coup attempt things were really bad. Most people felt that the MMD had turned things around and there was no justifiable cause for the army to overthrow the government.

The coup attempt was roundly condemned by Zambians who pointed out that in a democratic state like Zambia, the best way to change a government was through the ballot box and not through the barrel of the gun.[37] Further, a number of African leaders also condemned the coup and were "glad that the coup was foiled."[38] The reaction of the public in Zambia clearly indicated that people were not happy with the coup attempt, was a sad moment in the lives of Zambians. There were hardly any celebrations in the streets of Lusaka. Instead, when the announcement came on the radio that the coup had been crushed, there was jubilation and demonstrations in the streets. Students from the Copperbelt University in Kitwe and Evelyn Hone College in Lusaka openly showed their solidarity with the MMD government.

Lieutenant Mwamba Luchembe, leader of the June 1990 failed coup attempt, was among those who condemned the October 1997 coup attempt. He argued that the era for military takeovers was long gone. Lt. Luchembe, who described himself as a catalyst to the change that followed in 1991, added that "There was no cause for it because now democracy is in place. If they do not want the MMD government they should wait until 2001 or lobby Parliament to impeach the President and call for fresh elections instead of resorting to coups, that era is long gone."[39] Lieutenant Luchembe's views were echoed by most Zambians and foreign nationals who commended the Zambian soldiers for crushing the rebellion.

On 29 October 1997, the government declared a state of emergency to enable it to deal effectively with suspects in the failed coup staged by dissident soldiers. The Zambia Congress of Trade Unions (ZCTU) "hailed government's declaration of a State of Emergency [because that] was the only effective way of dealing with coup suspects and curb the high crime wave which was on the increase."[40] The ZCTU further added that workers' rights were going to be trampled upon had the coup succeeded.

The Unity Party for Democrats (UPD) supported the government's move to declare a state of emergency, but cautioned the government against abusing the state of emergency. A cross section of ordinary Zambians supported the declaration, which they felt was the only effective way the government would deal with the coup plotters. The feeling was that only those who were guilty were against the declaration of the state of emergency. Nonetheless, the state of emergency created a big dent in the democratic dispensation of the Third Republic.

UNIP and ZDC both felt that the state of emergency would be abused by the MMD government. UNIP also blamed the MMD for the coup.[41] National Party Vice President Daniel Lisulo considered the declaration of state of emergency "as most unfortunate and uncalled for."[42] While UNIP strongly condemned the declaration of the state of emergency, UNIP itself ruled Zambia for twenty-seven years under a state of emergency that was declared in 1964 and was lifted only when the MMD came to power in 1991. A second state of emergency was declared in 1993 following the Zero Option saga and was lifted three months later. The 1997 state of emergency was therefore the third since Zambia became independent in 1964. This third state of emergency was revoked by President Chiluba on 17 March 1998. Parliament ratified its revocation on 24 March 1998.

Meanwhile, at the close of the trial of the soldiers and civilians alleged to have participated in the coup attempt, all civilians were acquitted. A total of fifty-nine soldiers were found guilty and were sentenced to death hanging until pronounced dead. All the soldiers had their death sentences commuted to either life imprisonment or various years of imprisonment by President Levy Patrick Mwanawasa in February 2004. In exercising his prerogative of mercy, he told the Zambian people that he would never sign a death warrant for any person as long as he was president.

ETHNICITY AND REGIONALISM: CHALLENGES FOR THE THIRD REPUBLIC

Ethnicity and regionalism have been considered as the only lasting forms of political association in most of sub-Saharan Africa because the societies are culturally heterogeneous. Bertha Osei-Hwedie suggested that multiparty elections did not lead to social or ideological divisions. Instead, they emphasized the ethnic composition of the population and mutual hostility between ethnic groups.[43] Ethnicity and regionalism, with the behavior of the political elites, are said to account for the major difficulties in the process of consolidating democracy in Zambia. This observation is not new. As far back as the First Republic in 1967 Robert Rotberg, discussed the question of tribalism and politics in Zambia in which ethnicity was identified as the source of problems for multiparty politics in the country during the First Republic.

Many years later, Richard Sandbrook still was able to argue that communal cleavages complicated and undermined the give-and-take principle of democratic competition. He further argued that in societies where political parties are divided along ethnic or regional lines, people interpret victory of one party as victory of one ethnic or regional group.[44] While it is true that this undermines the future of democracy, there is need to reassess the question of ethnicity and regionalism in Zambian politics. Clinging to ethnicity or regionalism as concepts for understanding the political history of Zambia may not be justifiable in the Third Republic.

From a theoretical perspective, an ethnic group can be defined as a community of people with shared perceptions, common origins, historical memories, values and expectations. These people make a deliberate effort to collectively press for their political and socioeconomic interests. More often than not, ethnicity coincides with regionalism because ethnic groups are found in particular regions where the language of the dominant group is the lingua franca of the region. Consequently, therefore, ethnicity is politically significant in cases where a common culture is used to foster a common political agenda by an ethnic group. Osei-Hwedie suggests that in Zambia political ethnicity is forged by common language, and common experience.[45] According to H. Herzog, political ethnicity is a "natural expression of group affiliation, a heritage of the past and the future tradition."[46] Furthermore, political ethnicity requires an elite or leadership to articulate its common ethnic, political and socioeconomic interests to the central government. Thus, where political ethnicity was in place, a patronage culture based on ethnicity determined political behavior and support.

Those who subscribe to the primacy of political ethnicity in Zambian politics suggest that there is political rivalry between four groups based on language: the Bemba-speaking group, the Tonga-speaking group, the Nyanja-speaking group, and the Lozi-speaking group.[47] However, this analysis masks a deep-seated historical trend that has evolved, and one that Osei-Hwedie either deliberately ignores or is not aware of. Zambia's motto of "One Zambia One Nation" is not without its history. Since the founding of the colonial state at the beginning of the last century, people from various ethnic groups within the country and from neighboring countries migrated to the Copperbelt and other towns in search of employment.

Inadvertently, the cross-cultural contact that followed, and continues today, helped to build a culture of mutual acceptance. Lusaka's population has grown to 2 million and that of the Copperbelt towns has also grown to similar levels. The influence of these urban societies on the rest of the country is immense. Because of the high levels of urbanization, Zambia has experienced high levels of intertribal marriages whose offsprings are considered "proper" Zambians. Children of intertribal marriages do not usually align themselves to one ethnic group; they usually consider themselves as belonging to two ethnic groups and have loyalties to both. This is important because urbanization has rendered the traditional matrilineal or patrilineal influences less important in determining family heritage. Furthermore, language is no longer such an important criterion for political divide. There are many Bemba speakers on the Copperbelt who do not come from any one of the Bemba-speaking groups identified by Osei-Hwedie, just as there are many Nyanja speakers who also do not come from the groups she has identified. It is therefore plausible to suggest that political ethnicity in Zambia does not function in the manner that Osei-Hwedie describes.

It is also important that the analysis should examine the political profiles of leaders who are in intertribal marriages. President Chiluba's wife Vera is from Eastern Province, while the wife of former Vice President Lieutenant General Christon Sifapi Tembo, Nelly, is from Southern Province. There are several politicians, including members of Parliament, who are in intertribal marriages. There is no doubt that such politicians and parliamentarians are influenced by such unions in their political conduct. In fact, several politicians have never resided in their so-called home areas. The only home they have known are the areas where their fathers or grandfathers went to work.

While it is true that the political rhetoric in Zambia describes certain political parties as tribal parties, or regional political parties, the major political parties like the MMD, UNIP and the United Party for National Development cannot be seriously considered as tribal parties. They are national in character. An important development that defies the ethnic analysis of Zambian politics since 1996 is over the suspensions and expulsions that rocked the MMD. The most important of these expulsions was that of the National Treasurer and Minister of Environment Benjamin Mwila, for having declared his intention to stand for MMD presidency and republican presidency in 2001. When Mwila made the announcement in early 2000, he confirmed speculations that had been going on for months. Mwila was believed to be President Chiluba's uncle. Yet on the political scene, there was more conflict between them than proponents of political ethnicity care to understand. On 6 August 2000 heavily armed police sealed off Mwila's home in Lusaka's Chudleigh residential area, apparently to search for seditious material. The search yielded nothing, and was believed to have been conducted to intimidate him. Mwila had recently announced the formation of his own political party to challenge the MMD presidential candidate in 2001. He is president of the Zambia Republican Party (ZRP) which was born out of the merging of Mwila's Republican Party (RP), the Zambia Alliance for Progress (ZAP) and the New Republican Party (NRP).

The government's excessive use of violence and force against Mwila suggests that after 1996 political cleavages do not just happen between ethnic groups but within ethnic groups as well. Although it is too early to form a solid view about this new trend, there is some evidence that suggested a rethinking about political ethnicity as a major factor in Zambian politics. Nonetheless, the political elites from time to time appealed to ethnic affiliations to maximize political support. But those who did, risked being shunned by the electorates because Zambians (especially in urban areas) were generally not comfortable with politicians who subscribed to ethnic politics. Nonetheless, while there were clear signs that intertribal marriages were neutralizing ethnic feelings, especially in urban areas, it would be wrong to expect ethnicity to disappear from the political arena.

The third term debate, which among other things revitalized both racism and ethnic politics, created a political crisis in the nation that threatened peace and stability that existed since the country attained independence in 1964.

The above notwithstanding, the UPND has since its founding been struggling, and failed to address the tribal tag that has continued to haunt it. Sadly, as the the country was geared for the 2001 tripartite elections and all political parties were dressing themselves in national dress to gain support from all parts of the country, the UPND was sinking deeper in tribal campaigns. This was championed by the Tonga Traditional Association (TTA), which openly called upon all Lozis, Tongas and Nkoyas to back the UPND leader Anderson Mazoka for the republican presidency.[48] While it is incontestable that regional and ethnic interests do still play a role in the politics of Zambia, an open and blatant campaign on tribal lines as the UPND did was a sure way of losing the contest. Generally Zambians do not take kindly to political parties and indeed political leaders who subscribe and condone tribal and regional politics. During the run-up to the 2001 tripartite elections only two political parties, the Agenda for Zambia (AZ) and the UPND, entered the race with the tribal tag firmly stuck on them.

As a result of that, the AZ failed throughout its campaign period to attract membership and support outside the Western Province. On the other hand, the UPND experienced a decline in support when the TTA openly stated "we are not ashamed that ... Lozis, Nkoyas should support our choice.... All Southerners will support Mazoka."[49] Evidently, the experience of both the AZ and the UPND support our view that both at the theoretical and practical levels, it is futile to continue emphasizing political ethnicity as a major factor in the political process in Zambia. Yet, it is important to note that because of lack of clear class distinction in the Zambian society as a result of declining economic conditions of the people, there is a general tendency to resort to ethnic affiliations for political support instead of class affiliation. It is in this respect that scholars still find ethnic analysis to provide an explanation of the political behavior of most Zambian politicians in the political arena. Our view is that such an approach should be taken with some caution considering the changing character of the Zambian society arising from a very high rate of urbanization.

The results of the 27 December 2001 tripartite elections confirm the view that any political party that seeks to form a national government on the basis of ethnic stength cannot make it. This is why the UPND lost ground to the rulling MMD: It laid emphasis on ethnic support and won all seats in the Southern Province, but performed poorly in other provinces, except in North-Western Province. In a unitary state like Zambia, with its current constitution, a political party needs national support to win enough votes to form a government. Arguably therefore, ethnic and regional politics in Zambia cannot be used as a basis to seek national political office. That the MMD and Levy Patrick Mwanawasa emerged winers from tripartite elections confirms this observation.

THE THIRD TERM DEBATE: RETREAT FROM DEMOCRACY TO MOBOCRACY

This chapter opened with a quotation in which President Chiluba suggested that "the will and consent of the people is the basis of power and legitimacy of government." The third term debate in Zambia, which started soon after the appointment of district administrators (DAs) toward the end of 1999, raises serious questions over the nature of the concept of the will of the people. The third term debate was supposedly initiated by MMD party cadres who began to petition President Chiluba to consider standing for a third term during the 2001 presidential elections despite constitutional restrictions. *The Monitor* suggested that the campaign was funded by State House.[50]

The DAs mobilized scores of cadres to champion the cause and even brought some cadres who camped at Parliament Motel and vowed not to go back to their home provinces until President Chiluba had given in to their demand. These cadres were later moved from Parliament to the State Lodge following MP protests to the Speaker of the National Assembly. The manner in which the MMD handled the third term debate demonstrated the development of mobocracy within the MMD and the political arena in Zambia. The 2001 MMD provincial conferences were characterized by mobocracy in which concept of "the will of the people" was manipulated. There was no doubt that the attempted perversion of the constitution, and encroachment on the liberal democracy that the Zambian people fought for in 1991, was on the brink of chaos and mob rule. Arguably, a political system where one person, backed by a small group of people, sought to control the power of the state, and used that power in a self-serving manner, was a mobocracy. The MMD demonstrated that it was willing to do whatever it took to carry out its agenda of converting the republic, a government under the authority of the people it governed, into a mobocracy. A mobocracy is the passing of more and more laws by fewer and fewer people with less and less relevant information and less accountability.

However, the attempt received a sharp reaction from a cross section of the Zambia society, including the church and NGOs. The antithird term campaign received support when MMD Vice President Brigadier Godfrey Miyanda spoke out and called upon President Chiluba to open the campaign for the republican presidency.[51] It became apparent that mobocracy would be kept in check because the vast majority of Zambians decided not to tolerate the attempted perversion of the constitution.[52] Republican Vice President Lieutenant-General Christon Tembo added his voice to the anti-third term debate when he spoke at the rally organized by Law Association of Zambia (LAZ) on 21 April 2001. Several ministers including Minister of Legal Affairs Vincent Malambo, added their voices to the anti-third term debate. The two senior ministers regretted the fact that the republican president initiated a political crisis that pitted him against his ministers, which was yet another misfortune of multipartyism in the Third Republic.

The political crisis in the MMD came to a head during the party's 4th convention held at the Mulungushi Rock of Authority near Kabwe when republican Vice President Tembo, MMD Vice President Miyanda and several cabinet ministers and MPs were barred by party cadres from attending the convention. The convention was called to amend the MMD constitution to facilitate President Chiluba's bid for a third term. All members of the MMD National Executive Committee (NEC) opposed to the third term were barred from attending the convention, which took place from 28 April to 2 May 2001. The only member opposed to the third term who attended the convention was the party chairman, Sikota Wina.

His presence at the convention was strategic because the pro-third term members needed him to chair the proceedings of the meeting. It was evident during the convention that Wina went to the convention without the blessing of some of his closest allies, who included his wife Princess Nakatindi Wina who was conspicuously absent. Under normal circumstances she would have been by his side. Later there was speculation that Sikota Wina was forced to go to the convention and perform the role of chairman. After the convention both Sikota Wina and Princess Nakatindi Wina maintained an unusually long period of silence. They did not comment on the proceedings of the convention nor did they associate themselves with the expelled members of the MMD.

Meanwhile, the MMD Electoral Commission Chairman Chifumu Banda and two other members of the commission stepped down as preparations for MMD NEC elections were under way, citing serious irregularities over election procedures. The commission was denied lists of delegates who were qualified to vote at the convention. Chifumu Banda argued that he was too senior and respected a lawyer to be associated with the serious irregularities at the MMD convention and did not want to be associated with the manipulation of the country's democratic principles. Despite these revelations, the MMD convention continued and the elections were conducted, resulting in eighteen NEC members being returned unopposed. The only post that was seriously contested for was that of vice president, because Paul Tembo allegedly refused to give way to Enock K. Kavindere. Initial reports indicated that Paul Tembo beat President Chiluba's favorite candidate, but after more than four recounts Kavindere was declared the winner by 516 votes against Tembo's 515 votes. Tembo and his supporters immediately left the convention. Tembo later joined the Forum for Democracy and Development (FDD) before he was brutally murdered in July 2001.

At the close of the convention on 2 May 2001, twenty-two senior members of the party, including the republican vice president and party vice president, were expelled from the MMD. This was despite the a court injunction earlier obtained by those opposed to the third term restraining the MMD from expelling them from the party. Thus far, the spirit of mobocracy seemed to have succeeded and further demonstrated the intransigency of the MMD. The court injunction was extended on three occasions and remained in force for over a month. This meant that the expelled members of the MMD were legally members of the party.

Although President Chiluba suggested that by amending the MMD constitution the convention had made a great achievement, the convention actually left the MMD seriously divided and without a clear direction. This was especially so after his address to the nation that he would not seek reelection for a third term, but that the NEC would have to identify a republican presidential candidate. By the end of May 2001 it was not at all clear who the MMD presidential candidate would be. The newly appointed minister of information, Vernon J. Mwaanga, told a press briefing on 28 May that the MMD had began a serious search for a presidential candidate. It was only in early August that the first vice president in the Third Republic, Levy Patrick Mwanawasa, was elected by NEC as the MMD presidential candidate.

That the MMD amended its party constitution to enable President Chiluba to stand for a third term as MMD president clearly manifested the lack of political maturity in the MMD. The failure by senior politicians to acknowledge that the republican constitution was supreme and that party constitutions are subordinate to the republican constitution only served to complicate the constitutional crisis in the Third Republic.

Although the injunction obtained by Lieutenant General Christon Tembo and Brigadier General Godfrey Miyanda restraining the MMD from expelling them from the party remained in place, some of the twenty-two expelled members formed a new party clled the Forum for Democracy and Development under the chairmanship of Simon Zukas. Tembo formally resigned from the MMD and took up the position of interim vice president of the FDD. The other expelled members initially remained outside the FDD pending the High Court decision regarding the court injunction.

Simon Zukas pointed out that one of the fundamental pitfalls of party politics in Zambia was that the party president was all too powerful from the time of independence. He observed in a talkshow program on Radio Phoenix on 31 May 2001 that the MMD drifted along this line when President Chiluba and not party President Elias Chipimo began to chair NEC meetings. This rendered the party chairman irrelevant. In the process the party chairman became a passenger in the affairs of the MMD. Zukas suggested that the FDD would not allow a similar situation to develop in the new party, which would be more open and "embrace a broad section of Zambians going way beyond the expelled 22 MPs,"[53] There is no doubt that because all power rested with the president, party structures in the sections, wards and constituencies paid attention to what the party president wanted. This created a situation where the party president literally owned the party. Under this arrangement it was easy for the party president to manipulate the various organs of the party and begin to use mobs to effect his intentions and designs. Mobocracy became an attractive option in the name of democracy.

It is important to point out, however, that mobocracy did not only become a common feature within the MMD, but that it was becoming a national political phenomenon. The leadership wrangles in UNIP, the subsequent suspension of Francis Nkhoma from the presidency and his subsequent replacement by Tilyenji Kaunda reflected more the work of mobocracy than democracy. In December 2000 Rabbison Chongo who was acting UNIP president following the suspension of Francis Nkhoma was roughed up and thrown out of his office by Lusaka UNIP youths.[54] Arguably, therefore, mobocracy became a common political alternative to democracy, and there was a way in which politicians were subscribing more to mobocracy in the name of democracy and the will of the people.

However, the news that the MMD had amended the constitution to facilitate President Chiluba's bid for the third term resulted in mass demonstrations by students in higher learning institutions. The demonstrations grew when he was reelected party president unopposed. For the first time in many years, University of Zambia students peacefully demonstrated together with Evelyn Hone College students and those from Chainama College of Health Sciences. Although the demonstrations went on for several days, there were no reports of stone throwing or harassment of motorists. Undoubtedly, students understood exactly what they were demonstrating against. There were also very clear indications that the anti-third term demonstrations were supported by nearly all students.

Meanwhile, the third term debate was clouded by the birth of seemingly state-sponsored NGOs that began to champion the call for a referendum on the question of the constitution. Mike Zulu's National Organization for Civic Education (NOCE) conducted a controversial opinion poll over the issue and suggested that the Zambian population was split over the matter. NOCE, nonetheless, continued to call for a referendum as the only way forward. However, the outcome of the MMD convention, particularly the amendment of its constitution and the election of President Chiluba for a third term, galvanized the nation against the third term and President Chiluba's intention to amend the Republican constitution. Labor Day celebrations were characterized by anti-third term speeches by labor leaders, as well as by Labor Minister Edith Nawakwi.

Because of the mounting pressure from civil society and other interest groups, President Chiluba closed the 4th MMD convention without indicating one way or the other regarding his candidature for a third term as republican president. He stated that he would do so in a few days after taking into account national interests. The nation did not wait very long. In a late-night address on radio and television he told the nation that:

> Ten years ago when you the people of Zambia opted for popular government, I promised that I would serve faithfully and that when I had served my two terms, I would leave office. That has always been my position and that is the only statement that I have made. I have said nothing to repudiate that or contradicted my earlier pronouncements. I still stand by my word. I will leave office at the end of my term.[55]

President Chiluba made these revelations while blaming interest groups for derailing the third term debate, which he claimed started with public petitions for him to stand for another term of office. He bitterly lamented that the effort ended with a malicious campaign, and accused the anti-third term MMD members of ganging with opposition parties and mobilizing students to demonstrate against the amendment of the republican constitution.

Clearly, President Chiluba's pronouncement that he had no intention of seeking a third term as republican president was in response to the mounting pressure and the constitutional crisis that was unfolding in the nation. There is no doubt that he was trying to undertake a damage repair maneuver after presiding over an unpopular political situation that he initiated. However, because of mounting pressure, he sought to show that he was more concerned with national interests at the expense of party interests. Arguably, therefore, he dissolved cabinet and dropped all deputy ministers and provincial ministers. He argued that he took the decision to facilitate the constitution of a new government and a cabinet that would function in harmony.[56]

Evidently, the campaign by members of the civil society opposed to the third term, demonstrations by students and their demand that President Chiluba be removed, coupled with the stand taken by opposition parties and expelled MMD leaders to petition the Speaker to impeach President Chiluba,[57] forced him to reaffirm his earlier pronouncements that he would not seek a third term as republican president. Instead, he pointed out that the amending of the MMD constitution was to usher in a new era where the party president would not necessarily be the MMD republican presidential candidate. The MMD National Executive Committee would identity a candidate who would be sponsored to contest and win the republican presidency on behalf of the MMD. He likened the development to that of Tanzania in 1984 when the late President Julius Nyerere retired, but remained chairman of the ruling Chama Chamapinduzi Party.

However, it should be noted that President Chiluba's decision to remain party president resulted from the massive pressure against his intention to go for a third term. President Chiluba's scheme to run for a third term and secure an amendment of both the MMD and republican consitutions began in 1999 when he banned all MMD members from campaigning to take over the presidency of the party. The MMD began to split over the matter, especially when Benjamin Mwila, in an apparent defiance of the ban, announced his intention to contest the MMD presidency. He was subsequently expelled from the MMD. He founded the Republican Party (RP), which later merged with the Zambia Alliance for Progress (ZAP) to form the Zambia Republican Party (ZRP) of which he is president. In retrospect, it can be argued that Benjamin Mwila read President Chiluba's banning of MMD members from campaigning over the presidency correctly.

President Chiluba's intentions became clear only when he promoted the debate over the third term issue. The debate further split the MMD, especially when ministers and MPs opposed to the third term were barred from attending the 4th MMD convention and subsequently were expelled from the party. Although the MMD managed to amend its constitution and reelected President Chiluba unopposed, the massive pressure made him declare that he had no intention to seek a third term as republican president and also informed the nation that there would be no referendum over the issue. The debate was closed, but the MMD remained in a serious mess as it did not have a presidential candidate. Cadres who had campaigned for President Chiluba to seek a third term were frustrated and felt cheated. By June 2001, almost five months before the 2001 parliamentary and presidential elections, the MMD did not have a presidential candidate.

Resulting from the above, there were speculations that since the inception of the MMD the presidential candidate was elected at the party's national convention, the decision to allow the NEC to choose a presidential candidate was likely to lead to a further split of the party. A considerable number of MMD members argued that "if Chiluba knew that he was not going to stand for a third term, he should have let them choose a leader of their choice at the convention in Kabwe than leaving the matter to NEC."[58] However, what these MMD cadres failed to comprehend or deliberately ignored was the fact that President Chiluba had no intention in the first place to leave State House after only two terms. He was gunning for a third term, except for the massive anti-third term pressure.

That President Chiluba encouraged the third term debate and allowed the MMD to change its constitution to facilitate his election for a third term as MMD president, in conflict with the republican constitution, was a show of political immaturity by senior MMD politicians. They deliberately ignored the fact that the republican constitution was supreme and that a political party in Zambia should be guided by the clauses in it. Political parties are registered under the Societies Act and as such their constitutions should never be deliberately allowed to be at variance with the republican constitution, to which they are subordinate.

The MMD as the ruling political party should have learned some good lesson from Tanzania, where politicians in Zanzibar attempted to change the constitution to allow the president of Zanzibar to stand for a third term. However, Chama Chamapinduzi in Tanzania maintained that the Zanzibar constitution should not be at variance with that of the Union. That was a clear demonstration of political maturity by Tanzanian politicians over a similar issue. To be sure, the MMD unleashed a constitutional crisis both in the party itself and in the country. Small wonder that the search for a presidential candidate for the MMD became a source of conflict and instability in the party.

Yet it was not only the MMD that faced a leadership crisis. The United National Independency Party did not have an elected presidential candidate following the removal of Francis Nkhoma, nor did several other parties on the Zambian political landscape. Almost all the political parties were led by the founding leaders who were not elected. This gave the impression that the party positions were personal to holder. Worse still, most of the parties did not have party structures on the ground. It was therefore difficult to expect that these parties would form the next government. Evidently, the founding of the FDD was reminiscent of the founding of the Zambia Democratic Congress by Dean Mung'omba on the eve of the 1996 parliamentary and presidential elections. That the ZDC performed poorly in that year's election reflected lack of preparedness on the ground throughout the country.

As a reult of the third term debate, three political parties were born out of the MMD after its May 2001 convention: the Forum for Democracy and Development, the Heritage Party (HP) and the Patriotic Front. The birth of these political parties, especially that of the FDD, led to a temporary political decline of the MMD in the political arena. In fact, other political parties suffered in popularity as a result. One such political party that was directly affected by the birth of the FDD was the United Party for National Development, which lost some senior members to FDD.

POLITICAL VIOLENCE

Although Zambia, avoided the violence and war that ravaged the region from the 1960s, it did not escape politically motivated violence. Indeed, it was the incidence of politically motivated violence that accounted, among other things, for UNIP's decision to campaign for the establishment of the one-party state in 1972. In 1990 UNIP issued a document in which it outlined the level of politically motivated violence between 1946 and 1972. UNIP argued that plural politics would bring back interparty conflicts as was the case before 1972. The extent of interparty violence was substantiated by documentary evidence shown in the Table 8.

Table 8: Politically Motivated Violence, 1964-1972

Province	People Injured	People Killed	Villages Damaged
Northern	51	92	1
Eastern	73	127	27
Southern	5	27	1
Copperbelt	5	2	29
Western	17	0	0
Central	7	0	2
Lusaka	20	1	19
Luapula	1	0	0
North-Western	0	0	85

Source: Anonymous, "The Origins and Achievements of the One-Party Participatory Democracy," 13 August 1990.

While the one-party state era witnessed an end of interparty conflicts and politically motivated violence, the reestablishment of multiparty politics in 1991 did not lead to a resurgence of politically motivated violence. However, it was the third term debate that began in late 1999 that created conditions for politically motivated violence.

What was most disturbing was that this violence affected members of the ruling MMD. The violence was initially directed at those opposed to the third term. However, when the third term debate ended following the massive pressure on President Chiluba, MMD cadres turned their anger on members of the opposition political parties. The Zambia Police Service appeared helpless and did not arrest the perpetrators of this politically motivated violence, unless they were members of the opposition. MMD members were not arrested. The Zambia Police Service seemed to have been under extreme pressure and failed to professionally deal with the issue of politically motivated violence in the Third Republic. For example the deputy mayor of Lusaka was assaulted three times by MMD cadres, but the Police did not arrest the cadres. Worse still, the language used by senior MMD politicians encouraged violent behavior on the part of MMD cadres.[59] Meanwhile at another MMD gathering addressed by Minister of Information and Broadcasting Vernon J. Mwaanga, an MMD cadre told the minister that they would start beating up former ministers and MP expelled from the MMD one by one. The minister did not condemn this stand, but instead applauded it.

The MMD gave the impression that violent behavior was appreciated and encouraged. The MMD Lusaka province coordinator, Esther Nakawala, was promoted to that post following her violent behavior and abusive language against persons perceived to be against the republican president. Although several people reported her conduct to the Police, she was never charged nor cautioned. The culture of violence was so deep-rooted in the MMD that it appeared to be an accepted way of doing politics. Intimidation and haranguing of political opponents became a characteristic symbol of the MMD toward the run-up to the 2001 parliamentary and presidential elections.

Undoubtedly, therefore, politically motivated violence was not only a recipe for mobocracy, but was yet another mixed fortune of multipartyism in the Third Republic. On 15 June 2001 expelled MMD Kabwata Councilor Blandina Kamuzyu was shot in the stomach by an MMD Councilor in the presence of two Police Officers. The assailant told those Police that only the Police commissioner and Lusaka division officer commanding could talk to him. Meanwhile Blandina Kamuzyu underwent an emergency operation, but doctors at the University Teaching Hospital (UTH) failed to remove the bullet that was lodged in her stomach. She survived the shooting.

The worst incidence of politically motivated violence was in the Chawama Constituency during the by-elections that were held on 17 July 2001 following the resignation of Lieutenant General Christon Tembo. It was alleged that MMD National Secretary and Minister Without Portfolio Michael Sata "ordered MMD cadres to hack opposition parties supporters found monitoring the electoral process at polling stations in Chawama constituency."[60] The FDD won the by-election by a wide margin. The result angered the MMD, which began hacking people indiscriminately. On Wednesday 18 July 2001 *The Post* newspaper carried several pictures of people with deep cuts stitched at the Chawama Clinic waiting to be taken to the University Teaching Hospital. The Zambia National Broadcasting Corporation (ZNBC) Television evening news also showed several people with deep cuts sustained during the violence that took place the previous night. Government chief spokesperson and Minister of Information and Broadcasting Vernon J. Mwaanga condemned the violence. Although victims named some of the people involved in the violence, the Police made no arrests.

It is also important to point out that during the Third Republic Zambia witnessed several cases of politically motivated murders, which remain unresolved to date. They include the violent murder of former

Minister of Finance Ronald Penza in the MMD government, Wezi Kaunda of UNIP and former Deputy National Secretary of the MMD Paul Tembo. Tembo was murdered hours before he was to testify before a tribunal that was set up to investigate diversion of 2 billion kwacha from the National Assembly. It was alleged that the money was used to finance the MMD convention in May 2001. Anther person who died through mysterious circumstances was Baldwin Nkumbula, who died in a road traffic accident under suspicious circumstances. These cases raised serious questions regarding the security of politicians who took different positions in their political parties. Politically motivated violence was therefore a real threat to the democratization process in the Third Republic.

POLITICAL PARTIES AND THE 2001 TRIPARTITE ELECTIONS

By any measure, political parties that are defined as distinctive organizations whose principal aim is to acquire and exercise political power, that is, gain control of governmental apparatus, are undoubtedly a dominant feature of contemporary organized political systems. Political parties originated in their modern form in Europe and the United States in the nineteenth century. As formal organizations, they spread and became ubiquitous throughout the world. Currently political parties play a multiplicity of vital and indeed indispensable roles in the political arena, especially with regard to democratic governance. Political parties perform several essential functions: first, they act as agencies for the articulation and aggregation of different views and interests; second, they serve as vehicles for the selection of leaders for government positions; third, they organize personnel around the formulation and implementation of public policy; and fourth, they serve in a mediating role between individuals and their government. It is for this reason that political parties, in their various manifestations, attract unending intellectual and public policy interests, especially in developing regions like Africa where their strengths or weaknesses are crucial for the democratic project.

Today, most African governments, including those that are universally known to be autocratic, claim to be democratic. In justifying such claims there have been attempts to "racialize" democracy into brands of "African" democracy, which is then claimed to be different from brands of democracy elsewhere. An example has been the use of such "racialization" in rejecting competitive politics as un-African. Unfortunately, African experience with modern governmental systems has known little else but central executives so powerful that their claims to democracy, even "African" democracy, command little credence. Many African leaders accepted and participated in the democratic process after the collapse of the one-party systems of government as a means to an end: a vehicle or conduit for personal power. The situation is compounded by poverty. Most politicians in Africa see the state as the primary source of accumulation of personal wealth. This economic interest motivates the drive toward the monopolization of power by a single party and a narrow class of elites. This partly explains the multiplicity of political parties in Zambia. The call by some political parties that the state should fund opposition political parties seems to be informed by this economic motive.

Before we move to the next section of this discussion, let us look at the nine political parties that participated in the tripartite elections. They included the ruling MMD whose presidential candidate was Levy Patrick Mwanawasa, and eight opposition political parties, namely: UPND whose presidential candidate was Anderson Mazoka, UNIP whose presidential candidate was Tilyenji Kaunda, FDD whose presidential candidate was Lieutenant General Christon Tembo, ZRP whose presidential candidate was Benjamin Y. Mwila, HP whose presidential candidate was Brigadier General Godfrey Miyanda, NCC whose presidential candidate was Nevers Mumba, AZ whose presidential candidate was Dr. Inonge Mbikusita Lewanika, and ZAP whose presidential candidate was Dean Mung'omba. Of the nine political parties, UNIP was the oldest, having been first registered in 1959, and the Heritage Party was the youngest registered only on 9 July 2001. Below we attempt an analysis of these nine political parties and show their background and campaign strategies.

Agenda for Zambia (AZ)

AZ was formed just a week before the nomination dates for 1996 presidential and parliamentary elections and was led by Akashambatwa Mbikusita-Lewanika. It was registered on 23 October 1996. He participated as a presidential candidate and lost. The AZ fielded less than thirty parliamentary candidates in the 1996 parliamentary elections, out of which only two went through. As the country was preparing for the 2001 tripartite elections, AZ held elections in Livingstion and Dr. Inonge Mbikusita-Lewanika was elected AZ president to replace her brother Akashambatwa.

Since its formation in 1996, AZ has suffered from the general perception that it was an ethnically inspired political party. This perception was strengthened when its president supported the secession of Western Province from Zambia. As a result the party failed to attract membership in large enough numbers outside the Western Province. In fact the MPs who were elected in 1996 won in Western Province constituencies. The party therefore entered the race to Manda Hill in the 2001 tripartite elections with the tribal tag firmly stuck to it.

Forum for Democracy and Development (FDD)

The FDD was formed in June 2001 following the expulsion of twenty-two senior ministers and MPs from the MMD over their anti-third term views. The FDD was initially chaired by Simon Zukas, who had resigned from the MMD government in 1996 following his disagreement with the citizenship clause regarding presidential aspirants. It is considered to be a broadly based political party whose leadership reflects representation from all sections of the Zambian society. Although relatively new on the Zambian political scene, the FDD spread to every corner of Zambia within months of its formation and appeared comfortably set and ready for the 2001 tripartite elections. This was evident both during and after its convention held in October 2001.

The FDD held its convention at Mulungushi International Conference Center from 12 October to 16 October 2001. There were four presidential aspirants who included former Vice President Lieutenant General Christon Tembo, former Legal Affairs Minister Vincent Malambo, former MMD Lusaka Province Provincial Chairman Dr. Bornface Kawimbe and Kabwe Central Independent Member of Parliament Austin Chewe. Lieutenant General Christon Tembo was elected with a large majority to emerge as the FDD presidential candidate for the 2001 presidential elections. Prior to the convention the FDD contested in three by-elections and won the Chawama and Kabwata seats. The seats were previously held by Lieutenant General Christon Tembo and Brigadier General Godfrey Miyanda respectively. This was a clear indication that the FDD was emerging to be a threat the MMD

The FDD convention was hailed as a showpiece of the democratic process in Zambia. Unity and harmony characterized the five-day convention. Former First Lady Vera Chiluba addressed the convention and urged members of the FDD to remain united after the convention to ensure that the MMD was removed from power. After the convention the FDD emerged stronger and united, contrary to speculations from the ruling MMD that it would crumble. The FDD is the only political party whose presidential candidate won the party's presidency after beating three other contestants convincingly. In other opposition political parties, including the ruling MMD, presidential aspirants went unopposed at the conventions. The FDD therefore went into the tripartite elections with no hangovers of some leaders throwing their weight around because they "owned the party." The election procedures adopted ensured that the party emerged coherent and united as most founding members were elected to the National Policy Committee (NPC).

However, some delegates, particularly those from the Western Province, complained that their candidate for the vice presidency, William Harrington lost because he was not on a preferred list. Despite these complaints, there were no serious problems and at the end of the convention the FDD managed to maintain a sense of stability and unity in the party.

Heritage Party (HP)

The HP was founded by Brigadier General Godfrey Miyanda following his expulsion from the MMD over the third term debate. The party was registered on 9 July 2001. The party did not hold a convention before the tripartite elections, but its presidential candidate Brigadier General Miyanda took extensive campaign tours around the country. The party, especially its founding president, campaigned using the "village concept" as a strategy for developing the country and moving the country forward. However, because the party did not hold a covention to elect leaders, there was a general concern regarding its ability to practice democracy if the leaders were not willing to be subjected to an election within the party.

Movement for Multiparty Democracy (MMD)

The MMD as a movement was founded on 21 July 1990 and was registered as a political party on 4 January 1991. President Frederick Titus Jacob Chiluba was its founding president. It took part in the first democratic general elections in 1991 and convincingly beat UNIP. Because of its parliamentary majority the MMD government was a *de facto* one-party government that enacted laws with very little opposition. The MMD won the second democratic elections in 1996 convincingly, thanks to the decision by UNIP to boycott that year's general elections in protest against the citizenship clause and the issue of the Nikuv Voters' Register.

The MMD went to the 2001 tripartite elections with many difficulties despite being the ruling political party. The outgoing president precipitated a constitutional crisis within the MMD by allowing the amendment of the MMD constitution, but because of pressure from opposition political parties, NGOs and the donor community, he failed to do the same for the republican constitution. Consequently, although he was the MMD president, he was not eligible to seek reelection as republican president for a third term. The National Executive Committee organized elections and elected Levy Patrick Mwanawasa as MMD's presidential candidate. However, the election of Mwanawasa brought further constitutional crisis in the ruling MMD with the party's National Secretary Michael Sata, who had contested the party's presidency, arguing that the party contravened its constitution by electing Mwanawasa who was not an elected NEC member.

Sata wrote a protest letter to President Chiluba and resigned his position as minister without portfolio as well as his party position of national secretary. He was eventually expelled from the party. He founded the Patriotic Front (PF). The MMD campaigned heavily using all resources at its disposal to sell Mwanawasa to the electorate. Although it was the ruling party, the odds seemed to have been heavily against it in much the same way that in 1991 Zambians wanted UNIP out. In 2001 Zambians wanted the MMD out.

MMD presidential candidate Mwanawasa had an uphill battle during the campaign. When President Chiluba declared that he was not seeking a third term, a considerable number of district administrators and cadres were disappointed. Worse still, Mwanawasa was not too keen on the idea of DAs. As such, DAs who were part of the campaign machine for the MMD seemed not too keen to support Mwanawasa. The DAs were very instrumental in the third term campaign but were almost unheard of during Mwanawasa's campaign tours.

The party held a press conference on 26 October at the Mulungushi International Conference Centre at which the names of the adopted candidates for parliamentary elections were announced. When names for the Kanyama (Charles Muneku), Mandevu (Patrick Katyoka) and Matero (George Sazumbile) constituencies, were announced there was an uproar as cadres openly rejected the adopted candidates. Cadres who went to welcome President Chiluba from Gaborone displayed placards denouncing the adoption of Crispin Mushota as parliamentary candidate for Lusaka Central Constituency.[61] Similarly, on the Copperbelt the Kalulushi constituency MMD cadres rejected Chitalu Sampa who was adopted to contest in that constituency.

Meanwhile suspected MMD cadres in Ndola rural were reported to have set ablaze an MMD constituency vehicle on the same day in protest against the adoption of a candidate they did not support. There was therefore some sense of a repeat of what transpired in 1996 in Kabwe where Paul Tembo was openly rejected by Kabwe central constituency members in preference to Captain Austion Chewe, who later stood as an Independent and won the seat. However, this time the rejection of adopted MMD parliamentary candidates was widespread and threatened the smooth preelection campaign for the 2001 tripartite elections. In several constituencies MMD cadres threatened to vote for opposition political party candidates if their preferred candidates were not included. In Kwacha constituency, for example, MMD members openly said they would vote for the FDD candidate if Eugene Apple, whom they claimed was not among the interviewed candidates, was not dropped and replaced by their preferred candidate.

In Mansa MMD members in Mansa Central rejected J.S. Chilufya, whom they claimed was not among the candidates who were considered for the parliamentary seat. They requested the NEC to reconsider his adoption and replace him with a more popular candidate. The situation was the same in Livingstone where MMD members rejected former Mayor Coillard Chibbonta in preference to a female candidate. In Mpika Central the MMD rejected Edwin Mpongosa in preference to Blackson Mwaba. The Mpika district administrator, who was also the MMD provincial chairman for Northern Province, addressed the protesting cadres and indicated that the provincial committee would respect the wishes of the people on the ground. The adoption of parliamentary candidates by the MMD was as controversial as their convention in May. The process appeared to have created further rifts with the rank and file of the MMD and thus threatening the MMD's dominance in the political arena.

National Citizens Coalition (NCC)

The NCC was founded in 1998 and was registered on 23 July of the same year. It started as a pressure group, but was later registered as political party. Its founder and president is Pastor Nevers Mumba. The party seeks to champion Christian values in politics. It campaigned for the election of morally upright political leaders. Although the party came into being in 1998, it never won a single seat in all the by-elections it participated in. Its leader is not a politician and possesses no political experience, except that he founded the Victory Ministries International. The NCC therefore entered the race as an underdog in the political competition.

Social Democratic Party (SDP)

The SDP is the only political party in Zambia founded and led by a woman. The president is Gwendoline Konie, a long-standing diplomat. The party had been in existence only for a few months and had not taken party in any by-elections prior to the 1991 tripartite elections. It did not attract much attention from the electorate. The party president appeared on several television discussion programs organized by Coalition 2001. The SDP was easily forgotten as it did not seem to be assertive enough to challenge the other political parties.

United National Independence Party (UNIP)

UNIP is the oldest and largest political party, which was first registered on 24 October 1958. It fought for the independence of Zambia, won the 1964 elections and formed the first independent government in October 1964. It remained in power until October 1991 when it was voted out power by the MMD. Throughout its life in power its president was Kenneth David Kaunda. In 1996 UNIP boycotted the general elections in protest against some contentious clauses in the 1996 constitution.

Kaunda retired from politics in May 2000 and the party found itself in a deep leadership crisis. In his final speech as UNIP president, delivered when he opened the Third Extra-Ordinary Congress of the party at the Zambia International Trade Fair Grounds in Ndola, he said: "The first challenge that faces the party is that of management and administration. The party needs leaders to organize, and run the party so that in all its operations it is efficient, flexible and effective."[62]

Francis Nkhoma was elected party president, but he soon found himself rejected by some members of the Central Committee. He was eventually suspended from the party in November. He took the case to court, which after months of deliberation ruled in his favor. However, the party still rejected him and instead decided that Tilyenji Kaunda, son of former President Kaunda, be appointed president of UNIP. Tilyenji Kaunda began campaigning for the republican presidency as UNIP presidential candidate while Nkhoma insisted that he was the legitimate UNIP president. Thus for several months leading to the tripartite elections, UNIP was embroiled in the leadership wrangle. This worked against the party's campaign strategies, because its members were divided between two presidential candidates.

The leadership crisis in UNIP deepened when Muhabi Lungu at a press conference on 17 October 2001 said he would stop Tilyenji Kaunda from seeking the republican presidency on a UNIP ticket because he was not an elected president of UNIP. Lungu pointed out that the UNIP constitution did not allow Tilyenji Kaunda to skip positions to go to the top. He pointed out that it was unconstitutional for Tilyenji Kaunda to be campaigning for the republican presidency under a UNIP ticket when he was not the legally elected party president. Lungu argued that only Francis Nkhoma was qualified to stand as UNIP presidential candidate in the 2001 tripartite elections. Undoubtedly, this crisis worked against the campaign by the UNIP presidential candidate and was not at all helpful to UNIP.

United Party for National Development (UPND)

The UPND was founded in 1998 and was registered as a political party on 20 November of the same year. Its founder and president is Anderson Mazoka. Since its formation the UPND participated in several by-elections and won seven seats. This gave it the largest number of MPs during the 1996-2001 parliamentary session. While the UPND started very well and was a promising political party, it soon began to decline. The party has been struggling to deal with the tribal tag, which it has failed to address.

The tribal tag was confirmed by the Tonga Traditional Association, which openly campaigned for the UPND on tribal lines. As described earlier in this chapter, the TTA urged all Tongas, Lozis and Nkoyas to campaign for Anderson Mazoka and secure his election. This alienated UPND members who were not from the named tribes. As a result, the campaign message by TTA worked to the detriment of the party in the run-up to the 2001 tripartite elections. Sadly, the UPND made no attempt to deal with the negative impact of the political pronouncements by the TTA. However, the UPND further declined on the political scale following the founding of the FDD. It was in this respect that the UPND mounted a vigorous campaign to try to break the FDD, but without much success. The UPND saw FDD, not MMD, as the political party to beat in the 2001 tripartite elections.

Zambia Alliance for Progress (ZAP)

The ZAP was registered on 12 July 1999 following a merger of the Zambia Democratic Congress (ZDC), the National Lima Party (NLP) and the National Party (NP). Its president is Dean Mumg'omba. There is no doubt that it was the weakest party that entered the race for the tripartite elections. It commanded very little support among the electorate. Mung'omba stood against President Chiluba under the ZDC ticket in the 1996 general elections, which he lost by a very big margin. The party did not have any good prospects in the tripartite elections. It had temporarily joined the ZRP merger, but Mung'omba retraced his steps and refused to abolish the party. On 21 October 2001 he told the National Policy Council of the party that he would not stand as a presidential candidate in the tripartite elections because there were far too many presidential candidates. He argued that doing so would be going against what he stood for as a politician and that such a move would not help Zambians. He therefore decided that he would campaign for the MMD presidential candidate Levy Patrick Mwanawasa.[63]

Mung'omba's decision was condemned by some political parties and supported by others. Two NGOs-NOCE and ZIMT, which were generally believed to be pro-MMD-supported the decision by Mung'omba and ZAP. It is important, however, to observe that it is not unusual for weak political parties to align themselves with strong political parties. It is this same spirit that has prevented the emergence of a third strong political party in the United States. The electorate generally consider voting for a presidential candidate from a weak political party with little likelihood of winning as wasting one's vote. As such they tend to vote for their second-choice candidate. The battle for votes then is between two perceived strong parties. There is no doubt that in the political environment leading to the 2001 tripartite elections, ZAP was in a very weak position to field a presidential candidate. Mung'omba's decision, therefore, was in line with what is considered political agility.

Despite what appeared to be political agility on the part of Mung'omba, ZAP as a political party initially threw its weight behind the MMD presidential candidate Levy Patrick Mwanawasa in line with their president. However, following the announcement of MMD adopted parliamentary candidates, ZAP spokesperson Makungo told the press on 31 October that ZAP had revisited its decision and had decided to withdraw its support for Levy Mwanawasa. ZAP argued that the adoption of Peter Machungwa, Golden Mandandi, Katele Kalumba and Patrick Katyoka meant that Levy Mwanawasa would end up with a cabinet of corrupt leaders if elected. In their view Mwanawasa would therefore not meaningfully and positively contribute to the political process of the country while surrounded by such leaders.

Zambia Republican Party (ZRP)

The ZRP was registered as such on 9 August 2000 following a merger of the New Republican Party, the Republican Party founded by Benjamin Y. Mwila in 1998 and the ZAP. Mwila assumed the presidency of the ZRP because his RP was the strongest at the time of the merger. Mwila founded the RP following his expulsion from the MMD for openly declaring his intention to stand for the MMD presidency when President Chiluba's second and final term came to a close. President Chiluba was not happy with that development. Unknown to most people at the time, President Chiluba was nursing ideas about changing the MMD and republican constitutions to facilitate his reelection to both MMD and republican presidency. President Chiluba therefore banned members of the ruling MMD from campaigning for party presidency.

Mwila decided to defy President Chiluba and declared that he would stand and started preparing for the elections. He was therefore expelled from the party, and they formed the RP. In retrospect and following the third term debate, it is arguable that Mwila had sensed President Chiluba's intentions when he banned MMD members from beginning to campaign for the MMD presidency. It was only when the third term debate was well under way that most people understood what the ban was all about. Mwila had shown rare courage by defying party president in 1998.

Unfortunately, since its formation the RP and later the ZRP never won a single seat in the various by-elections. Equally disappointing is the fact that the ZRP has shied away from contesting in some by-elections. Although its presidential candidate has conducted extensive country-wide campaign tours in preparation for the 2001 tripartite elections, its popularity and standing in the political arena will be seen only after the elections.

LACK OF INSTITUTIONALIZATION OF POLITICAL PARTIES

It is evident from the above that Zambian political parties lack a serious sense of institutionalization. This means defining, creating, developing and maintaining social institutions and the extent or degree of institutional characteristics at any given time. It is not therefore surprising that because of little institutionalization, political parties are easily manipulated by the government. Moreover, the ruling party circumscribed the activities of opposition political parties if not completely outlawing them. What is behind this?

The answer seems to come from the fact that although political parties first appeared on the Zambian political scene as far back as 1948, they are still in a state of flux. The state of flux has continued because, unlike in the American political system where two strong political parties emerged,[64] in Zambia two strong political parties that can meaningfully determine the political future of the country have not yet developed.

Both during the First Republic and the Third Republic, the regimes employed a wide range of tactics to hinder opposition activities, including imposing tight restrictions on legal sources of funding. Meanwhile the ruling party was largely unhindered in its use of public funding. The private sector, the only potential source of funding, thus resorted to covert funding of opposition political parties to avoid punitive actions by the government such as loss of government contracts and harassment by the tax authorities. As a result, opposition political parties became antagonistic to the ruling party and opposed everything it did. They saw their role in governance as ensuring that the ruling party fell from power by whatever means. Yet, from time to time political leader and those in the middle ranks constantly defected to either the ruling party or the party that appeared most promising to offer rewards to individual leaders. This constant shift of political leaders and their quest for personal achievement maintained that state of flux of the opposition political parties in Zambia, especially during the run-up to the 2001 tripartite elections.

Arguably, therefore, this lack of institutionalization of political parties became even more evident in other important respects. Modern party systems are invariably involved in interlocking relationships with other political institutions as controllers of the military and other national bureaucracies, as recruiters of judicial personnel, as coalition builders among organized interest groups, as civic educators and as managers of election systems. Because power is distributed among the institutions of a political system, it is usually the party system that must draw together the dispersed units of power to enable the country to achieve working consensus on public policies and legitimacy for its leaders and institutional operations. This, however, has not been the case in Zambia, where transparent adherence to the "rules of the game" has not been the norm. As a result, opposition political parties have generally assumed an antagonistic relationship with the ruling party. Worse still, opposition political parties have been characterized by frequent movement of party leaders and ordinary party members from one political party to another. This is because most political leaders and supporters alike lack commitment and are merely opportunists seeking government positions in a party that was promising to form the next government.

CONCLUSION

The manifestations of various views over the issues discussed in this chapter clearly show the mixed fortunes of multipartyism in the political history of Zambia. Consensus is the last thing to expect. Issues that those in Western democracies take for granted are a cause of much debate and controversy in a developing country like Zambia. That Zambia was democratizing and reforming its political institutions was unquestionable. Yet the participants in this process did not agree entirely. Part of the reason was that a third world democratizing country like Zambia was usually judged too harshly by both those in the West and even by its own citizens in the opposition. In Zambia the private media, while enjoying the freedom of a democratic nation, was the most critical of the political reform process in the country. The *Post Newspaper* is a good example in this case. The paper's editorials were critical and were perceived to be anti-MMD government. This should be understood in light of high expectations from most stakeholders in the country. Because the Third Republic was born out of a highly restrictive, paternalistic and autocratic state, the citizens had very high expectations in the Third Republic.

Consequently, the democratic process was constantly under attack. The opposition political parties operated in this democracy, but were constantly suggesting that it did not exist. Opposition political party leaders felt that the party in power was undemocratic and went to extremes to test the party in power. UNIP, for example, was involved in some most undemocratic practices, hoping to provoke the government to take action that it could then use to claim that the MMD government was repressive. The UNIP leadership would never have left the MMD leaders free if they were involved in the burning of voter cards. But, because the MMD government adhered to the rule of law, it allowed UNIP the freedom to practice its civil disobedience campaign.

Yet, the greatest threat to Zambia's liberal democracy remained the lack of a credible opposition. Opposition parties were generally weak and most serious candidates tended to gravitate toward the MMD. Consequently this produced " the usual maladies of *de facto* one-party state government with some mild degree of corruption, presumption and bureaucratic malaise, although certainly mild by regional standards."[65] UNIP, which was generally expected to produce a credible opposition, was itself undergoing a major leadership crisis. As one prominent UNIP member observed during an interview, UNIP was suffering from a leadership crisis because no one in UNIP was bold enough to challenge former president Kaunda for the leadership of the party.[66] He noted that defying former president Kaunda was suicidal for most UNIP members, some of whom were capable of leading the party. This crisis was further compounded by the view that UNIP was "owned" by the Kaunda family. The election of Kaunda's son as UNIP president did not help matters.

UNIP's woes continued even after the 1996 elections. A top-secret letter to UNIP president Kaunda, written by UNIP Secretary General Sebastian S. Zulu, leaked to the press clearly highlighted continuing conflicts in the former ruling party. The letter was subsequently published in full in the *Times of Zambia* of Friday 28 April 1998.[67] In that letter, Zulu was advising Kaunda to retire from active politics. However, the major controversy in the letter arose from his desire to see some issues pointing to Major Wezi Kaunda's activities in the party addressed. It was generally believed that Major Wezi Kaunda had a strong desire to take over the leadership of the party from his father. He was murdered under very mysterious circumstances. Undoubtedly, therefore, the squabbles and power struggles within UNIP, primarily, and within other opposition parties, negatively affected their capacity to provide credible opposition and consequently their contribution toward the enhancement of the liberal democratic process in the country.

Thus far it can be safely concluded that Zambia's fledgling democracy during the first ten years of the Third Republic was largely a result of the weak opposition as well as the Movement for Multiparty Democracy's intransigence toward other political parties in the country. While there was much debate on the role of the ruling party to create an enabling environment for other stakeholders in the political arena, it was evident that the opposition was too weak to make a positive impact and strengthen liberal democracy in Zambia. The MMD, like UNIP before it, was also becoming intransigent and President Chiluba faced mounting criticism of authoritarianism and corruption. As President Chiluba was coming toward the end of his second term, there were clear signs that the MMD was facing serious challenges and its future as a ruling party was in doubt. Consequently, the MMD and President Chiluba in particular resorted to using district administrators to campaign for a change of constitution to facilitate his bid for a third term. Undoubtedly, the use of DAs and mobs to force a change of the constitution was a clear demonstration of Zambia's attempted retreat from liberal democracy to mobocracy. Yet, as noted above, mobocracy had become an attractive political phenomenon, which political parties used to deal with political opponents.

The 2001 tripartite elections were the most contested in terms of numbers of presidential, parliamentary and ward councilor candidates and political parties. The interest of the people in exercising their civic right to select leaders of their own choice was unmistakable. Unlike in the 1996 general elections where the people had to choose candidates from only MMD and ZDC, UNIP having boycotted the elections, or in 1991 when they had only a choice between UNIP and the MMD, they were now faced with a wider choice between a total of fifteen political parties, eleven of which sponsored presidential candidates. There were also at least eighty independents parliamentary candidates. The voters looked at the candidates closely and selected their candidates because of the party affiliation, ethnic background, level of education, status in society and articulation of issues, or promises of what will be achieved. The tripartite elections were held on 27 December 2001.

The selection of the candidate, after all the campaigns and promises, was left to the voter using the secret vote. A lot of contentious issues were raised and discussed openly in the press and at public meetings and in the compounds, townships and workplaces. They ranged from the eligibility of the presidential candidates; the issues surrounding the birthplace and citizenship of FDD presidential candidate Lieutenant General Christon Tembo and development issues; the state of the roads; marketing of agricultural produce, especially maize; unemployment, provision of social services, education, health and community services and many more. The source of campaign funds also became a major campaign subject with both the ruling MMD and opposition political parties accusing each other of using funds from dubious sources to finance their political campaigns.

Some issues were localized while others took a national perspective. Each issue provided the voter with a reason for choosing a candidate who it was hoped would bring development and assistance to the village constituency and district. The election was a participation in the electoral process. It was also the establishment of a covenant between the voters and the person elected as a member of parliament. If the trust and confidence is kept he or she is assured of reelection. If not, a new member will be elected. That is the beauty of the elections. They provide an environment for continuity or change.

The role of NGOs such as the Law Association of Zambia, and church organizations such as the Episcopal Conference of Zambia, the Evangelical Fellowship of Zambia and the Christian Council of Zambia; the Monitoring groups, ZIMT, FODEP, Afronet, Coalition 2001, NOCE, the women's organizations, and the various political parties helped to strengthen the democratic process. The actions of these and other groups helped to sensitize the public about the need for political reform, accountability, transparency and free and fair elections. The role of these groups was crucial to observance, upholding and continuance of the democratic process in Zambia. Elections will continue to be part and parcel of this exercise.

Another conclusion that can be drawn from this study is that political parties in Zambia need to rethink the process of adopting parliamentary candidates. That several adopted candidates from the MMD and other political parties were rejected by various constituencies where they were to stand was a clear indication that the processes used were not in line with democratic principles. Democracy is an expensive venture. It is therefore expected that political parties opt for cheaper processes of adopting candidates. Yet the more expensive process of holding primary elections to determine who gets adopted to stand against opponents from other political parties, would undoubtedly contribute significantly to the consolidation of the democratic process in the country. This would also ensure that the adoption of candidates reflects the wishes of the people on the ground, unlike the current situation, where the final decision rests with the highest organ of the party. As it happened with the MMD, some adopted candidates were not even interviewed resulting in their being rejected by constituency officials.

Primary elections would surely enhance transparency, which has been a major concern and, indeed, an essential ingredient for the consolidation of the democratic process in the country. The interview method has undoubtedly proved highly contentious and unsatisfactory as a means of democratically deciding who stands in parliamentary and ward elections. The experience of the 2001 tripartite elections and past general elections has shown that the interview method tends to strengthen instead of weakening patronage. Elected officials tend to look to higher organs of the party for support instead of the lower organs that give them the voters. Thus our democracy in the past has been top-down instead of bottom-up. As a result, once elected, official almost forget the electorate until the next round of elections and count on the higher organ of the party to adopt them. All they need to do is show up for the interview. This is why in some cases the MMD adopted candidates who did not even feature in the interviews during the 2001 tripartite elections, resulting in open rejection by members in the lower organs of the party.

On reflection, the lack of clear guidelines regarding campaign financing is yet another problem that affected the democratic process, especially the electoral process. The ruling MMD committed unlimited amounts of money toward the tripartite elections to the disadvantage of opposition political parties. A more disturbing development as a result of this lack of guidelines was the misuse of public funds by the ruling MMD. The diversion of 2 billion kwacha from Parliament to finance the MMD convention is a case in point. Perhaps less known are cases where the MMD made requests for funds from institutions such as the Ministry of Finance and the Zambia Revenue Authority (ZRA) to finance the campaign without the authority of Parliament. This prompted Emmanuel Kasonde, chairman of the ZRA Board, to resign his position when the MMD government requested K500 million without following the normal procedures and without explaining what the money was for.

Weeks later a ZRA employee who led a team of ZRA officers to Pilatus Engineering to demand duty on a fleet of vehicles that had been brought into the country without paying duty was locked up by the Police because as it turned out the vehicles were brought by Pilatus Engineering on behalf of the MMD and were all registered under the State House. There is therefore a case for developing clear guidelines for campaign financing in Zambian elections. While cases of this nature seem to affect the ruling political party, evidence suggests that even opposition political parties spend large sums of money buying votes. For example, *The Monitor* reported that "money exchanged hands in an effort to woo support from delegates, a development that has been cited as corruption contrary to the electoral code of conduct in a democratic nation."[68] On the other hand, other political parties traversed the country during their campaign trail with loads of bundles of *salaula* (second hand clothes) for distribution to the electorates. Undoubtedly, this amounted to vote buying and in a country where poverty was rife the practice influenced voters.

From the number of political parties that participated in the 2001 tripartite elections, and the results that emerged at the end of the exercise, it can be safely concluded that despite several difficulties experienced during this process, Zambia once again demonstrated that it was building a democratic political system. Indeed, as Larry Diamond and Dennis Galvin noted, democracy, especially mature democracy takes long to develop and the path toward it is not a smooth one.[69] With each election that takes place, democracy moves a step further toward maturity.

Notes

1. Donald Chanda, *Democracy in Zambia: Key Speeches of President Chiluba 1991-92* (Lusaka: Africa Press Trust, 1993), p.1.
2. John M. Mwanakatwe, *End of Kaunda Era* (Lusaka: Multimedia Publications, 1994), p. 36.
3. Mwanakatwe, *End of Kaunda* Era, p. 36.
4. *New African*, March 1991, p.18.
5. *New African*, March 1991, p.18.
6. Alfred W. Chanda, "Zambia's Fledgling Democracy: Prospect for the Future," *Zambia Law Journal*, 25-28 (1993-96), p.142.
7. Tenthani Mwanza, in *The Post*. He referred to President Chiluba as a fool and that all who voted for him are fools. That he got away with it shows the level of tolerance under MMD. In the UNIP era Mwanza would have been detained for similar remarks on the president.

8.   A.W. Chanda, Zambia's Fledgling Democracy, p. 135.

9.   *Times of Zambia*, Tuesday 19 November 1996.

10.   *Zambia Daily Mail*, Friday October 1996.

11.   *Times of Zambia*, Tuesday 29 July 1997.

12.   *Times of Zambia*, Tuesday 29 July 1997.

13.   Republic of Zambia, *Report of the Constitutional Review Commission* (Lusaka: Government Printer, 1995), Section 12:12:1, p. 52.

14.   Mwanakatwe, *End of Kaunda Era*, p.185.

15.   *The Post*, Tuesday 12 November 1996.

16.   *The Post*, Tuesday 12 November 1996.

17.   *Times of Zambia*, Friday 25 July 1997.

18.   *Summary of the Recommendations of the Mwanakatwe Constitutional Review Commission and Government Reaction to the Report*, Government White Paper No. 1 1995, pp. 104-06.

19.   Chanda, "Zambia's Fledgling Democracy," p. 145.

20.   Mwanakatwe, *End of Kaunda Era*, p. 219.

21.   Fr. Ives Chituta Bantungwa, "The Role of the Church in the Democratisation Process in Africa: The Zambian Experience," *The Courier*, No. 134 (July-August 1992), p. 70.

22   Mwanakatwe, *End of Kaunda Era*, p. 220.

23.   Mwanakatwe, *End of Kaunda Era*, p. 220.

24.   *National Mirror*, 26 February- 4 March 1995.

25.   Chanda, "Zambia's Fledgling Democracy", p. 146.

26.   *Zambia Daily Mail*, Friday 5 September 1997.

27.   *Zambia Daily Mail*, 5 September 1997.

28.   *Times of Zambia*, 4 September 1997.

29.   *Zambia Daily Mail*, 5 September 1997.

30.   *Times of Zambia*, 8 September 1997.

31.   *Times of Zambia*, 9 September 1997.

32.   Chanda, "Zambia's Fledgling Democracy," p. 135. A.W. Chanda is the president of the Forum for Democratic Process (FODEP) which has been generally very critical of the MMD government.

33.   *The Post*, 2 October 1996. By the end of 2000 the privatisation programme was almost complete.

34.   This part of the book was drafted as the coup attempt was in progress.

35.   "*KK Warns of an Explosion*," *The Post*, Monday 27 October 1997.

36.   Zambia National Broadcasting Corporation, Announcement by Captain Solo at 06:00 on Tuesday 28 October 1997.

37.   *Times of Zambia*, 30 October 1997 and 31 October 1997.

38.   *Zambia Daily Mail*, 30 October 1997.

39.   *Times of Zambia*, 30 October 1997.

40. *Zambia Daily Mail*, 31 October 1997.

41. *The Post*, 30 October 1997.

42. *The Post*, 30 October 1997.

43. Bertha Osei-Hwedie, "The Role of Ethnicity in Multi-Party Politics in Malawi and Zambia," *Journal of Contemporary African Studies*, 16, 2 (1998), p. 228.

44. Richard Sandbrook, *Politics of Africa's Economic Recovery* (Cambridge: Cambridge University Press, 1993), p. 96.

45. Osei-Hwedie, "The Role of Ethnicity in Multi-Party Politics," p. 229.

46. H. Herzog, "Social Construction of Reality in Ethnic Terms: The Case of Political Ethnicity in Israel," *International Review of Modern Sociology*, 15, 1-2 ((1985), p. 46.

47. Osei-Hwedie, "The Role of Ethnicity in Multi-Party Politics," p. 231.

48. *The Post*, Friday 12 October 2001.

49. *The Post*, Friday 12 October 2001.

50. "Chiluba Funds Third Term Bid," *The Monitor*, Online Issue Number 133, URL http://www.afronet.org.za/monitor133/headline1.htm.

51. *Times of Zambia*, Friday 2 March 2001; *Zambia Daily Mail*, Friday 2 March 2001.

52. Gideon Thole, "Zambians Gang Up Against Chiluba's Third Term," Information Dispatch Online, Thursday 22 February 2001, URL http://www.dispatch.co.zm/news. See also "We Pray That Chiluba Comes To His Senses, Says Mwanakatwe," Information Dispatch Online, Thursday 22 February 2001, URL http://www.dispatch.co.zm/news.

53. *The Post*, Monday 28 May 2001.

54. *The Post*, 28 December 2000.

55. *Zambia Daily Mail*, Saturday 5 May 2001.

56. *Zambia Daily Mail*, Saturday 5 May 2001.

57. *The Post*, Friday 4 May 2001.

58. "The Barometer: MMD Face Another Split Over Presidential Candidate," *Elections Digest*, 1-6 June 2001.

59. *The Post*, Thursday 14 June 2001. Minister Without Portfolio Michael Sata told MMD cadres that he was ready to "throw punches" if he was insulted.

60. *The Post*, Wednesday 18 July 2001.

61. *Zambia Daily Mail*, Saturday 27 October 2001.

62. "The Zambian Crisis" *The Monitor*, Issue No. 109 Friday 2-Thursday 8 June 2000.

63. *The Post*, Tuesday 23 October 2001.

64. For details see John F. Bibby, "Political Parties in the United States," in George Clark (ed.), *United States Elections 2000* (Washington, DC: US Department of State, 2000), pp. 2-7.

65. Wayne C. Johnston, "Zambia: Eye of the Political Storm," http://www.chalcedon.edu/report/97oct/so6.htm.

66. Anonymous Interview Lusaka, July 1997. However, when President Kaunda finally retired from active politics in 2000, UNIP was plunged into a deep leadership crisis.

67. *Times of Zambia*, Friday 28 April 1998.

68. *The Monitor*, October 19-25, 2001.

69. Diamond, Larry and Dennis Galvin. "Sub-Saharan Africa," in Robert Wesson (ed.), *Democracy: A World Survey 1987* (New York: Praeger Publishers, 1987), pp. 64.

CONCLUSION

Sir John S. Moffat's suggestion, that "democracy ... can only flourish in a mature and stable society with a stability established by a long tradition,"[1] summarizes the burden of this study. It has been shown that colonial Zambia did not have a long tradition of liberal democracy during the colonial period. In contrast to the white dominions of Australia, Canada and New Zealand, or even the neighboring colony of Southern Rhodesia, colonial Zambia never experienced a period of responsible government during which different parties took turns in forming the government under the tutelage of the Colonial Office. Indeed, until five years before independence, the country did not even experience party politics. Between 1962 and 1964 three constitutions were written.[2] The 1964 constitution placed power in an executive president. This represented a change from the form of parliamentary government as a dependency to presidential government at independence.

The transition from colonial rule to independence did not provide any experience of liberal democracy. The crucial elements of liberal democracy never developed. Instead, the educated elite who dominated the postcolonial state proceeded to behave exactly as seventy years of colonialism had taught them. Michael Crowder argued that "if the colonial state provided a model for its inheritors it was that government rested not on consent but force." This was to later provide the fertile ground for mobocracy, particularly in the Third Republic.[3] African nationalists had never experienced liberal democracy. They were products of their history and governed much the same as the British before them had. During the decolonization period, the "government-in-waiting"[4] was not an opposition party *per se*, but an African nationalist movement propelled by the search for pigmentational self-determination. Indeed, "democracy, for nationalist forces in the era of decolonization, was a theory of challenge to the colonial order, a vehicle to contest its hegemony and accelerate its departure."[5] A "government-in-waiting" was no longer desirable after independence. Evidently the commitment to liberal democracy was a transitory one.

Because colonial Zambia came into being in only 1911 when North-Eastern Rhodesia and North-Western Rhodesia were amalgamated in response to the financial—not political—concerns of the British South Africa Company, the country remained politically fragmented. The Colonial Office takeover of the administration of the country in 1924 did not significantly alter the political orientation of the territory. The use of chiefs and their village headmen as units of the colonial state continued the political fragmentation of the country. It was only after the creation of the African Representative Council in 1946 that colonial officials began to reorient emerging African politicians to think of themselves as Northern Rhodesians. Africans soon took advantage of this process and founded the African National Congress, which sought to unify Africans in the territory and push for political liberation.

The absence of political pluralism during the colonial period benefited African nationalists in their struggle for political power. Africans were able to respond, almost in unison, to the British desire to see a well-organized nationalist movement that commanded mass support under an undisputed leader. Desiring to make their withdrawal easy and as painless as possible, the British almost demanded unanimity among Africans, a one-party state in waiting, before they handed over power. This encouraged Africans to coalesce around one political movement.[6] Kaunda's exposition that "the mass of the people supported one party and were prepared to trust that party with the task of guiding the new nation,"[7] is reminiscent of Ernest Gellner's perceptive observation that "nationalism is not the awakening of nations to self-consciousness: it *invents* nations where they did not exist."[8] However, in the colonial Zambian context, as in other former British colonies, the imagined or invented nation reflected the colonial state that the African political elites sought to protect and preserve. As Anderson argued, the magic of colonization and later "of nationalism turn[ed] chance into destiny."[9] Colonialism provided the frontiers that later signified UNIP's "One Zambia One Nation" slogan. Also, as Young stated, "the model of the constitutional state utilized as the exemplary vision of the ideal polity to be replicated in the structure of decolonization was the metropolitan state".[10] However the metropolitan parliamentary model lasted only two years (1962-1964), and the liberal democracy model only eight years until the one-party state in 1972. Once independence had been achieved, the metropolitan model faded rapidly as clinging to power became the dominant aim and new models became attractive. Over much of the continent the new and fashionable model was the one-party state or military dictatorship.

The dream of the metropolitan model was shared by all who believed that colonial Zambia was their home. The process of decolonization, however, brought to light several realities of the shared dream. While there was no desire to change the frontiers of the postcolonial state, there was nonetheless disagreement over its political orientation and who should control it. These issues were reflected in the debate between liberals and African nationalists and the civil society. Since most liberals were white, they were associated with the colonial state in the minds of most African nationalists. Thus, while the Capricorn Africa Society genuinely sought to preserve and consolidate the crucial elements of liberal democracy, it was heavily suspected of working to preserve white supremacy. Political pluralism and liberal democracy were considered the greatest threat to a unified nationalist movement by radical African nationalists. In the end, liberalism as an alternative approach for the decolonization of colonial Zambia was rejected by most African nationalists.

While the African educated elites initially found common cause with white liberals, the alliance for most elites was short-lived. The slow pace of economic and political liberalization, and especially the politics that preceded the formation of the Federation of Rhodesia and Nyasaland in 1953, radicalized African political thought. Liberalism lost ground as most African nationalists took to militant politics as the quickest way of achieving political results. White liberals made a serious political error when they supported the Federation despite African opposition. For the small settler communities of colonial Zambia and Nyasaland, federation was less about economics (the main propaganda in its favor) than it was about saving a substantial degree of white power. Liberals should not have been a part to such a scheme. However given their belief in economic development before political responsibility, particularly by more conservative liberals, they fell easy prey to the propaganda for federation. As a result, they became suspect among most Africans. They were never able to shake the image that they were white first and liberals a long way second.

Yet, nationalism itself was never a monolithic political movement. It represented several interests loosely held together by the desire to get rid of white rule. The very fragility of unity of the nationalist movement made it fear and resent liberal democracy. Many Africans were either coerced or persuaded into believing that African unity of expression was essential until white rule was replaced. Only after independence would dissent—liberal democracy—be permitted. However, the independent government felt no more secure than it had as a nationalist movement. Since the nationalists had been held together by fear that colonialism might remain should they quarrel, they felt quite uncomfortable when it was gone. They thus invented fears of multinational companies conspiring or the South Africans plotting to replace British colonialism.

Despite the apparent common objective, there were disagreements on how best to proceed. This led to the split of the ANC in 1958, after which the nationalist movement remained divided. While the 1958 split could have formed a base for political pluralism, the brief period of colonial tutelage did not make this possible. More important, "the ephemeral nature of the graft cuttings of parliamentary democracy upon the robust trunk of autocracy,"[11] during the terminal colonial state proved to serve only as a legitimating myth for the power transfer process. The autocratic and hegemonic impulses of the colonial state that had a more enduring legacy were replicated in the postcolonial state. The dominant political party became intransigent and sought to eliminate the opposition, first through the ballot box and later, when this proved impossible, through legislation. Because the masses had never experienced liberal democracy during the colonial period, they were easy prey for UNIP rhetoric. It was not as if the masses were losing something that they had enjoyed and came to value. In so doing UNIP behaved exactly like the colonial state. By 1969 Zambia was *de facto* a one-party state. Three years later the country was *de jure* a one-party state. This represented a failure of liberal democracy in postindependence Zambia. More important, perhaps, the one-party state was President Kaunda's contribution to dealing with political ethnicity that was threatening the political future of Zambia.

In both South Africa and colonial Zambia, the failure of "political liberalism" has been attributed to the belief by liberals in the power of persuasion. It has been suggested that liberals sought to direct the white minority towards a "universal truth, morality or humanity" *vis-à-vis* an alternative that guaranteed the material benefits of their power and privilege.[12] It is true that many liberals had reservations about handing over political power to Africans before Africans were "ready." In fact, many white settlers believed that liberalism provided too many compromises with Africans and would eventually lead to lowering standards in government. Yet in the case of colonial Zambia, liberalism was anathematized by most Africans because of its insistence on gradualism in order to consolidate the crucial elements of liberal democracy.

By the early 1960s it was evident that multiracialism—the strategic platform of liberal ideology—had almost faded away because of the ability of nationalists to ridicule liberals into silence. In colonial Zambia however, liberals managed "to become the Government and ... [tried], in the desperately short time available to ... ruthlessly ... abolish all distinctions based on color alone and to start a crash program to obliterate difference and inequalities between races."[13] That brief interlude (February to November 1961) of liberal government did very little to reassure African nationalists or, for that matter, provide enough experience for liberal democracy in the country. Nonetheless, "liberals had already adjusted to a world where they were no longer "the Baas." More important, they may have been defeated, but at least they had tried".[14] Thus at independence they resolved to rally behind the triumphant nationalist party—the United National Independence Party.

The triumph of UNIP signaled the rejection of the liberal ideology that advocated multiracialism. Liberalism in Central Africa recognized that divisions in society were inevitable, but that where and when such divisions were necessary, the criteria should be material and educational progress. In other words, Central African liberals accepted and encouraged the creation of economic and social classes.

Yet in the circumstances of colonial Zambia, liberals were weakened by their ambivalent class position. Because they wanted to give democratic power to everyone gradually while maintaining European values, they were accused of seeking to preserve the status quo. UNIP adopted the convergence theory and thereby neutralized political-class differentiation that liberals were keen to maintain. Furthermore, liberals were weakened by being absorbed into the more radical mobilizational party that secured a dominant electoral position at independence. UNIP used the convergence theory as an ingredient in its campaign for national unity. In the end, through coercion, persuasion and even economic blackmail Zambia became a one-party state in December 1972.

In its day Capricorn propounded three major ideas.[15] It argued for a qualitative and not universal franchise, in opposition to both the white settler nationalism influenced by South African ideology and "Africanism" of black nationalists influenced by ideas from further north. Its hope was the creation of a racially fluid and expanding ruling middle class elite. From this flowed the idea of a multiparty liberal constitutionalism deemed essential in an open society. Capricorn also looked to the formation of a wider East and Central African Federation and supported the campaign to establish the Central African Federation, abandoning federation only when it appeared to be terminally ill.

Until recently it seemed as if these goals were fleeting illusions, even in the lifetime of Capricorn. Surely they were all swept away irrevocably in the triumph of African nationalism. The qualitative franchise lasted only so long as settlers were able to prevent universal suffrage, and looked increasingly like the last desperate attempts to stop the flow of history. When UNIP came to power it seemed to assume that it was an axiomatic political aim to get rid of all other parties, first by sweeping them away through its electoral support, and when that failed, by making them illegal. Pan-East-Central Africanism was a nonstarter. The Central African Federation was swept away as the preliminary, not the climax, of the transfer of power into African hands in colonial Zambia and Nyasaland. Nothing, it seemed, was left of Capricorn's ideas and concepts.

Recently, however, these same concepts have had a renaissance in new form, spoken through African mouths. The one-party state in Zambia became bankrupt and the postcolonial regime gave way to a multiparty political system accompanied by freedom of association and of the press and a renewed emphasis on the freedom of the individual.[16] The government scheduled multiparty presidential and parliamentary elections for October 1991 where the main political contender was Frederick Chiluba's Movement for Multiparty Democracy.[17] These events were certainly a revival of liberal democracy, without the restrictions suggested by liberals in the 1960s. Since 1991 Zambia was under a political system that facilitated the formation of over thirty-five political parties. The political reform process is still in progress, but it is under severe stress from opposition political parties and some NGOs. Even under these conditions, it is evident that Zambia became an example in the subregion that it is possible in Africa to change governments peacefully through the ballot box.

Undoubtedly, the major issue that threatened Zambia's democracy in the Third Republic was the weak opposition, which was too divided to provide any meaningful checks and balances to the ruling MMD. During the first ten years of the Third Republic, Zambia witnessed major splits and fragmentation in the opposition parties, as well as the ruling MMD itself. These events were not healthy for a developing democracy, for they led only to the development of a *de facto* one-party state. A majority of the opposition political parties never held elections. Most existed only on paper. Party posts were held by appointed leaders. Such political parties could not be expected to effectively participate in national democratic elections, let alone form a democratic government if elected into office.

Thus for democracy to flourish in the country, it is expected that political parties practice democracy within themselves and minimize the tendency to form splinter groups at the slightest incident of disagreement. Politicians, both in the ruling MMD and the opposition, should learn to agree to disagree.

Perhaps a major threat to Zambia's multiparty democracy in the Third Republic was people's disillusionment with democracy and the MMD government. As Alfred W. Chanda observed, "citizens have withdrawn from the political process because they are disillusioned with the activities of politicians."[18] This withdrawal was reflected in the low turnout at by-elections that were held since the 1991, and the presidential and parliamentary elections held in 1996. Of the 4.6 million eligible voters who were expected to register for the 1996 elections, only 2.3 million voters registered. Worse still, women who since independence were leading in the voters' registration exercise stayed away, resulting in few appearing on on the voters roll, prompting the Women's Lobby Group to call upon women to register as voters.

Events of mid 2000 and 2001 where the ruling MMD witnessed massive suspensions and expulsions of prominent party members signified serious problems in the party. What was most puzzling was that the suspensions and expulsions did not conform to theories of political ethnicity. This is because some of the people at the center of the conflict were members of Chiluba's ethnic group and some were known close relatives. It is from this perspective that this study suggests a rethinking about the continued use of political ethnicity as a useful tool for analyzing politics in Zambia. It is plausible to suggest that individual greed, coupled with personal glorification, contributed to conflicts in the political arena. There is no doubt that the showdown between Benjamin Y. Mwila and the MMD was a case in point.[19] For how else would one explain the political confrontation between an uncle and a nephew? Certainly not political ethnicity.

As we conclude this study it should be noted that "the character of society is determined by the action of individuals, who, while acting on their own, must remember that they are part of a society in which collective action is necessary."[20] Dickson A. Mungazi further suggests that individual action and collective action both require observance of rules of conduct and behavior that have evolved over a long period of time. Accordingly, individuals are either liberal, conservative or moderate. However, to this list of political behavior can be added radical, as was the case in Zambia and Zimbabwe. Thus in Zambia, multiparty politics have had to contend with radicals who are not favorably disposed to democracy, hence the emergence of a one-party dictatorship.

White liberals in colonial Zambia subscribed to liberal political philosophy like their counterparts in colonial Zimbabwe. Undoubtedly, they contributed to the transformation of the Zambian society. It is equally important to point out that resulting from the activities of liberals and civil society, Zambians demand that they must be involved at every stage and phase of developing a national policy.

While liberalism in both South Africa and Zambia failed to achieve constitutional nationalism, it contributed significantly to moderating political dialogue in the sense that liberals played a crucial role in mitigating against violence. There is no doubt that in colonial Zambia as in South Africa, the rhetoric of nationalism, liberalism and pluralism formed the basis for dealing with ethnicity and group rights. This is why although President Kaunda was not a liberal, he was guardedly attracted to white liberals.

There are also undeniable parallels between colonial Zambian liberalism and South African liberalism. Both were engaged in an unending struggle to define their own position in relation to African nationalism and white nationalism during the era of decolonization and struggle for majority rule. In both South Africa and colonial Zambia, neither African nationalists nor white nationalists trusted liberals. In the case of South Africa, Afrikaner nationalist saw liberalism as a threat because it demanded equal rights for black people.[21] On the other hand, African nationalists saw liberalism as a drawback because it insisted on gradual peaceful change and guarantees for all individuals and minorities. In the Zambian context, Capricorn and other liberal organizations were shunned by both whites and African nationalists for precisely the same reasons.

The fragility of democracy in Zambia became more noticeable as mobocracy took a centre stage in the political arena. Both the ruling MMD and opposition UNIP appeared to embrass the mobocracy ideology by allowing the mob to dictate the direction of their respective parties and the political process in the country. This process engineered a serious political crisis that was manifested in the call for the amendment of the constitution to facilitate President Chiluba's bid for a third term. It should be pointed out that the pro-third term campaigners were strong belivers in a party strongman and had a fanatical faith in the leader principle in same way that UNIP supporters campaigned for President Kaunda. They were convinced that only President Chiluba would ensure continued rule by the MMD. It was for that reason that they vehemently sponsored and secured the amendment of the MMD constitution. Only the massive opposition by the civil society, opposition political parties and members of the MMD opposed to the third term made President Chiluba change his mind regarding running for a third term.

UNIP on the other hand continued to suffer from a leadership crisis since former President Kaunda retired from active politics. Since 1991 when former President Kaunda lost to President Chiluba, UNIP did not have a strongman and by 2001 it was still facing a leadership crisis. Undoubtedly, democracy in Zambia seems to be under serious stress. While the anti-third term campaigners relied on the power of pursuasion like liberals before them, the pro-third term campaigners relied on intimidation and the mobs, variously called party cadres or party militants. It is in this respect that there was a sense in which democracy seemed to have given way to mobocracy in the first ten years of the Third Republic. However, unlike liberals in colonial Zambia who lost to militant nationalists, the anti-third term campaigners aided by student demonstrations and civil society kept mobocracy in check.

The 2001 tripartite elections seemed to provide yet another building block in the process of consolidating democracy in Zambia despite the many hurdles experienced since 1991. Despite the challenges of multipartyism experienced since 1991, the democratization process, and consolidation of democracy in Zambia appeared to be on course in 2001.

Notes

1. NAZ, SEC 5/270, Sir John S. Moffat, Text of the speech given during the presentation of the Moffat Resolution in the Northern Rhodesia Legislative Council on 29 July 1954.

2. M.G. de Winton, "Decolonization and the Westminster Model," in A.H.M. Kirk-Greene (ed.), *The Transfer of Power: The Colonial Administration in the Age of Decolonization* (Kidlington Oxford: Oxford University Press, 1979), p. 189.

3. Michael Crowder, "Whose Dream Was It Anyway?: Twenty-Five Years of African Independence," *African Affairs*, 86, 342 (1987), p. 13.

4. Kenneth D. Kaunda and Colin Morris, *A Humanist in Africa: Letters to Colin Morris from Kenneth D. Kaunda* (London: Longmans, 1966), p. 107.

5. Crawford Young, "The African Colonial State and Its Political Legacy," in Donald Rothchild and Naomi Chazan (eds.), *The Precarious Balance: State and Society in Africa*, (Boulder, CO: Westview Press, 1988), p. 53.

6. Kaunda and Morris, *A Humanist in Africa*, p. 107. This was hardly the case for Northern Rhodesia where the nationalist movement split in 1958. Yet when faced with the choice of forming a coalition government with either the UFP or UNIP in 1963, Nkumbula chose to go with UNIP.

7. Kaunda and Morris, *A Humanist in Africa*, p. 107.

8. Ernest Gellner, *Thought and Change* (London: Weidenfeld and Nicholson, 1964), p. 169, cited in Benedict Anderson, *Imagined Communities: Reflections on the Origins and Spread of Nationalism* (London: Verso, 1983), p. 15.

9. Anderson, *Imagined Communities*, p. 19.

10. Young, "The African Colonial State," p. 53. However, it ought to be pointed out that in reality the actual experience of colonial rule was autocratic, and never functioned in the way that the model state was imagined.

11. Young, "The African Colonial State," p. 57.

12. Heribert Adam, "The Failure of Political Liberalism," in Heribert Adam and Hermann Giliomee (eds.), *The Rise and Crisis of Afrikaner Power* (Cape Town: David Philip, 1979), p. 266.

13. Sir John Moffat, "The Role of the Liberal in Rhodesian Politics," *Central African Examiner*, (24 September 1960), p. 12.

14. Ian Hancock, *White Liberals, Moderates and Radicals in Rhodesia 1953-1980* (London: Croom Helm, 1984), p. 216. The term "baas" is a South African (Afrikaans) word for "boss". In Central Africa, as in South Africa it was used by Africans in addressing Europeans. Among Africans in Northern Rhodesia, "baas" became "bwana".

15. For details see Chapters Two and Three.

16. *Africa Confidential*, 31, 20 (12 October 1990), p. 6.

17. Frederick Chiluba was, until his election as president of the MMD, chairman-general of the Zambia Congress of Trade Unions, which championed the cause for multiparty politics.(*Africa Confidential*, 32, 5 [8 March 1991]), p. 5).

18. Alfred W. Chanda, "Zambia's Fledgling Democracy: Prospects for the Future," *Zambia Law Journal*, 25-28 (1993-96), p.148.

19. See Chapter Seven.

20. Dickson A. Mungazi, *The Last British Liberals in Africa: Michael Blundell and Garfield Todd* (Westport, CT: Praeger Publishers, 1999), p.2.

21. Johan Degenaar, "Nationalism, Liberalism, and Pluralism", in Jeffrey Butler, Richard Elphick, and David John Welsh (eds.), *Democratic Liberalism in South Africa: Its History and Prospect* (Middletown, CT: Wesleyan University Press, 1987), p. 240.

APPENDICES

APPENDIX I: THE SALISBURY DECLARATIONS: 1952

We, the sponsors of the Capricorn Declarations, affirm the beliefs which have guided us in their preparation and which will inspire us in their fulfilment.

We hold that all men, despite their varying talents, are born equal in dignity before God, and have a common duty to one another. We hold that the differences between men, whether of creed or colour, are honourable differences. We emphasise this simple precept of Christian teaching because it is fundamental to our beliefs, and also because we wish to dissociate ourselves from the barren philosophy which determines racial legislation in lands beyond our boundaries.

We believe in the destiny of the British East and Central African territories and their peoples. We believe that the colonies of Southern Rhodesia, and Kenya, the protectorates of Uganda, Nyasaland and Northern Rhodesia, the territory of Tanganyika, should be bound in a single self-governing federation under the British Crown, wherein men of all races may live side by side in harmony, sufficiency and freedom.

We believe that to strive towards such a goal will provide a sense of shared purpose and dedication transcending racial differences; and that its attainment will bring untold benefits to Africa and its people, to the British Commonwealth of Nations and to mankind.

Bound by these convictions, we submit that:

1. Africa South of the Sahara is comparable in natural resources with other continents of the world. The extent of mineral, agricultural and

industrial potentialities is only being established by research and development.

2. The peoples of Europe have two responsibilities in Africa, and these are complimentary to one another. They have an obligation to mankind to develop that continent jointly with the Africans, so that it shall contribute from its great resources to the wealth of the world. They have an equal obligation to give to the African both incentive and opportunity to achieve higher standards of life, and so make possible a true partnership between the races.

3. The African peoples as yet lack the technical skill, the industrial maturity and indeed the numbers to secure by themselves the timely development of the continent. The twofold responsibility of the European cannot be discharged by reserving all Africa's sparsely populated areas for gradual development at a pace determined by the African's birth rate. It can be discharged, and Africa's development quickened, by an increasing combination of western immigration and technology with the latent capacity of the African and other races.

4. British East and Central Africa is divided into many separate territories with separate administrations. The divisions are for the most part arbitrary and are seldom based on considerations of geography, economics or race. They deny the urge, increasingly felt among all races, to become part of a greater communion, racially and economically. In a larger political and economic unit, problems which are obstinate of solution within individual territories can be more readily resolved.

The consequent economic expansion might well create a nucleus so strong that in time the neighbouring non-British territories would desire to negotiate customs union and other commercial and security arrangements with the Federal Government. The achievement now of Central African Federation should thus be seen as the first step in the unfolding history of a continent's integration.

5. The Federal Government of East and Central Africa proposed in the Declarations must have the legal authority and moral force to weld the six territories into a single economic entity and to become the focus of loyalty for all its citizens. The allocation of powers between the federation and the territories must be made with this end in view.

6. Sustained social and economic progress for any race in the Federation demands sound administration and political stability, which at the outset will call for European leadership and guidance in federal and territorial government. This leadership can be claimed only by right of administrative ability and experience, not of colour. It will not endure, nor deserve to endure, unless it encourages the participation of other races.

7. The successful federation of the six territories will depend essentially upon a policy of race relations which is flexible enough to meet the special requirements of each territory; and broad and liberal enough to face with confidence the scrutiny of enlightened opinion throughout the world. The Federal Government must hold in trust the interest of all Africa's peoples, and its constant duty must be to ensure that the federal structure corresponds to the growing capacities of all sections in the community.

It must promote the spiritual, economic, cultural and political progress of the African. All Africans who have attained the necessary social and educational standard must be accorded the responsibility of franchise and be given no less opportunity than their European fellow citizens to play their part in an expanding, civilised community. At the same time the Federal Government must help those Africans who are unable or unwilling to accommodate themselves to the new economy and way of life to develop in their own ares at a pace consistent with their abilities.

In conclusion, we submit that the leaders of all races in all six territories must be called upon to establish a standing convention to press for the attainment of the objects set out in these Declarations. The Society will convene the first assembly, and place before it the more detailed proposals which follow.

Article 1
The three fundamental aims of policy are to:
(a) Promote the spiritual, economic, educational, cultural and political progress of the African.
(b) Provide full opportunities for those Africans who are unable or unwilling to accommodate themselves to the European way of life, to develop in Reserves and other Native areas, at a pace consistent with their abilities. In these areas, Native interests would be paramount.
(c) Encourage European immigration on a scale required to meet the needs of the developing, economy, but consistent with the legitimate land requirements of the African population.

Article 2

To achieve these objectives, each of the three territories should be divided into two main areas—the Native areas, and the European or Open areas. (In the case of Kenya, cognisance must be further taken other areas, such as the coastal belt protectorate.)

In the Native area, no non-African would be permitted to own land, reside or carry on any business except in an official capacity, or if that business resulted in the furthering of African interests. (From this provision mining and existing trading rights, subject to proper safeguards, would be excluded.)

In the Open areas, the rights of the non-European to own land would be limited to ownership of residential and trading sites in certain urban areas. Apart from this limitation, the paramount interest in this area would be that of civilisation and progress, not the interests of any race, colour or creed.

Certain restrictions on the movement of Africans between the areas might be necessary to prevent social evils arising from the growth of "shanty" towns in the Open areas, and likewise to avoid undue pressure on the lands of the Native areas.

Article 3

In the Open areas, the State Government would be permitted to lay down conditions which would ensure European standards of living and proficiency for any trade or calling. All achieving those standards would have the right to seek employment in those trades.

Political rights would be enjoyed by those Africans who desire them and who had reached the standards of culture and civilisation judged to be requisite for the exercise of such rights.

To avoid all risk of lowering the standards of European civilisation, it would be necessary to constitute a Federal Authority to lay down the principles which would determine the granting of political rights and also the merits of individual claimants. To ensure justice in this matter, any claimant who considered that his application had been unfairly refused, would have the right of appeal to the courts.

Article 4

The policy requires that active development of native areas for the benefit of their inhabitants as the first consideration.

The State would encourage industries financed from outside the Native areas; the natural growth of Trade Unions to protect workers' interests; the flow of revenue to the Native Authority, creation, where desired, of cooperative societies; and the steady development of an African middle class.

The Africans in these areas would have communal representation and an increasing degree of self-administration.

8. Certain areas of reasonable or good economic prospect within the six territories, which have a substantial African population and a relatively small European settlement, should be designated "Native States". The electorate of such states would, in due time, have representation on the federal Government and a full measure of state autonomy.

The Federal Government and state and territorial legislatures should accept the principle that the political advance of the African must be kept in line with, and not ahead of, his economic and cultural advance.

9. Unrestricted Asiatic immigration would, however, be damaging to the aim of encouraging the African to achieve European standards and moulding East and central Africa into a modern democratic state. Many Asiatic people would gladly participate in the federation's cultural and political life, provided their attachment to Asia was not encouraged by fresh Asiatic immigration.

10. In order to maintain administrative continuity the Colonial service should be gradually merged into a new federal civil service. The officials should take, as soon as the federal proposals have been carried out, their directive from the Federal Government.

11. Constitutional changes, which are now being considered in any of the six territories, should not be put into effect if they are in any way liable to prejudice the federation of East and Central Africa, or conflict with the spirit of these Declarations.

12. The leaders in all six territories of all races should be called upon to establish a Standing Convention to press for the attainment of the objectives set forth in these Declarations.

We sign these Declarations as individuals in the conviction that we are furthering a movement capable of great benefit to Africa and the British Commonwealth of Nations.

The following signed the Declarations:

Sir Godfrey Huggins

Sir Roy Welensky

Ian Wilson (Speaker, S.R.)
J. W. Keller (MP, S.R.)
L. M. Hodson (Deputy Speaker, S.R.)
A. S. Soffe (CAS)
N. H. Wilson (CAS)
G. M. Ellman Brown (CAS)
Bavus A. Baker (United Party, CAS)
C. J. Bowden
Stainley S. Cooke (UCAA)
Hugh Wheeler
Geoffrey Beckett
Hon. Humphrey Gibbs
H. St. L. Green fell (CAS)
Albert Keyser
F. A. P. Schmid
Major General G. R. Smallwood
C. Kenneth Archer
Michael Blunden (Kenya Legco)
Gerald Hopkins (Kenya Legco)
Wilfred B. Havelock (Kenya Legco)
T. C. C. Lewin
Major Kendal Ward
Stainley Ghersie
Clive Salter
R. W. Miller
The Earl of Portsmouth
Lady Sidney Farrar (CAS, Kenya)
R. V. Stone
G. W. Caregie (Tanganyika)

Note: The published version of the Declarations was signed by David Stirling
(President) and Arthur Stokes (Secretary).
Source: CAS Papers.

APPENDIX II: DRAFT STATEMENT ON PARTNERSHIP

(Prepared by the government of Northern Rhodesia as a basis for local discussion with reference to paragraph 6 of the Victoria Falls Conference on the Closer Association of the Central African Territories.)

Part I: The Policy

1. The ultimate political objective for the people of Northern Rhodesia is self-government within the British Commonwealth; self-government must take full account of the rights and interests of both Europeans and Africans and include proper provisions for both.

2. The only satisfactory basis on which such provision can be secured is economic and political partnership between the races, and this is the approved policy for Northern Rhodesia.

3. The application of such partnership in practice must ensure that Africans are helped forward along the path of economic, social and political progress on which their feet have already been set so that they may take their full part with the rest of the community in the economic and political life of the territory. Africans for their part must be willing to accept the responsibilities as well as the privileges which such advancement entails.

There can be no question of the Government of Northern Rhodesia subordinating the interests of any section of the community to those of any other section.

The application of the policy of partnership is not in any way inconsistent with, and does not in any way interfere with, the territory's present status.

It imposes on each of the two sections (Europeans and Africans) an obligation to recognise the right of the other section to a permanent home in Northern Rhodesia.

4. In the political sphere partnership implies that any constitutional arrangement must include proper provision for both Europeans and Africans and proper safeguards for their rights and interests.

5. Generally, partnership implies that Europeans and Africans will pay due regard to each other's outlook, beliefs, customs and legitimate aspirations and anxieties.

Part II: Putting the Policy into Progressive Operation

6. In the political sphere Africans will be able to advance until ultimately (so long as representation on racial grounds remains) they have the same number of representatives as Europeans in both Legislative and Executive Councils when they are fit for this. It is hoped to make early progress towards this end and it is proposed that there should be an increased number of representatives of African interests in the next Legislative Council.

7. In the economic field every individual must be free to rise to the level that his ability, energy, qualifications, and character permit. In accordance with its declared policy that Africans in Northern Rhodesia should be afforded opportunities for employment in more responsible work as and when they are qualified to undertake it, the Government will continue to provide more and better facilities for training Africans for such work.

8. In the educational field the Government will, in cooperation with Native Authorities and Missions, continue to work steadily towards universal literacy for all African children of school-going age and it will, in accordance with long-term plans already made, provide expanded facilities for both secondary education and vocational training. The question of building in Central Africa a higher college for Africans is being actively pursued in consultation with the other two Governments concerned, and expert advice on the subject is being sought.

9. In the field of Local Government the Government is training Africans to take a larger and more effective part in the administration of rural areas. In the towns African membership of African affairs sub-committees of Municipal Councils and Township Management Boards is extending and it is to be expected that, as Africans gain the necessary knowledge and experience, they will become members of such councils and boards.

10. In the Government service Africans are being trained for and promoted to more responsible positions as they show themselves capable of assuming heavier duties and increased responsibilities.

11. At the present stage of the development of Africans the repeal of all differential legislation would not be in their best interests; much of it is designed to protect them and some of it grants them special privileges. It has been the policy of the Government to remove or relax the differential provisions in legislation according as the advancement of Africans

renders such provisions no longer necessary. The Government will keep this matter under close review and propose to the Legislature from time to time such further amendments as it may consider appropriate.

12. Discriminatory practices based on racial distinctions are incompatible with the policy of partnership, and the trend of public opinion in Northern Rhodesia is towards a clearer recognition of this fact. Such practices are diminishing in Northern Rhodesia and will diminish still more rapidly as Europeans and Africans recognise each other's needs as well as their own obligations in this matter. The Government has taken and is taking steps to encourage in both races a sympathetic and helpful approach to this problem.

A. T. WILLIAMS.
ACTING CHIEF SECRETARY.
The Secretariat,
LUSAKA.
April 1952.
Source: PRO CO 1015/553/47.

APPENDIX III: AFRICAN REPRESENTATIVE COUNCIL DRAFT STATEMENT ON PRINCIPLES OF INTER-RACIAL POLICY

1. The ultimate objective for the people of Northern Rhodesia is self-government within the British Commonwealth, based on a truly democratic franchise.

2. No one race must ever be in a position to dominate another for its selfish interests. The only way for this to be done is for each to have equal power in the Legislative and Executive Councils.

3. Each individual in Northern Rhodesia shall have the right to advance in every sphere, according to his energy, character, ability and qualifications, without any regard to colour, race or religion.

4. The only satisfactory means by which such provision can be secured is economic, political and social equality between the races, and this is the proposed policy for Northern Rhodesia.

5. The application of such a policy of equality in practice must ensure that Africans are helped forward along the path of economic, social and political progress on which their feet have already been set so that they must take their full part with the rest of the community in the economic and political life of the Territory.

6. In the meanwhile there must be no question of the Government of Northern Rhodesia subordinating the interests of any section of the community to those of any other section and the application of this policy is not in any way inconsistent with, and does not in any way interfere with, the Territory's present protectorate status.

7. In the political sphere equality implies that meanwhile a constitutional arrangement must include proper provision for both Europeans and Africans and proper safeguards for their rights and interests.

Source: PRO CO 1015/554/72 Enc.

APPENDIX IV: THE CAPRICORN CONTRACT, 1956

Part One

We affirm our faith in the greatness of common destiny and resolve to reject the barren doctrine of racial nationalism. We believe that our purpose of uniting the races in one patriotism and one allegiance has the power to provide the stability essential to the orderly development of Africa. We resolve to work for the establishment of a society free from racial discrimination and declare our determination to secure, as a condition of full self-government and the adoption separately in each of the six territories of a written constitution embodying the following Precepts:

Precept One

All men, despite their varying individual talents and differences of race and colour are born equal in dignity before God and have a common duty to one another.

Precept Two

Man's fulfilment of his responsibilities to his fellow men is the essential foundation for a community and for the assertion and enjoyment of his rights as an individual. The state has the obligation to secure justice in the case of conflict of interests between individuals.

Precept Three

The state is under obligation to protect and advance the moral, material and cultural standards of its peoples.

Precept Four

All who were born in Capricorn Africa or live within their boundaries are entitled to equal standing before the law and, subject to the law, to freedom of movement, speech, religion and association and the right to acquire and enjoy property. They are entitled, without distinction of race or colour, to access to public service and institutions and practice any trade and profession.

Precept Five

Membership of the state has responsibilities and duties, and the citizen is under obligation to live by the rule of law and to defend the state.

Precept Six

The right to elect members of the Legislature would be open to all who have attained the statutory qualifications and would be registered on one common roll.

Part Two. Provisions

1. The Electoral System. [See Chapter Four for details on this issue].

2. Land Reform

(a) The state would allow and encourage the conversion of all land into areas open to purchase by all persons irrespective of race. All existing individual rights in land would be recognised and confirmed by law.

(b) Land would not be reserved in perpetuity for members of one race or tribe to the exclusion of others. Legislation to implement these principles would involve the abrogation of treaties and of solemn pledges to various communities. The state would control any further transfer of land resulting from this legislation. It would also take steps to ensure that transfer of particular lands were made only to experienced farmers.

(c) All land occupied by Europeans would gradually become available for purchase or lease by all races, and land occupied on a communal basis by Africans would be gradually made open for purchase or lease by Africans and would later be made open for transfer to persons of any race.

(d) Where land was to be released from exclusive African reservation, the state would encourage and make provision for land units of a size capable of sustaining a farmer or pastoralist and his family on a reasonable standard of living and would encourage the consolidation of these units into a size which an African farmer could purchase and manage.

(e) Any un allocated land in areas reserved exclusively for members of one race would be allocated in the first instance to members of that race, after which it would be freely transferable to persons of any race.

3. Labour Relations

(a) Standards of living would be maintained and protected and everything possible would be done to bring all workers up to those standards and to raise standards in respect of output and quality of work, responsibility and rewards.

(b) Individuals holding positions of equal responsibility and producing work equal in quality and quantity would be entitled to equal rates of pay.

(c) Members of a trade organisation would not be denied any person on grounds of race.

(d) The opportunity of trade apprenticeship would be open to members of all races on the same terms. To enable all workers to achieve a progressively higher rate and quality of work, the creation of training facilities at every level would be encouraged.

4. Education

To hasten the fulfilment of this provision, we agree that the following steps be taken:

(a) The establishment of inter-racial teacher training centres.

(b) The extension of out-of-school activities of all kinds on an inter-racial basis.

(c) The extension of inter-racial education at university and technical college level.

(d) The extension of educational facilities of all kinds for women and girls of all races.

(e) The establishment of courses on citizenship and civic responsibilities in all secondary schools and in all forms of adult education.

5. Immigration

Immigration of Asiatic people would have to be restricted to avoid lowering of European standards.

Source: CAS Papers.

Bibliography

PRIMARY SOURCES

Archival Manuscripts
Colonial Office Archives: Public Record Office (PRO), Kew Gardens, London.
Series CO 537, CO 795, CO 959, CO 1015, CO 4690 and DO 35
National Archives of Zambia (NAZ), Lusaka
Historical Manuscripts (HM)
>   HM 11 The '48 Club
>   HM 47 Harry Henry Franklin Papers
>   HM 53/1-6 Edward Geden Nightingale Papers
File Series NR and SEC
>   NR 8/1 Partnership, 1952
>   NR 8/4-7 Closer Association, 1949-56
>   NR 9/16 African Representative Council, 1957-58
>   NR 11/44-47, Closer Association: Central African Federation, 1949-56
>   NR 11/118-122, Closer Association: Conferences and Meetings, 1951-52
>   NR 11/135, Central African Independence Association, 1951
>   NR 11/158, African National Congress, 1953-58
>   NR 11/162, Unity League, Northern Rhodesia, 1954
>   SEC 5/10, African National Congress Boycott, 1956
>   SEC 5/43-46, African Representative Council Proceedings, 1946-58
>   SEC 5/67, Lusaka African Urban Advisory Council, Central Province, 1957-59
>   SEC 5/112, Closer Association White Paper No. 1, 1952
>   SEC 5/113, Closer Association, The Kabalata Affair, 1952
>   SEC 5/185, Godwin A. Mbikusita Lewanika, 1950-56
>   SEC 5/434-441, Race relations in Northern Rhodesia, 1949-60
>   SEC 5/197, Integration of Native Policy, 1951-55
>   SEC 5/270, The Moffat Resolutions, 1954-55

United National Independence Party Archives (PA), Lusaka

> ANC 3/24, African Condemnation of federation, 1950-1958
>
> ANC 3/13-14, African Civil Servants, Political Activities, 1959-63
>
> ANC 5/11 Conclusion of Federation Debate: Central African Convention Party, 1954
>
> ANC 5/22, The African Bureau Correspondence with ANC
>
> ANC 7/3, Official Press Statements on Dissolution of Federation
>
> ANC 7/23, Northern Rhodesia Constitution with regard to Independence Proposals, 1964-68
>
> ANC 7/31, African National Congress Week-by-Week Publications, 1960-69
>
> ANC 7/63, Northern Rhodesia Society, General Correspondence, 1958-63
>
> ANC 7.79, ANC Protests to the United Nations against Federation, (n.d.)
>
> ANC 7/83, Correspondence on the Capricorn Africa Society: Race Relations Policy, 1952
>
> ANC 7/108-109, ANC Boycotts, 1952-1970

Private Papers

Special Collections, University of Zambia

> Papers of Eileen Haddon
>
> Papers of Fergus MacPherson

Center for Research Library, Chicago

> Microfilms of The Capricorn Africa Society Papers held at the University of York (20 reels)

Published Official Sources

Northern Rhodesia Government Publications

Northern Rhodesia African Representative Council Proceedings, Bound copies, 1946-1958

Northern Rhodesia Legislative Council debates, 1948-63

Newspapers and Periodicals

Africa Confidential

Africa Report

Africa Research Bulletin

Central African Post

The Central African Examiner

East Africa and Rhodesia

The Economist

Equinox

Keesing's Contemporary Archives
Manchester Guardian
The Monitor
National Mirror
New African
Rhodesia Herald
The Listener
The Northern News
Trunza
The Post
Times of Zambia
UZ Spokesman
Zambia Daily Mail
Zebra

Personal Communication
Terence Ranger, 3 January 1989

Oral Interviews
Gabriel Musumbulwa, at Luanshya (Zambia), 15 May 1989.

SECONDARY SOURCES

Books

Almond, Gabriel A. and Bingham Powel *Comparative Politics: A Developmental Approach* (Boston: Little, Brown & CO., 1966).

Anderson, Benedict. *Imagined Communities: Reflections on the Origins and Spread of Nationalism* (London: Verso, 1983).

Anglin, Douglas G. and Timothy M. Shaw *Zambia's Foreign Policy: Studies in Diplomacy and Dependence*, (Boulder, CO: Westview Press, 1979).

Austin, Dennis. *Politics in Africa* (Hanover: New Haven, 1978).

Baker, Donald G. *Race, Ethnicity and Power* (London: Routledge & Kegan Paul, 1983).

Barnes, J.A. *Politics in a Changing Society* (London: Oxford University Press, 1954).

Bates, R.H. *Unions, Parties and Political Development: A Study of Mineworkers in Zambia* (New Haven CT: Yale University Press, 1971).

Berger, Elina L. *Labour, Race and Colonial Rule: The Copperbelt From 1924 to Independence* (Oxford: Clarendon Press, 1974).

Bowman, Larry W. *Politics in Rhodesia: White Power in African State* (Cambridge: Harvard University Press, 1973).

Bull, Theodore. *Rhodesia, Crisis of Colour* (Chicago: Quadrangle Books, 1967).

Burdette, M.M. *Zambia: Between Two Worlds* (Boulder, CO: Westview Press, 1988.

Buttler, Jeffrey, Richard Elphick and David John Welsh (eds.), *Democratic Liberalism in South Africa: Its History and Prospect* (Middletown, CT: Wesleyan University Press, 1987).

Chanda, Donald (ed.) *Democracy in Zambia: Key Speeches of President Chiluba, 1901-92* (Lusaka: Africa Press Trust, 1993).

Chanock, Martin. *Unconsummated Union: Britain, Rhodesia and South Africa 1900-1945* (Manchester: Manchester University Press, 1977).

Chidzero, Bernard T.G. *Partnership in Practice* (London: Sword of the Spirit Press, 1960).

Chiluba, Frederick J.T. *Democracy: The Challenge of Change* (Lusaka: Multimedia Publications, 1995).

Chipungu, Samuel N. (ed.) *Guardians in Their Time: Experiences of Zambians Under Colonial Rule, 1890-1964* (London: Macmillan, 1992).

Chishala, Beatwell *Lt Luchembe Coup Attempt* (Lusaka: Multimedia Publications, 1991).

Clements, Frank. *Rhodesia: A Study of the Deterioration of White Society* (New York: Praeger Publishers, 1969).

Cloete, J.J.N. *Emergent Africa: Political and Administrative Trends* (Pretoria: Africa Institute, 1966)

Cox, Richard. *Pan-Africanism in Practice: An East African Study: PAFMECSA 1958-1964* (London: Oxford University Press, 1964).

Creighton, T.R.M. *The Anatomy of Partnership: Southern Rhodesia and the Central African Federation* (London: Oxford University Press, 1960).

Davidson, J.W. *The Northern Rhodesia Legislative Council* (London: Faber and Faber, 1967).

Diamond, Larry, Juan L. Linz and Seymour M. Lipset (eds.) *Democracy in Developing Countries: Vol. 2 Africa* (Boulder, CO: Lynne Rienner Publishers, 1988).

Dunn, Cyryll. *Central African Witness* (London: Victor Gollancz, 1959).

Fisher, Monica. *Nswanga-The Heir: The Life and Times of Charles Fisher a Surgeon in Central Africa* (Ndola: Mission Press, 1991).

Fraenkel, Peter. *Waileshi* (London: Weidenfeld and Nicolson, 1959).

Franck, Thomas M. *Race and Nationalism: The Struggle for Power in Rhodesia and Nyasaland*, (London: George Allen & Unwin, 1960).

——(ed.). *Why Federations Fail: an Inquiry Into the Requisites for Successful Federations* (New York: New York University Press, 1968).

Franklin, Harry. *Unholy Wedlock: The Failure of the Central African Federation* (London: George Allen and Unwin, 1963).

Gallagher, John Jack. *The Decline, Revival and Fall of the British Empire* (Cambridge: Cambridge University Press, 1982).

Gann, L.H. *The Birth of a Plural Society: The Development of Northern Rhodesia Under the British South Africa Company 1894-1914* (Manchester: Manchester University Press, 1961).

Gann, L.H. *A History of Northern Rhodesia: Early Days To 1953* (London: Chatto and Windus Press, 1964).

Gann, L.H. and Peter Duignan *White Settlers in Tropical Africa* (London: Penguin Books, 1962).

Gertzel, Cherry, Carolyn Baylies and Morris Szeftel (eds.). *The Dynamics of the One-Party State in Zambia* (Manchester: Manchester University Press, 1984).

Gibbs, Peter. *Avalanche in Central Africa* (London: A. Baker, 1961).

Gifford, Prosser and W.R. Louis (eds.). *The Transfer of Power in Africa: Decolonization 1940-1960* (New Haven: Yale University Press, 1982).

Goldsworth, David. *Colonial Issues in British Politics 1945-1961* (London: Clarendon Press, 1970).

Hailey, Lord. *An African Survey: A Study of Problems Arising in Africa South of the Sahara* (London: Oxford University Press, 1957).

Hall, Richard. *Kaunda: Founder of Zambia* (London: Longmans, 1964).

——*Zambia* (New York: Praeger, 1965).

—— Zambia 1890-1964: The Colonial Period (London: Longmans, 1976).

—— *The High Price of Principles: Kaunda and the White South* (New York: Africana Publishing, 1969).

Hancock, Ian. *White Liberals, Moderates and Radicals in Rhodesia 1953-1980* (London: Croom Helm, 1984).

Hargreaves, John D. *Decolonization in Africa* (London: Longmans, 1986).

Harries-Jones, Peter. *Freedom and Labour: Mobilization and Political Control on the Zambian Copperbelt* (Oxford: Basil Blackwell, 1975).

Hatch, John. *Two African Statesmen: Kaunda of Zambia and Nyerere of Tanzania* (London: Secker & Warberg, 1976).

Hazelwood, Arthur (ed.) *African Integration and Disintegration* (London: Oxford University Press, 1967).

Hodder-Williams, Richard. *An Introduction to the Politics of Tropical Africa* (London: George Allen and Unwin, 1984).

Holderness, Hardwicke. *Lost Chance: Southern Rhodesia 1945-1958* (Harare: Zimbabwe Publishing House, 1985).

Hyam, Ronald. *The Failure of South African Expansion 1908-1948* (London: Oxford University Press, 1972).

Ihonvbere, Julius. *Economic Crisis, Civil Society and Democratization in Zambia* (Lawrenceville, NJ: Africa World Press, 1996).

Jones, A. Creech and Rita Hinden *Colonies and International Conscience* (London: Fabian Publications, 1945).

Kaunda, Kenneth D. *Zambia Shall Be Free,* (London: Heinemann 1962).

Kaunda, Kenneth D. *Humanism in Zambia and a Guide to Its Implementation* (Lusaka: Government Printer, 1974).

Kaunda, Kenneth D. and Colin Morris. *Black Government?: A Discussion Between Colin Morris and Kenneth Kaunda* (Lusaka: United Society for Christian Literature, 1960).

——*A Humanist in Africa: Letters to Colin Morris from Kenneth Kaunda* (London: Longmans, 1966).

Kay, George. *A Social Geography of Zambia: A Survey of Population Patterns in a developing Country* (London: University of London Press, 1967).

Keith, George. *The Fading Colour Bar* (London: Robert Hale, 1966).

Kenneth, Dane Keith. *Islands of White: Settler Society and Culture in Kenya and Southern Rhodesia, 1890-1939* (Durham, NC: Duke University Press, 1987).

Kuper, L. *Race, Class and Power: Ideology and Revolutionary Change in Plural Societies* (London: Duckworth Publications, 1974).

Kuper L. and M.G. Smith *Pluralism in Africa* (Los Angeles: University of California Press, 1969).

Legum, Colin (ed.). *Zambia: Independence and Beyond, the Speeches of Kenneth Kaunda* (London: Oxford University Press, 1966).

Leys, Colin. *European Politics in Southern Rhodesia* (London: Oxford University Press, 1959).

Leys, Colin and Cranford Pratt (eds.), *A New Deal in Central Africa* (London: Heinemann, 1960).

Lewin, Julius (ed.). *The Struggle for Racial Equality* (London: Longmans, 1967).

Livingston, W.S. *Federalism and Constitutional Change* (London: Oxford University Press, 1956).

Loney, Martin. *Rhodesia: White Racism and Imperial Response* (Harmondsworth: Penguin Books, 1975).

MacPherson, Fergus. *Kenneth Kaunda of Zambia: The Times and the Man* (Lusaka: Oxford University Press, 1974).

Makasa, Kapasa. *Zambia's March to Political Freedom* (Nairobi: Heinemann, 1985).

Marquard, Leopold. *Liberalism in South Africa* (Johannesburg: South Africa Institute for Race Relations, 1965).

—— *A Federation of Southern Africa* (London: Oxford University Press, 1971).

Mason, Philip. *Year of Decision: Rhodesia and Nyasaland in 1960* (London: Oxford University Press, 1960).

Mazrui, Ali A. *Towards A Pax-Africana: A Study of Ideology and Ambition* (London: Oxford University Press, 1967).

Meebelo, Henry S. *Reaction to Colonialism: A Prelude to the Politics of Independence in Northern Rhodesia 1893-1939* (Manchester: Manchester University Press, 1971).

Mphaisha, Chisepo J.J. (ed). *The State of the Nation: Volume I. Politics and Government* (Lusaka: Kenneth Kaunda Foundation, 1988).

Mulford, David C. *The Northern Rhodesia General Election 1962* (London: Oxford University Press, 1964).

——*Zambia: Politics of Independence 1957-1964* (London: Oxford University Press, 1967).

Mungazi, Dickson A. *The Last British Liberals in Africa: Michael Blundel and Garfield Todd,* (Westport, CT: Praeger Publishers, 1999).

Mutambirwa, James A.C. *The Rise of Settler Power in Southern Rhodesia, 1898-1923* (Rutherford, NJ: Fairleigh Dickinson University Press, 1980).

Mwanakatwe, John M. *End of Kaunda Era* (Lusaka: Multimedia Publications, 1994).

Mwangilwa, Goodwin. *Harry Mwaanga Nkumbula: A Biography of the "Old Lion" of Zambia* (Lusaka: Multimedia Publications, 1982).

Omer-Cooper, J.D. et al. *The Making of Modern Africa: Volume 2 The Late Nineteenth Century to the present Day* (London: longmans, 1971).

Oldham, J.H. *New Hope in Africa* (London: Longmans, 1955).

Palley, Claire. *The Constitutional History and Law of Southern Rhodesia 1880-1965* (Oxford: Oxford University Press, 1966).

Parpart, Jane L. *Labour and Capital on the African Copperbelt* (Philadelphia: Temple University Press, 1983).

Pearce, Robert D. *The Turning Point in Africa: British Colonial Policy 1938-48* (London: Frank Cass, 1982).

Pettman, Jan. *Zambia: Security and Conflict* (Sussex: Julian Friedmann Publishers, 1974).

Phiri, Bizeck J. *The Crisis of an African University: A Historical Appraisal of the University of Zambia* (Denver: International Academic Publishers, 2001).

Porter, A.N. and A.J. Stockwell (eds.). *British Imperial Policy and Decolonization 1938-1964,* (London: Macmillan, 1987).

Rich, Paul B. *White Power and the Liberal Conscience: Racial Segregation and South African Liberalism, 1921-1960* (Manchester: Manchester University Press, 1984).

Roberts, Andrew. *A History of Zambia* (New York: Africana, 1976)

Robertson, Janet. *Liberalism in South Africa 1948-1963* (London: Clarendon Press, 1971).

Rotberg, Robert I. *The Rise of Nationalism in Central Africa: The Making of Malawi and Zambia 1873-1964* (Harvard MA: Yale University Press, 1965).

——*Black Heart: Gore-Browne and the Politics of Multiracial Zambia* (Berkeley: Yale University Press, 1977).

Sachikonye, Lloyd. (ed.). *Democracy, Civil Society and the State: Social Movements in Southern Africa* (Harare: SAPES, 1995).

Sandbrook, Richard. *Politics of Africa's Economic Recovery* (Cambridge: Cambridge University Press, 1993).

Sanger, Clyde. *Central African Emergency* (London: Oxford University Press, 1960).

Sartori, G. *Parties and Party Systems* (Cambridge: Cambridge University Press, 1976).

Seliger, Martin. *The Liberal Politics of John Locke* (London: George Allen and Unwin, 1968).

Short, Robin. *African Sunset* (London: Johnston, 1973).

Sichone, Owen B. and Bornwell C. Chikulo (eds). *Democracy in Zambia: Challenges for the Third Republic* (Harare: SAPES Books, 1996).

Sikalumbi, Wittington K. *Before UNIP: A History* (Lusaka: Neczam, 1977).

Somjee, A.H. *The Democratic Process in a Developing Society* (New York: St. Martin's Press, 1979).

——*The Political Society in Developing Countries* (New York: St. Martin's Press, 1984).

Stirling, David and N.H. Wilson, *A Native Policy for Africa* (Salisbury: Capricorn Africa Society, 1950).

Tembo, Nephas *The Lilian Burton Killing: The Famous Trials of Zambian Freedom Fighters* (Lusaka: Apple Books, 1986).

Tembo, Trywell Z. *The Road to Multi-Party Democracy in Zambia and its Consequences* (Livingstone: Sanisani Chemist, 1996).

The Capricorn Africa Society Handbook for Speakers (Salisbiury: CAS, 1955)

Tordoff, William (Ed.). *Politics in Zambia* (Manchester: Manchester University Press, 1974).

Van der Post, Lawrence. *The Dark Eye in Africa* (London: Hogarth Press, 1955).

Vickery, Kenneth P. *Black and White in Southern Zambia: The Tonga Plateau Economy and British Imperialism 1890-1939* (Westport CT: Greenwood Press, 1986).

Virmani, K.K., *Zambia: The Dawn of Freedom* (Delhi: Kalinga Publications, 1989).

Wele, Patrick M. *Kaunda and Mushala Rebellion: The Untold Story* (Lusaka: Multimedia Publications, 1987).

Wele, Patrick M. *Zambia's Most Famous Dissidents: From Mushala   t   o Luchembe* (Lusaka: PMW, 1995).

Wilson, N.H., Abel Nyirenda and T.J. Hlazo *Federation and the African* (Salisbury: Capricorn Africa Society, 1952).

Wina, Sikota. *A Night Without A President* (Lusaka: Multimedia Publications, 1985).

Wood, Anthony St. John. *Northern Rhodesia: The Human Background* (London: Pall Mall Press, 1961).

Wood, J.R.T. *The Welensky Papers: A History of the Federation of Rhodesia and Nyasaland* (London: Oxford University Press, 1984).

ARTICLES

Adam, Heribert. "The Failure of Political Liberalism," in Heribert Adam and Hermann Giliomee, *The Rise and Crisis of Afrikaner Power* (Cape Town: David Philip Publishing, 1979).

Aihe, David O. "The Issue of Closer Association with Southern Rhodesia in Zambia's Constitutional History," *Odu*, 8, (October 1972), pp. 33-60.

Albinski, H.S. "The Concept of Partnership in the Central African Federation," *Review of Politics*, 19, 2 (April 1957), pp. 186-204.

Allen, Robert. "Reassessing African Political Activity in Urban Northern Rhodesia," *African Affairs*, 80, 317 (1981), pp. 238-258.

Atmore, Anthony and Nancy Weslake. "A Liberal Dilemma: A Critique of the *Oxford History of South Africa*," *Race*, 14, 2 (October 1972), pp.107-136.

Austin, D. "White Power," *Journal of Commonwealth Political Studies*, 6, 2 (1968), pp. 95-106.

——"What Happened To the Colonial State?" *The Round Table*, 295 (1985), pp. 206-216.

Austin, Reginald. "White Response to New Pressures," *African Perspectives*, 1 (1976), pp. 81-90.

Baker, C. "The Non-African Population of the Federation of Rhodesia and Nyasaland," *Geography*, (1957), pp. 132-134.

Balsvik, Randi R. "Student Life at the University of Zambia: Strikes, Closures and Disruption of Learning, 1965-1992," (1995), pp. 1-20.

Bantungwa, Fr. Ives Chituta. "The Role of the Church in the Democratisation Process in Africa: The Zambian Experience," *The Courier* 134 (July-August 1992),

Baylies, C. and M. Szeftel. "The Fall and Rise of Multi-Party Politics in Zambia," *Review of African Political Economy*, No. 54 (1992).

Baxter, G.H. and P.W. Hodges, "The Constitutional Status of the Federation of Rhodesia and Nyasaland," *International Affairs*, 33, 4 (October 1957), pp. 442-452.

Bennett, George. "Paramountcy to Partnership: J.H. Oldham and Africa," *Africa*, 30, 4 (October 1960), pp. 356-360.

——"British Settlers North of the Zambezi, 1920 to 1960," in L.H. Gann and P. Duignan (eds.). *Colonialism in Africa*, Volume 2, (Cambridge: At the University Press, 1970), pp. 58-91.

Bibby, John F. "Political Parties in the United States," in George Clerk (ed.), *United States Elections 2000* (Washington, DC: US Department of State, 2000), pp. 2-7.

Bratton, Michael. "Beyond Autocracy: Civil Society in Africa," Beyond Autocracy in Africa: the Inaugural Seminar of the African Governance Program (The Carter Center of Emory University Working Paper Series, Atlanta, February 17-18, 1989), pp. 29-34.

——"Economic Crisis and Political Realignment in Zambia," in J. Widner (ed.), *Economic Change and Political Liberalisation in Sub-Saharan Africa* (Baltimore: John Hopkins University Press, 1994).

Bratton, Michael and Beatrice Liatto-Katundu, "A Focus Group Assessment of Political Attitudes in Zambia," *African Affairs*, 93, 373 (1994), pp. 535-563.

Burawoy, M. "Another Look at the Mine-worker," *African Social Research*, 14 (1972), pp. 239-287.

Burnell, Peter. "The Party System and Party Politics in Zambia: Continuities Past, Present and Future," *African Affairs*, 100, 1 (2001), pp. 239-263.

Caplan, Gerald I. "Barotseland: The Secessionist Challenge to Zambia," *Journal of Modern African Studies*, 6, 3 (1968).

Chanaiwa, D. "The Premiership of Garfield Todd in Rhodesia: Racial Partnership versus Colonial Interests, 1953-1958," *Journal of Southern African Affairs*, 1, 1 (1976), pp. 83-94.

Chanda, Alfred W. "Zambia's Fledgling Democracy: Prospects for the Future," *Zambia Law Journal*, 25-28 (1993-96), pp. 125-154.

Chanda, Donald. "The Movement for Multi-Party Democracy in Zambia: Some Lessons in Democratic Transitions," in Lloyd M. Sachikonye (ed.). *Democracy, Civil Society and the State: Social Movements in Southern Africa* (Harare: SAPES Books, 1995), pp. 114-128.

Chidzero, Bernard T.G. "Central Africa: The Race Question and the Franchise," *Race*, 1, 1 (1959), pp. 53-60.

Chikulo, Bornwell C. "Elections in a One-Party Participatory Democracy," in Ben Turok (ed.) *Development in Zambia: A Reader* (London: Zed Press, 1979), pp. 201-213.

Chona, Mainza "Northern Rhodesia's Time for Change," *Africa South*, 5, 2 (1961).

Clay, Gervas "African Urban Advisory Councils in Northern Rhodesia: Copperbelt," *Journal of African Administration*, 1 (1960).

Coleman, J.S. "Economic Growth and Political Reorientation," in Melville J. Herskovits and Mitchell Harwitz (eds.). *Economic Transition in Africa* (Evanston, IL: Northwestern University Press, 1964), pp. 377-396.

Cooper, Frederick. "From free Labor to Family Allowances: Labor and African Society in Colonial Discourse," *American Ethnologist: The Journal of the American Ethnological Society*, 16 4 (November 1989).

Crookenden, Henry. "The Capricorn Contract," *African Affairs*, 55, 221 (1956), pp. 297-302.

Crowder, Michael. "Whose Dream Was It Anyway?: Twenty-Five Years of African Independence," *African Affairs*, 86, 342 (1987), pp. 7-24.

Datta, Kusum. "Farm Labour, Agrarian Capital and the state in Colonial Zambia: The African Labour Corps, 1942-52," *Journal of Southern African Studies*, 14, 3 (April, 1988), pp. 371-392.

Day, John. "The Creation of Political Myths: African Nationalism in Southern Africa," *Journal of Southern African Studies*, 2, 1 (1975)

De St. Jorre, John. "Race Tension on the Copperbelt: Rhodesia Infects her Northern Neighbour," *The Round Table*, 225 (January 1967), pp. 75-80.

De Winton, M.G. "Decolonization and the Westminster Model," in A.H.M. Kirk-Greene (ed.). *The Transfer of Power: The Colonial Administration in the Age of Decolonization*, (Kidlington Oxford: Oxford University Press, 1979), pp. 183-192.

Diamond, Larry and Dennis Galvin. "Sub-Saharan Africa," in Robert Wesson (ed.), *Democracy: A World Survey 1987* (New York: Praeger Publishers, 1987), pp. 63-104.

Flint, John E. "The Failure of Planned Decolonization in British Africa," *African Affairs*, 82, 328 (1983), pp. 389-411.

Flint, John E. "Scandal at the Bristol Hotel: Some Thoughts on Racial Discrimination in Britain and West Africa and its Relationship to the Planning of Decolonization, 1939-1947," *Journal of Commonwealth and Imperial History*, 12 1 (October 1983), pp. 74-93.

Friedland, Elaine A. "The Southern African Development Co-ordination Conference and the West: Co-operation or Conflict?," *The Journal of Modern African Studies*, 23, 2 (1985), pp. 287-314.

Gann, L.H. "Lord Malvern (Sir Godfrey Huggins): A Reappraisal," *Journal of Modern African Studies*, 23, 4 (1985), pp. 723-728.

Gann, L.H. and P. Duignan. "Changing Patterns of a White Elite: Rhodesian and Other Settlers," in L.H. Gann and P. Duignan (eds.). *Colonialism in Africa* (Cambridge: At the University Press, 1970), pp. 92-170.

Garbett, G. Kingsley. "The Rhodesian Chief's Dilemma: Government Officer or Tribal Leader," *Race*, 8, 2 (1966), pp. 113-128.

Gifford, Prosser. "Misconceived Dominion: The Creation and Disintegration of Federation in British Central Africa," in Prosser Gifford and W.R.

Louis (eds.). *Transfer of Power in Africa: Decolonization, 1940-1960*, (New Haven: Yale University Press, 1982), pp. 387-416.

Glickman, Harvey. "Frontiers of Liberal and Non-Liberal Democracy in Tropical Africa," *Journal of Asian and African Studies*, 23, 3-4 (1988), pp. 234-254.

Good, Kenneth. "Settler Colonialism: Economic Development and Class Formation," *Journal of Modern African Studies*, 14, 4 (December, 1976), pp. 597-620.

——" Settler Colonialism in Rhodesia," *African Affairs*, 73, 290 (1974), pp. 10-36.

Gordon, D.F. "Mau Mau and Decolonization: Kenya and the Defeat of Multiracialism in East and Central Africa," *Kenya Historical Review*, 5, 2 (1977), pp. 329-348.

Gray, Richard. "Race Relations in Central Africa," *African Affairs*, 62, 249 (1963), pp. 333-340.

Gupta, Anirudha. "The Zambian National Assembly: Study of an African Legislature," *Parliamentary Affairs*, 19, 1 (1965-66), pp. 48-55.

Gutteridge, W.P. "The Debate on Central African Federation in Retrospect," *Parliamentary Affairs*, 10, 2 (1957), pp. 210-219.

Hancock, Ian R. "The Capricorn Africa Society in Southern Rhodesia," *Rhodesian History*, 9 (1978), pp. 41-63.

Hellen, J.A. "Independence or Colonial Determinism?: The African Case," *International Affairs*, 44, 4 (October, 1968), pp. 691-708.

Henderson, Ian. "The Economic Origins of Decolonization in Zambia, 1940-1945," *Rhodesian History*, 5 (1974), pp. 49-66.

——"The Limits of Colonial Power: Race and Labour Problems in Colonial Zambia, 1900-1953," *Journal of Imperial and Commonwealth History*, 2, 3 (1974), pp. 294-307.

——"Wage-Earners and Political Protest in Colonial Africa: The Case of the Copperbelt," *African Affairs*, 72, 287 (1973), pp. 288-299.

—— "White Populism in Southern Rhodesia," *Comparative Studies in Society and History*, 14, 4 (1972), pp. 387-393.

Hertzog, H. "Social Construction of Reality in Ethnic Terms: The Case of Political Ethnicity in Israel," *International Review of Modern Sociology* 15, 1-2 (1985).

Hill, Christopher, R. "Regional Co-operation in Southern Africa," *African Affairs*, 82, 327 (April 1983), pp. 214-239.

Horowitz, Dan. "The British Conservatives and the Racial Issue in the Debate on Decolonization," *Race*, 12, 2 (1970), pp. 169-187.

Hyam, Ronald. "The Geopolitical Origins of the Central African Federation: Britain, Rhodesia and South Africa, 1948-1953," *The Historical Journal*, 30, 1 (1987), pp. 145-172.

Ihonvbere, Julius O. "Democratization in Africa", *Peace Review*, 9, 3 (1997), pp.371-378.

—— "The 'Irrelevant' State, Ethnicity, and the Quest for Nationhood in Africa," *Ethnic and Racial Studies*, 17, 1 (January 1994), pp. 42-60.

——"Political Pluralism and Crisis in Africa: The Case of Zambia," *Hemisphere*, No. 10 (1995).

Izuakor, Levi I. "Kenya: The Unparamount African Paramountcy, 1923-1939," *Transafrican Journal of History*, 12 (1983), pp. 33-50.

Jackson, Robert H. and Carl G. Rosberg. "Democracy in Tropical Africa: Democracy Versus Autocracy in African Politics," *Journal of International Affairs*, 38, 2 (1985), pp. 293-305.

Joseph, Richard. "The Challenge of Democratization in Africa: Some Reflections," *African Governance in the 1990s: Objectives, Resources and Constraints*, The Second Annual Seminar of the African Governance Program (The Carter Center of Emory University Working Paper Series March 23-25, 1990), pp. 17-21.

Kanogo, Tabitha M.J. "Politics of Collaboration or Domination?: A Case Study of the Capricorn Africa Society," *Kenya Historical Review*, 2, 2 (1974), pp. 127-142.

Kaunda, Kenneth. "Zambia's Economic Reforms," *African Affairs*, 67, 269 (1968), pp. 295-304.

Kinloch, G.C. "Changing Black Reaction to White Domination," *Rhodesian History*, 5 (1974), pp. 67-75.

Kuper, Hilda. "The Colonial Situation in Southern Africa," *Journal of Modern African Studies*, 2, 2 (1964), pp. 149-164.

Leys, Roger, and Arne Tostensen. "Regional Co-operation in Southern Africa: the Southern African Development Co-ordination Conference," *Review of African Political Economy*, 25, (January-April, 1982), pp. 52-71.

Llewellin, Lord. "Some Facts About the Federation of Rhodesia and Nyasaland," *African Affairs*, 55, 221 (1956), pp. 266-272.

Lonsdale, John. "The Emergence of African Nations: A Historiographical Analysis," *African Affairs*, 67, 266 (January 1968), pp. 11-28.

——"States and Social Processes in Africa: A Historiographical Survey," *The African Studies Review*, 24, 2/3 (June/September 1981), pp. 139-225.

Lucan, Lord. "Capricorn African Society," *Venture*, 7, 9 (February 1956), pp. 6-7.

MacAdam, A. "The Limits of Dissent in Rhodesia," *Race Today*, 3, 5 (1971), p. 151-152.

——"Rhodesian Phantom Liberalism: Imperialism, Federation and Rebellion in British Central Africa," *African Perspectives*, 1 (1976), pp. 47-54.

McKee, Major H.K. "Northern Rhodesia and Federation," *African Affairs*, 51, 202 (1952), pp. 323-335.

Mason, Philip. "Prospects and Progress in the Federation of Rhodesia and Nyasaland," *Africa Affairs*, 61, 242 (1962), pp. 17-28.

Mazrui, Ali A. "Pluralism and National Integration," in Leo Kuper and M.G. Smith (eds.). *Pluralism in Africa* (Berkeley: University of California Press, 1969), pp. 333-349.

Molteno, Robert. "Cleavage and Conflict in Zambian Politics: A Study in Sectionalism," in William Tordoff (ed.), *Politics in Zambia* (Manchester: Manchester University Press, 1974), pp. 62-106.

——"Zambia and the One-Party State," *East Africa Journal*, 9, 2 (February 1972), pp. 6-8.

Moffat, Sir John. "The Role of the Liberal in Rhodesian Politics," *Central African Examiner* (24 September 1960).

Molteno, Robert and William Tordoff. "Conclusion, Independent Zambia: Achievements and Prospects," in William Tordoff (ed.) *Politics in Zambia* (Manchester: Manchester University Press, 1974).

Morris-Jones, W.H. "Dominance and Dissent: Their Interrelations in the Indian Party System," *Government and Politics*, 1, 4 July-September 1966).

Moyana, H.V. "British Complicity in Rhodesia, 1923-1970," *Pan-African Journal*, 8, 1 (1975), pp. 45-74.

Mulford, David C. "Northern Rhodesia: Some Observation on the 1964 Election," *Africa Report*, 9, 2 (February 1964), pp. 13-17.

Musambachime, Mwelwa C. "Dauti Yamba's Contribution to the Rise and Growth of Nationalism in Zambia 1941-1964," *African Affairs*, 90, 359 (1991), pp. 259-281.

——"The Impact of Rumour: The Case of the Banyama (vampire men) Scare in Northern Rhodesia, 1939-1964," *The International Journal of African Historical Studies*, 21, 2 (1988), pp. 201-215.

——"Rural Political Protest: The Case of the 1953 Disturbances in Mweru-Luapula," *International Journal of African Historical Studies*, 20, 3 (1987), pp. 437-453.

Ngwenyama, N.M. "Rhodesia Approaches Collapse: A Study of Settler Residence to African Nationalism," *Ufahamu*, 5,3 (1975), pp. 11-16.

Nyerere, Julius K. "The Entrenchment of Privilege," *Africa South*, 2, 2 (1958), pp. 85-89.

Osei-Hwedie, Bertha. "The Role of Ethnicity in Multi-Party Politics in Malawi and Zambia," *Journal of Contemporary African Studies*, 16, 2 (July 1998), pp. 227-247.

Palmer, Robin. "European Resistances to African Majority Rule: The Settlers' and Residents' Association of Nyasaland, 1960-1963," *African Affairs*, 72, 288 (1973), pp. 256-272.

Parpart, Jane L. "Class and Gender on the Copperbelt: Women in Northern Rhodesian Copper Mining Communities, 1926-1964," in Claire Robertson and Iris Berger (eds.), *Women and Class in Africa*, (New York and London: African Publishing, 1988), pp. 141-160.

Pearce, Robert D. "The Colonial Office and Planned Decolonization in Africa," *African Affairs*, 83, 330 (1984), pp. 77-93.

Pettman, S. "Zambia's Second Republic: the Establishment of a One-Party State," *Journal of Modern African Studies*, 12, 2 (1974), pp. 231-244.

Phiri, Bizeck J. "The Capricorn Africa Society Revisited: The Role and Impact of 'Liberalism' in Zambia's Colonial History," The *International Journal of African Historical Studies*, 24, 1 (1991), pp.65-83.

——"Colonial Legacy and the Role of Society in the Creation and Demise of Autocracy in Zambia, 1964-1991," *Nordic Journal of African Studies*, Vol. 10, 2 (2001), pp. 224-44.

——"Coping With Contradictions—Class, Ethnicity and Nationalism: the Case of Godwin A. Mbikusita Lewanika and Zambian Nationalism," *Transafrican Journal of History*, Vol. 29 (1999).

——"Decolonization and Multi-Racial Liberalism in Northern Rhodesia: A Reassessment," *Zambia Journal History*, No. 5, (1992), pp. 14-35. .

——"The Failure of Multi-Racial 'Liberal' Parties in Northern Rhodesia/ Zambia: a Prelude to One-Party State?," *Asian and African Studies*, Vol. 25, 1 (1991), pp. 55-80.

——"The Mixed Fortunes of Multipatyism in Zambia's Third Republic: Democracy or Mobocracy?," *Journal of Humanities*, Volume 3, 2001, pp. 84-109.

——"The Myth and Realities of 'One-Party Participatory Democracy': A Study in the Failure of Liberal Democracy in Post-Independence Zambia," *Geneva-Africa*, Vol. 29, 2 (November, 1991), pp. 9-24

——"Zambians of Indian Origin: A History of Their Struggle for Survival in a New Homeland," Communications of the Centre for Advanced Studies of African Society, *Occasional Paper* No. 12 (2001).

Phiri, Isaac "Media in 'Democratic' Zambia: Problems and Prospects," *Africa Today*, 46, 2 (1999), pp. 53-65. http://www.press.jhu.edu/journals/africa_today/v046/ 46.2phiri.html

——"Why African Churches Preach Politics: The Case of Zambia," *Journal of Church and State* (Spring 1999) http://www. britannica.com/bcom/maga-zine/article/ 0,5744,255864,00.html

Pillay, P.D. "White Power in Southern Rhodesia," *African Quarterly*, 10, 1 (April-June 1970), pp. 32-39.

Prain, Sir Ronald L.. "The Problem of African Advancement on the Copperbelt of Northern Rhodesia," *African Affairs* 53, 211 (April 1954), pp. 91-103.

Pratt, R. Cranford. "Partnership and Consent: The Monckton Report Examined," *International Journal*, 16 (Winter 1960-61), pp. 37-49.

Ranger, Terence. "The Politics of the Irrational in Central Africa," *The Political Quarterly*, 34 (1963), pp. 285-291.

——"Making Northern Rhodesia Imperial: Variations on a Royal Theme, 1924-1938," *African Affairs*, 79, 316 (1980), pp.349-373.

Rasmussen, Thomas. "Political Competition and One-Party Dominance in Zambia," *The Journal of Modern African Studies*, 7, 3 (1969), pp. 407-424.

——"The Popular Basis Of Anti-Colonial Protest," in William Tordoff (ed.), *Politics in Zambia*, (Manchester: Manchester University Press, 1974), pp. 40-61.

Rea, F.B. "Rebirth of a Nation: Can Capricorn Rise From Its Ashes?," *Central African Examiner*, 2, 26 (23 May, 1959), pp. 14-15.

Robert, Andrew D. "White Judges Under Attack: Growing Pressure for a One-Party State," *The Round Table*, No. 236, (October 1969), pp. 423-426.

Robinson, Ronald. "Andrew Cohen and the transfer of Power in tropical Africa, 1940-1951," in W.H. Morris-Jones and George Fischer (eds.). *Decolonization and After: The British and French Experience* (London: Frank Cass, 1980).

Roll, Alistair. "The Capricorn Africa Society and European Reaction to Nationalism in Tanganyika, 1949-1960," *African Affairs*, 76, 305 (1977), pp. 519-535.

Rosberg, Carl G. "The Federation of Rhodesia and Nyasaland: Problems of Democratic Government," *The Annals*, 306 (July 1956).

Rotberg, Robert I. "Colonialism and After: The Political Literature of Central Africa — A Bibliographical Essay," *African Forum*, 2 (Winter 1967), pp. 66-73.

——"The Federation Movement in British East and Central Africa, 1889-1953," *Journal of Commonwealth Political Studies*, 2, 2 (1964), pp. 141-160.

——"Race Relations and Politics in Colonial Zambia: the Elwell Incident," *Race*, 7 (1965), pp.17-29.

——"Tribalism and Politics in Zambia," *Africa Report*, 12 (December 1967), pp. 29-35.

Rothchild, Donald. "African Federations and the Diplomacy of Decolonization," *Journal of Developing Areas*, 4, 4 (July 1970), pp. 509-524.

——"Force and Consent in African Region-Building," *Makerere Journal*, 11 (1965), pp.23-38.

Sandbrook, Richard. "Liberal Democracy in Africa: A Socialist-Revisionist Perspective," *Canadian Journal of African Studies*, 22, 2 (1988), pp. 240-267.

Seliger, Martin. "Locke, Liberalism and Nationalism," in John W. Yolton (ed.), *John Locke: Problems and Perspectives, A Collection of New Essays* (Cambridge: At the University Press, 1969), pp. 19-33.

Shaw, Timothy M. and Sandra J. MacLean "Civil Society and Political Economy in Contemporary Africa: What Prospects for Sustainable Democracy?," *Journal of Contemporary African Studies*, 14, 2 (July 1996), pp. 247-264.

Shepperson, George. "The Literature of British Central Africa," *Human Problems in British Central Africa*, 23 (1958), pp. 12-46.

Slinn, Peter. "The Role of the British South Africa Company in Northern Rhodesia, 1890-1924," *African Affairs* 70, 281 (1971)

Small, N.J. "The Northern Rhodesia Policy and Its Legacy," *African Social Research*, No. 27 (1979), pp. 523-539.

Sills, H.D. "The Break Up of the Central African Federation," *African Affairs*, 73, 290 (1974), pp. 50-62.

Soremekun, Fola. "The Challenge of Nation-Building: Neo-Humanism and Politics in Zambia, 1967-1969," *Geneva-Africa*, 9,1 (1970), pp.3-41.

Stabler, John B. "The British South Africa Company Proposal for Amalgamation of the Rhodesias 1915-1917: Northern Rhodesian Reaction," *African Social Research*, 7 (June 1969), pp. 499-528.

——"Northern Rhodesian Reaction to 1948 Responsible Government Proposals: the Role of Sir Stewart Gore-Browne," *Journal of South African Affairs*, 3, 3 (July, 1978), pp. 295-317.

Stirling, David. "The Capricorn Africa Contract," *African Affairs*, 56, 224 (1957), pp. 191-199.

Sumaili, Fanuel K.M. "The Self and Biographical Writings in Zambia," *Zango*, 3, 1 (1988), pp. 72-115.

Tembo, Mwizenge S. "Zambia By Zambians," *Canadian Journal African Studies*, 22, 1 (1988), pp. 149-151.

Todd, Garfield S. "White Liberals and the Future," *Central African Examiner* (13 August 1960), p. 12.

——"The Meaning of Partnership in the Rhodesia Federation," *Optima*, (December 1967), pp. 174-180.

Tordoff, William "Political Crisis in Zambia," *Africa Quarterly*, 10, 3 (December 1970).

Tordoff, Wiliam and Ian Scott. "Political parties: Structures and Policies," in William Tordoff (ed.). *Politics in Zambia* (Manchester: Manchester University Press, 1974).

Trapido, Stanley. "Liberalism in the Cape in the 19th and 20th Centuries," *The Societies of Southern Africa in the 19th and 20th Centuries*, Vol. 4 (1974), pp. 53-66.

Vaughan, Megan. "Exploitation and Neglect: Rural Producers and the State in Malawi and Zambia," in David Birmingham and Phyllis M. Martin (eds), *History of Central Africa: The Contemporary Years Since 1960* (London: Longmans, 1998), pp. 167-201.

Voegelin, Eric. "Liberalism and its History," *Review of Politics*, 36, 4 (October 1974), pp. 504-520.

Vickery, Kenneth P. "The Second World War Revival of Forced Labor in the Rhodesias," *The International Journal of African Historical Studies*, 22, 3 (1989), pp. 423-437.

Wallance, I.A. "The Beginning of Native Administration in Northern Rhodesia," *Journal of the African Society*, 21 (1922).

Welensky, Sir Roy. "Development of Central Africa Through Federation," *Optima*, (December 1952), pp. 5-10.

Westcott, N.J. "Closer Union and the Future of East Africa 1939-48: A Case Study in the Official Mind of Imperialism," *Journal of Imperial and Commonwealth History*, 10, 1 (1981), pp. 67-88.

Wetherell, H.I. "Britain and Rhodesian Expansionism: Imperial Collusion or Empirical Carelessness," *Rhodesian History*, 8 (1977), pp. 115-128.

——"N.H. Wilson: Populism in Rhodesian Politics," *Rhodesian History*, 6 (1975), pp. 53-76.

——"Settler Expansionism in Central Africa: The Imperial Response of 1931 and Subsequent Implications," *African Affairs*, 78, 311 (1979), pp. 210-227.

Williams, Geoffrey J. Zambia: Physical and Social Geography," in *Africa South of the Sahara, 1990* (London: Europa Publications, 1990).

Young, Crawford. "The African Colonial State and its Political Legacy," in Donald Rothchild and Naomi Chazan (eds.). *The Precarious Balance: State and Society in Africa* (Boulder CO: Westview Press, 1988), pp. 25-66.

Unpublished Theses

Burawoy, M. "The Roles of the University Student in the Zambian Social Structure," MA Dissertation, University of Zambia 1972.

Keet, Dot L. "The African Representative Council 1946-1958: A Focus on African Leadership and Politics in Northern Rhodesia," MA Thesis, University of Zambia, Lusaka, 1975.

Mahoso, Tafataona Pasipaipa. "Between Two Nationalism: A Study in Liberal Activism and Western Domination, Zimbabwe 1920-1980," PhD Thesis, Temple University, 1987.

Mandaza, Ibbotson D.J. "White Settler Ideology, African Nationalism and the 'Coloured' Question in Southern Rhodesia/Zimbabwe, Northern Rhodesia/Zambia and Nyasaland/Malawi 1900-1976," DPhil University of York, (UK), 1976.

Phiri, Bizeck J. "The Capricorn Africa Society: A Study of Liberal Politics in Northern Rhodesia/Zambia, 1949-1972," PhD Thesis, Dalhousie University, Halifax, 1991.

Sondashi, Harris B. K. "The Politics of the Voice: an Examination and Comparison of British Pressure Groups (the Capricorn Africa Society, the Africa Bureau and the Movement for Colonial Reform) which Sought to Influence Colonial Policies and Events: The Case of Central Africa, 1949-1962," M Ph University of York (UK), 1980.

Watson, Joan Lorraine. "The Capricorn Africa Society and Its Impact on Rhodesian Politics," PhD Thesis, St. John's University, New York 1981.

Unpublished Papers

Flint, John E. "The Colonial Office and White Settler Nationalism in Central Africa, 1923-39," History Seminar, Dalhousie University, 1989.

——"The Colonial Office and the 'South African Menace', 1940-43," (n.d.).

SACCORD 2000 Report, "Conflict in Zambia and Beyond," (Lusaka: SACCORD, March 2001).

Vickery, Kenneth. "Roy Welensky and the World of Central African Labor," History Staff Seminar, University of Zambia, 15 February 1989.

Young, Crawford. "The Colonial State and its Connection to Current Political Crises in Africa," Draft paper given at a Conference on *African Independence*, University of Zimbabwe, Harare, January, 1985.

Index